Measuring Development

MEASURING DEVELOPMENT

The Role and Adequacy of Development Indicators

Edited by

NANCY BASTER

FRANK CASS : LONDON

First published 1972 in Great Britain by
FRANK CASS AND COMPANY LIMITED
67 Great Russell Street, London WC1B 3BT, England

and in United States of America by
FRANK CASS AND COMPANY LIMITED
c/o International Scholarly Book Services, Inc.
P.O. Box 4347, Portland, Oregon 97208

ISBN 0 7146 2967 7

This collection of papers first appeared in April 1972 as a Special
Issue on Development Indicators of the *Journal of Development Studies*,
Volume 8 No. 3, published by Frank Cass and Company Limited.

Printed in Great Britain by
Billing & Sons Limited, Guildford and London

Contents

Development Indicators: An Introduction

By Nancy Baster*

SUMMARY

Development is seen as multi-dimensional, involving changes in structure and capacity, as well as output. Three different, but overlapping, approaches to the definition of indicators are distinguished first, the definition of indicators in the context of theoretical models of development, socio-political as well as economic; second, the use of indicators in the empirical study of interrelations between economic and non-economic factors; third, the development of indicators for policy and planning. The integration of economic, social and political variables, and the identification of systematic relations between them depends on progress along each of these three dimensions.

INTRODUCTION

This issue is concerned with development (and development indicators) in a particular period of time and in a particular historical context—namely in the context of the changes that are taking place in the less-developed or low-income countries of the third world in the period since World War II.

It is one of the assumptions underlying the issue that the actual historical development of the countries of the third world is multi-dimensional, that this development has political, social and economic dimensions, however these are defined. It clearly makes nonsense to talk about the development of a newly independent country in Africa or Asia without, for example, taking into consideration the fact of political independence with all its ramifications, or the fact of social stratification in a multi-racial society, with all its implications. In fact, the extent to which, not only amongst economists, development tends to be subsumed under economic development is a constant source of surprise. For example, there is no entry under 'Development' in the *International Encyclopaedia of Social Sciences*. Under the entry 'Developing countries' the reader is referred to economic growth; industrialization; modernization; nationalism; power transition; stagnation; technical assistance. If the reader follows through under "Modernization", he or she finds this by D. Lerner: 'modernization is therefore the process of social change in which development is the economic component'. However important the economic dimension of development, it is dangerous to use it as a proxy for development.

* Lecturer, Overseas Courses, Social Administration Department, University College of Swansea. I should like to thank the United Nations Research Institute for Social Development in Geneva for providing hospitality in summer 1971, making it possible for me to prepare a first draft of this paper. I also have to thank former colleagues at UNRISD and present colleagues at Swansea, as well as Dudley Seers. Michael Lipton, and Richard Jolly of the Institute of Development Studies at the University of Sussex, for helpful comments on the earlier draft. My debt to those who contributed articles to this issue is reflected, I hope not too inadequately, in this introductory paper.

Another assumption running through the issue is that development involves changes in structure and institutions as well as growth, or output. Changes in structure in this context refer to changes in the relation between parts making up the whole, e.g. changes in the pattern of production, changes in the occupational structure of the population, changes in the social structure and pattern of distribution. Structural changes can also refer to organizational changes which affect efficiency and responsiveness to new demands. Structural change can also be broadly interpreted to include changes in institutions, such as property, legal and religious institutions. In the low-income countries which are involved in the complex process of building national independence, political, social and economic development *implies* changing structures, establishing new ways of doing things, and developing new organizations. In other words, the choice of components and indicators of development should reflect changes in the capacity to attain development objectives, as well as the extent to which the objectives are attained.

Tied up with this emphasis on changes in structure and institutions is the fact that the development of the previously dependent countries has to be seen within the context of an international system dominated by the rich industrialized countries. Growth of national independence is an important aspect of development; the demand for independent political status, for indigenous personnel in key positions, for greater control of foreign investment, for the development of indigenous technology, for a change in the structure of trade, is part of this desire for national autonomy seen as a major element in development.

The point of these introductory remarks is to emphasize certain characteristics of development in the context of the less-developed countries, which appear relevant to the discussion of development indicators. The first is the multidimensional character of development. The second is the need to take into account structural and institutional change as well as expansion (or capacity as well as output). The third is the position of a country within the international system.

DEVELOPMENT VALUES

There is an underlying assumption running through the previous paragraphs that development to be meaningful is not just change but is related to development values. A distinction is made in this paper between development as a normative concept, and development as an empirical process of change. It is argued that development is necessarily a normative concept, and involves values, goals and standards which make it possible to compare a present state against a preferred one. This raises immediately the question of whose values and goals are to be taken into account in assessing development. Planners' values or people's values? Market values or politically determined values? Most national 'welfare functions', as far as they are explicitly stated, are a mixture of these different elements.

The analysis of development goals is part of the analysis of development. Gunnar Myrdal, for example, starts his analysis of development in South Asia by making explicit [*Myrdal, 1968, Vol. 1, Part 1, Ch. 2*] a number of modernization ideals which are taken to be *relevant* and *significant* in the Asian context, meaning that they are relevant in that they reflect actual values held by people who are concerned with the problems being studied, and significant in that these people are influential in moulding public policy. Others have emphasized the importance of development plans for indicating preferences. Rosenstein-Rodan has written in a recent paper (*Rosenstein-Rodan, 1969, p. 4*) 'National planning is a method that provides additional information which the normal market mechanism cannot provide, not only about means, but also about ends. National development objectives are revealed which reflect the society's scale of values, or value judgments incorporated in a social welfare function. These objectives relate not only to a rate of growth of income, but also to income distribution and other social goals.' Both these approaches assume that it makes sense to talk about a generally accepted core of development values. Both tend to minimise problems arising from differences in the degree of articulation of the values of different social groups, and from the possibility of conflict of values between the élite and the mass of the population.

The same questions arise when it comes to the value premises implicit in cross-national measures of development. It is usually assumed that these are related to values about which there is a general consensus reflected in the recommendations and programmes of the international organizations. For example, the components and indicators recommended for the international definition and measurement of levels of living are based on the 'generally accepted aims for social and economic policy as determined by national or international agencies' [*United Nations, 1954, p. 7*]. The strategy elements which provide the framework for evaluating progress [*United Nations, 1971a*] during the Second Development Decade are derived from the International Development Strategy [*United Nations, 1971b*], which is the action programme agreed by the General Assembly. This again assumes that there is an internationally agreed 'welfare function' which represents a commonly accepted set of values. The assumption is that these values, which include a more equitable distribution of opportunities between countries, are accepted in spite of historical and cultural differences between countries, and in spite of conflicts of values between the rich and the poor countries.

These problems are not avoided, but arise in different form when monetary measures are used to measure development within countries, and to make comparisons between countries. Figures on national product and national income have the enormous advantage of being expressed in homogeneous units which can be aggregated. Theoretically, the exchange prices which provide the weights reflect the economic cost of producing the goods and services which go to make up the national product, and the value which people put on the goods and services produced. But as Myrdal and many others have pointed out, the use of market prices to express value itself involves a value judgement which is often not made explicit. For example, the demands (needs, goals) of different social groups are weighted according to the distribution of income, wealth and power. Prices do not reflect the real value of community services provided through the public sector, but only their costs. Many aspects of the quality of life and of the environment fall outside the market calculus. Development policy and planning is concerned almost by definition with issues where market prices provide an inadequate guide, and where values are determined through the political process rather than through the market.

A number of the contributors to this issue have dealt forthrightly with this question of development values, in some cases taking quite different positions from the one expressed here and from each other. Dudley Seers argues that 'Development is inevitably a normative concept, almost a synonym for improvement'. Development is concerned with the fulfilment of the necessary conditions for the realization of human personality, including, in the poor countries, a minimum income needed to provide basis necessities, employment opportunities, and a lessening of inequality. Value judgements about human needs and distribution are inherent in Jan Drewnowski's system of welfare indicators, although he would give greater weight to the political determination of preferences in his suggested welfare function. Donald McGranahan on the other hand takes a more empirical point of view, and suggests that a distinction might be made between development and progress: 'This conception of development as progress toward a collection of desiderata . . . or an ideal picture of the future raises a fundamental question whether development is purely a matter of progress towards ideals, or is to be conceived as an objective process that may even exclude certain ideals that are impractical to achieve at the moment, and may embrace various changes, including structural changes and changes in attitude that are not values in themselves, but are a necessary part of that process.' These differences partly reflect the point made in Charles Taylor's paper, where he suggests that the question of 'whose values' has to be looked at in two contexts, that of the people undergoing the process, and that of the scholar observing it.

THE NATURE AND PURPOSE OF INDICATORS

A development indicator represents some aspect of development, such as industrialization, health, equality, participation. It may be a direct measure of an economic or social variable in the sense that G.N.P. measures the output of goods and services, or, more often, an indirect measure of some non-measurable phenomenon. Most of the commonly accepted indicators of levels of living, for example, are indirect measures of different aspects of welfare. Opinions differ as to the boundaries of indicators. Drewnowski, for example, argues in his paper that indicators should be limited to observable and measurable phenomenon. Irma Adelman and Cynthia Taft Morris on the other hand make a case for a more flexible approach to the measurement of institutional phenomena, which would rely on expert judgement on qualitative rankings on reasonably explicit criteria of complex phenomena such as the degree of political participation.

Indicators may be disaggregated, composite (aggregated) or representative. In the first case a complex phenomenon is broken down into a number of elements or components, and indicators are selected to represent these different components. Ideally, these elements should be homogeneous, mutually exhaustive, and mutually exclusive. In the second case a single indicator is constructed by combining a number of indices, involving some system of weighting. In the third case, a representative indicator is selected as the 'best' measure of a particular phenomena on the basis of some criteria such as closeness of correlation with other indicators of the same phenomenon.[1] In all three cases the validation of the indicator depends on its reliability, sensitivity and accuracy, and on the consistency of its relation to other development indicators. In the final analysis however, the justification for particular indicators, and for particular selection processes will depend on the purpose for which they are to be used.

Development indicators are used—or needed—for a number of different purposes. They may be used to describe trends and to diagnose a particular development situation (and to compare these trends and situations); they may be used to analyse interrelations between variables; they may be used for prediction; and they may be used for planning, both for measuring targets and objectives, and for evaluating progress. To a certain extent the indicators required for these different purposes overlap, although McGranahan in his paper has provided a useful warning of the dangers of confusing indirect measures of particular phenomena with specific planning objectives. There is an emphasis in this paper (and in this issue) on the development of indicators for policy and planning, but some of the papers are focused more directly on the use of indicators for the analysis of interrelations between development variables. This difference of emphasis corresponds to the distinction made earlier between those who give greater weight to the normative aspect of development, and those who stress the empirical process of development. (In other words, it is the use of the indicator that is normative, not the indicator itself.)

THE SYSTEMATIZATION OF INDICATORS

The systematization of development indicators can be approached from two directions. It is possible to start from existing collections of data that seem relevant, and look for systematic relations between the variables, or to start with some analytical model or models in mind, and to proceed from there to the selection of indicators, and the collection of data. In practice these two approaches are not unrelated, since some sort of model, however vaguely articulated, is implicit in a systematic classification of data, and in seeking data to test an analytical model some attention has to be paid to what is available.

A vast amount of effort and resources is currently being put into the collection of statistical data both at the national and international level. Regular official statistical series are collected and published by national governments and then by international organizations. Data banks of cross-national data, and time-series going back over more than a hundred years are being collected by scholars at universities and research institutions. The focus of these various collections is rather different. Official government series have tended to concentrate on basic demographic data derived from the census, and economic series on trade, production, and consumption, and, increasingly, on information concerning those public sectors where the government has some administrative responsibility, transport, education, health, housing, perhaps social security. The same classifications tend to reappear in the international statistical yearbooks, with greater emphasis in recent years on the collection and standardisation of social statistics.[2] The non-governmental data banks built up by universities and research organisations on the other hand, have been broader in scope, and have given more weight to political series, as well as social indicators. It is interesting that political scientists in particular have played an active role in this connection.[3]

There is therefore an accumulating wealth of statistical data throwing light on economic, demographic, and to a lesser extent, on social and

political trends, although anyone who has worked with the data knows that
their availability and reliability vary directly with the level of development. Statistical information systems are still in their infancy in the majority of the less-developed countries. In spite of this the classification and
statistical analysis of the cross-national data slowly becoming available
has begun to transform our understanding of empirical trends and patterns of interrelations between these statistical series at different levels of
development.

Yet it is arguable whether these statistical series are in themselves indicators of development. Some further process of selection is required
which will depend on the purpose for which the data are needed. They
cannot all be equally useful even in describing trends, and even less in providing development indicators in the normative sense suggested earlier.
And it may very well turn out that existing statistical series do not provide
meaningful indicators for those dimensions of development which are
most significant from a theoretical or operational point of view. The systematization of development indicators depends on the prior conceptualization of the relevant components or dimensions of development, in either
a theoretical or an operational context. This point is emphasized in a number of the contributions to this issue.[4] Adelman and Morris, for example,
talk about 'the weak link between theoretical constructs and empirical
definitions', and Taylor in his paper on indicators of political development
suggests that indicators will be selected in response to theory-building:
'Good explanation cannot be found without informed perspective, and
data cannot be collected without some *a priori* notion of what to collect.'

In the three sections which follow the systematization of development
indicators will be discussed briefly within the context of (1) development
theory, (2) empirical cross-national analysis, and (3) policy and planning
(problem solving).

THEORETICAL MODELS

To what extent is it possible to draw on theoretical models in order
to define the relevant categories or components of development? The
difficulty is, of course, that while there is no shortage of models or partial
models at the present time (economic, social and political) there is no
agreement (and perhaps never can be), about a general model of development. It is impossible in a few pages to attempt an adequate review of
different theoretical models; this would require another issue of this
Journal (and another editor). What can be done is to indicate briefly the
main focus of the different disciplinary approaches, the kind of variables,
or sub-sets of variables,[5] with which each are dealing, and to consider the
possibility of integrating these different approaches in a broader theoretical model which would facilitate the specification of indicators.

Economists have, of course, developed a number of clearly specified
models of economic development involving such variables as income and
expenditure, consumption and savings, investment and output, production
and foreign trade. There is considerable agreement about a central core of
indicators of economic development. These are reflected, for example, in
the economic growth targets for the second Development Decade, which
include the annual rate of growth of national product, gross and *per capita*,
and related targets of expansion in the agricultural and industrial sectors,

in the ratio of gross savings to gross product, and expansion of exports and imports [*United Nations, 1971b, pp. 3-4*]. These are the conventional economic indicators, derived from economic theory, and integrated in the system of national accounts. To this central core could be added other national accounting variables which reflect the structural changes which are associated with the modernization and diversification of the economy, such as the structure of industrial production, or the structure of exports.[6]

Still within the boundaries of economic theory much is being done to improve national accounting (monetary) measures of national product and national income as indicators of economic welfare, and to improve comparability over time and between countries.[7] Sametz [*1968*] has argued the case for a new set of accounts for measuring economic growth, which would include upward adjustments to allow for improvement in the quality of products and the introduction of new products, and for increased leisure (less effort), and downward adjustments to allow for the decrease in non-marketed products, and for the costs of increasing urbanization and development, which include occupational costs (cost of getting to work, etc.), other social costs associated with the deterioration of the environment, and much of government expenditure on infrastructure. Issues such as distribution and employment, which have tended to fall through the net of both development theory, and national accounting, are being brought back in again. The relation between income and satisfaction of needs is being reexamined. These two last dimensions are the central themes of the papers in this issue by Dudley Seers and Riad Tabbarah. I shall be returning to them later.

At the same time the boundaries of economic analysis are being pushed outwards to include the analysis of the components of levels of living, such as education, health, housing, both as 'outcomes of expenditure', and as 'inputs' in the economic process. And finally the economic analysis of development is being stretched to include components relating to the capacity of the system to carry out the policy measures to facilitate economic development. Rosenstein-Rodan, for example, in the article mentioned earlier [*Rosenstein-Rodan, 1969*], has outlined four criteria of development, the capacity to restructure the economy, the capacity to mobilize savings, and the capacity to repay foreign loans. The categories include institutional and non-economic factors which lie outside the traditional sub-set of economic variables, where concepts and indicators are less clearly defined, and the links with economic variables less clearly specified. There is clearly an overlap with other conceptual frameworks, and other subsets of indicators.

Although levels of living and social indicators generally do not fall into any neat disciplinary niche, they play an important role in development policy (as they have in the whole history of social reform), and call for separate discussion here. As defined internationally, levels of living refers to the satisfaction of needs or wants in certain well-defined and quantifiable aspects of the total life situation. The internationally recommended components include health, food consumption and nutrition, education, employment and conditions of work, housing, social security, clothing, recreation, human freedoms, together with a number of 'background' conditions, including demographic conditions, aggregate consumption and savings and transportation and communications. Indicators have been recommended under most of the components [*United Nations, 1961*].

In practice there is a good deal of confusion about the place of level of living indicators within development models. In the broadest interpretation improvement in level of living becomes synonymous with development, a challenge to national income as an indicator of welfare. It is argued by Drewnowski, for example, in the paper he has contributed to this issue and elsewhere, that development should be measured in terms of the final aims of development, that is in terms of an improvement of level of living, or welfare. His level of living index provides an illustration of such an approach. Others take a rather narrower sectoral approach in which indicators of health, education, social security, etc., are linked with the appropriate public expenditure programmes. A third interpretation, somewhere in between these two, takes the point of view that improvement in health, levels of education, etc., are development objectives in themselves, in the same way that a higher rate of economic growth and expansion of employment are development objectives, and should be included along with other development values as part of an interdependent system.[8] In the International Development Strategy [*United Nations, 1971b*] the improvement in levels of living is seen as both 'determining factors and end results in development'. Indicators of education, health, nutrition, housing and social welfare are included both amongst the criteria of achievement and as conditions.

Indicators of levels of living are intended to represent dimensions of welfare. They have recently been caught up in what has come to be known as the 'social indicator movement', which is concerned with a much wider range of social phenomena. Discussions of social indicators have ranged from the welfare dimensions included in the levels of living indicators, to a wider range of social relations and social problems, including such dimensions as social stratification and social mobility, inequality and poverty, participation in social and political life, and social cohesion and social conflict.[9] Clarification of concepts and the definition of components and indicators has proceeded much further in some of these areas than others. It may be useful in the present context, as Drewnowski suggests in his paper, to make a distinction between the welfare aspects, and the social relations dimensions, the latter falling more directly within the boundaries of political and sociological theory.

Political scientists have been concerned with a quite different theoretical framework, and with a different subset of variables. Almond and Coleman [*1960*] developed a functional analysis of the political system, stressing such functions as the communications function, the authoritative function, interest articulation, political socialization function. Political development was associated with the extent of complexity and specialization of national political institutions. Organski [*1965*] stressed the role of national integration, and the improvement in government efficiency in utilizing the human and material resources of the polity for national goals. More recently more attention has been given to problems of measuring the performance and capability of the political system. In a review article, L. Pye [*1968*], drawing on an earlier article by Almond [*1965*], outlined three dimensions of political development: *equality*, which includes the transition in attitude from subject to active citizens, greater reliance upon achievement rather than ascription, universalistic and impersonal rules and laws rather than particularistic; *capacity*, meaning the rational organization of administration, and increase in the capabilities of the political system; *differentiation*, which involves structural specialization, and the integration of roles and structure. Each of these structural dimensions in turn affects the functions of the political system.

Within the field of political theory it seems therefore that there has been a shift from a functional to a more developmental approach, and from a more theoretical to a more operationally orientated approach, with a consequent shift in emphasis in the kind of indicators needed. This link between concepts and indicators is discussed by Taylor in his contribution to this issue. The problems involved in conceptualizing a complex phenomenon such as 'participation in the political process' (an aspect of political equality), and translating this concept into components and indicators is discussed at some length in the paper by Adelman and Morris. As will be seen later 'the extent of political participation' was one of the indicators of political development included by the same authors in their earlier quantitative analysis of economic, political and social indicators [*Adelman and Morris, 1967*].

Sociological theories of development have a strong 'organic' tradition, going back particularly to the parallels drawn by the classical sociologists in the nineteenth century between development of society, and organic growth, or evolution. Society was seen as advancing from a simple to a complex state through a process of differentiation and adaptation.

Nisbet [*1969*] has argued that this metaphor of growth, drawn from the analogy of change in society to change in the growth processes of the individual organism, and intended to explain the 'natural' growth of abstract entities, lies behind much of the sociological analysis of the development of the countries of the third world since World War II. Development and modernization have been interpreted as a unilinear movement between two ideal-types, with the highly industrialized western country at one end, and the traditional agricultural society at the other.[10] The sociology of development then becomes a question of identifying and analysing the social, cultural, and psychological changes associated with economic development and industrialization in terms of such dimensions as social values (communally orientated values versus individualistic achievement orientated values), social organization (extended family versus nuclear family), occupational structure, social class and social mobility, urbanization, communications. This suggests a particular set of relatively conventional dimensions and indicators of social change.

There is another strand of sociological theory which is focused more directly on the relations between social groups and between societies, and on such issues as social cohesion and social conflict, and on the capacity of society to integrate and organize the interests and pressures of different social groups. This approach, which brings the interests of sociologists close to those of political scientists, is reflected for example in Deutsch's theory of social mobilization and political development [*Deutsch, 1961*] where he put forward the hypothesis that development is the result of the balance between the increased pressure on governments resulting from social mobilization, reflected in such indicators as exposure to modernity, mass media, voting participation, literacy, geographical mobility, population growth, and the increasing capacity of governments to cope with these pressures, reflected in such indicators as the occupational shift out of agriculture, urbanization, cultural and political assimilation and income growth. Further work on the concept of the capacity of society to respond to pressures and to function efficiently, would probably show significant overlap with the dimensions of political development mentioned earlier (equality or participation, capacity or efficiency, and differentiation of structure and roles), and with the 'non-economic' dimensions of economic development suggested in Rosenstein-Rodan's 'capacity to restructure the economy', 'capacity to use capital productively', and so on.

From these and other approaches (psychological theories, for example, have been omitted altogether from the discussion), it would be possible conceptually to construct subsets of variables, or components and indicators, relating to different dimensions of development. Such classifications have in fact guided the selection of indicators used in recent cross-national studies of development, as will be seen in the following section. Although each theoretical approach is concerned with a particular set of variables, there is considerable overlap, as we have seen, amongst the subsets used in the different approaches.

However, although some of the elements are common to the different approaches, the way in which they are combined depends on the theoretical approach. To an economist, literacy is an outcome of expenditure on literacy programmes; it may also be considered as a factor contributing to productivity. To the political scientist literacy is an aspect of political socialization. To the sociologist it is an aspect of social mobilization, or agent of social change. It is very difficult to see how these different approaches can be homogenized into an integrated theory of development which will make it possible to define an agreed set of components and indicators. The predominant tendency from a theoretical point of view is to try to combine the different sets of variables within a broad economic framework. This is so even when the framework is as broad as that suggested by Myrdal [*1968*] for example, where the conditions or dimensions of development include, besides the more conventional economic dimensions, categories relating to levels of living, values and attitudes, and social institutions.[11] However it is possible to envisage alternative integrating frameworks. One would be a political-sociological framework, developing further along the lines suggested earlier. Another would be the 'system' approach proposed by McGranahan in his paper in this issue. It will be argued later that more progress is likely to be made in integrating variables from different subsets within an operationally-orientated approach.

THE EMPIRICAL MEASUREMENT OF DEVELOPMENT:
CROSS-SECTORAL COMPARISONS

This brief analysis of different theoretical approaches provides a background for an equally brief review of some recent quantitative studies of development indicators. These have been selected in order to illustrate different approaches and different methodologies.

A study made by Beckerman and Bacon [*1966*] may be used to illustrate a method of using non-monetary development indicators to estimate national income measures for purposes of making international comparisons of income levels. The essence of the method, as they describe it, is to find the 'best' statistical relationship, on the basis of inter-country comparisons for such countries for which independent estimates of relative real income or consumption levels exist, between relative real income or consumption and selected non-monetary indicators for which data are readily available in most countries, and then to use these statistical relationships to predict, from data on the non-monetary indicators, the relative real income levels of all countries for which such data exist.

This method was used to predict the real private consumption per head from a number of non-monetary indicators. A preliminary selection of indicators was made on the basis of their correlation with independent observations of real consumption per head. The final equation used to predict real private consumption per head included seven variables which were found to provide the highest correlation coefficients. These variables were:

> annual apparent crude steel consumption per head
> annual cement production per head
> annual number of domestic letters sent by head
> stock of radio receivers per head
> stock of telephones per head
> stock of road vehicles per head
> annual meat consumption per head

The authors of this study are not questioning the validity of national accounting measures of output and income. The non-monetary indicators have no independent significance, they are simply indicators of consumption income in situations where reliable income data are not available. In fact in another publication one of the authors [*Beckerman, 1966*] expresses a good deal of scepticism about what he calls arbitrary collections of disparate indicators which are not linked with national accounting measures, and which have no precise theoretical meaning.

In contrast to this illustration we may cite the study of the contents and measurement of development carried out by UNRISD [*1970*] which is referred to in McGranahan's paper, but not described there in any detail. This study, quite different in purpose from the previous one, is intended as an exploratory study of ways of analysing and measuring development in its combined economic and social aspects. It is concerned with the selection of the most appropriate indicators of socio-economic development, with the analysis of relationships between these indicators at different levels of development, and the construction of a synthetic index of development which is more representative and sensitive than *per capita* G.N.P. to general development levels.

The study started with seventy-three social and economic variables (including structural variables, such as indicators of demographic structure or labour force structure) which were eventually reduced to forty-two and then eighteen highly correlated core variables. The selection was based on the assumption that variables with high intercorrelations on the average with other development variables are better development indicators than those with low correlation. Consideration was also given to maintaining some balance between indicators representing different dimensions of development. Thus the core indicators (which are listed in Table 1), included nine social (mainly levels of living) indicators, and nine economic indicators. Thirteen of the indicators are developmental, in the sense that they reflect commonly accepted development values, such as health, or agricultural productivity, while the remaining five are structural, includ-

TABLE 1

UNRISD LIST OF CORE INDICATORS OF SOCIO-ECONOMIC DEVELOPMENT

1 Expectation of life at birth
2. Percent population in localities of 20,000 and over
3. Consumption of animal protein, *per capita*, per day
4. Combined primary and secondary enrolment
5. Vocational enrolment ratio
6. Average number of persons per room
7. Newspaper circulation per 1,000 population
10. Percent economically active population in electricity, gas, water, etc,
11. Agricultural production per male agricultural worker
12. Percent adult male labour in agriculture
13. Electricity consumption, kWh *per capita*
14. Steel consumption, kg. *per capita*
15. Energy consumption, kg. of coal equivalent *per capita*
16. Percent G.D.P. derived from manufacturing
17. Foreign trade *per capits*, in 1960 U.S. dollars
18. Percent salaried and wage earners to total economically active population

Source: UNRISD, *Contents and Measurement of Socio-economic Development*, Geneva, 1970, p. 63.

ing those indicators of economic and social structure which are closely correlated with development values.

The method of best-fitting curves was used to establish the empirical correspondence between the eighteen core indicators at different levels of development, on the basis of cross-national comparisons. The system of correspondence points was also used to determine critical points for converting the indicators to a common scale. A general index of development was then constructed, using a system of shifting weights derived from the degree of correlation of each indicator with other indicators at each level of development. The resulting index of socio-economic development was found to correlate more highly with individual economic and social indicators than the more conventional index of *per capita* G.N.P.

The UNRISD study is based on the assumption of interdependence between all the variables, and reflects a system approach to development, in contrast to the Beckerman and Bacon study, which is placed squarely within the context of economic theory.

The quantitative study of development indicators made by Adelman and Morris [*1967*], differs in a number of respects from the two previous illustrations. The purpose of the study as described by the authors was to gain more precise empirical knowledge about the interdependence of economic and non-economic (particularly institutional) aspects of the development process. It was intended to provide 'semi-quantitative' insights into the behaviour of a range of variables which are considered by sociologists and political scientists to play an important role in the early stages of development, and yet which are not usually dealt with systematically because they are difficult to quantify.

Seventy-four developing countries were classified according to forty-one variables, which are listed in Table 2. The variables were of three types: those for which classification could be based on published statistics, those for which it was necessary to combine statistical and qualitative elements, and those which were purely qualitative in nature. This use of qualitative indicators in a quantitative study was one of the innovations in the analysis which is discussed in a paper by the authors in this issue.

TABLE 2

SOCIAL, POLITICAL AND ECONOMIC VARIABLES: ADELMAN AND MORRIS

Size of the traditional agricultural sector
Extent of dualism
Extent of urbanization
Character of basic social organization
Importance of the indigenous middle class
Extent of social mobility
Extent of literacy
Extent of mass communication
Degree of cultural and ethnic homogeneity
Degree of social tension
Crude fertility rate
Degree of modernization of outlook
Degree of national integration and sense of national unity
Extent of centralization of political power
Strength of democratic institutions
Degree of freedom of political opposition and press
Degree of competitiveness of political parties
Predominant basis of the political party system
Strength of the labour movement
Political strength of the traditional élite
Political strength of the military
Degree of administrative efficiency
Extent of leadership commitment to economic development
Extent of political stability
Per capita G.N.P. in 1961
Rate of growth of real *per capita* G.N.P.: 1950/51–1963/64
Abundance of natural resources
Gross investment rate
Level of modernization of industry
Change in degree of industrialization since 1950
Character of agricultural organization
Level of modernization of techniques in agriculture.
Degree of improvement in agricultural productivity since 1950
Level of adequacy of physical overhead capital
Degree of improvement in physical overhead capital sonce 1950
Level of effectiveness of the tax system
Degree of improvement in the tax system since 1950
Level of effectiveness of financial institutions
Degree of improvement in human resources
Structure of foreign trade

Source: Adelman and Morris, [1967, pp. 16, 17.]

Factor analysis was used to throw light on the interdependence between the social and political variables and the level of economic development, and to analyse the relation between various aspects of social, political and economic change and economic growth and modernization in terms of a smaller number of independent factors at three different levels of socio-economic development. Levels of socio-economic development were defined by using scores or factor loadings on a factor representing varied aspects of socio-economic structure. The rationale for the use of factor analysis in this and other studies and a brief note on some of the findings can be found in a recent article by the same authors [*1971*]. The authors argue there that these 'empirical procedures may be more fruitful than hypothesis testing for the initial exploration of those wider interactions involved in economic modernisation' [*1971, p. 91*].

Finally, a brief reference may be made to the quantitative analysis of human resource development made by Harbison and his colleagues at Princeton University [*1970*]. The purpose of the study was to explore and apply various methods of ranking, classifying and comparing countries or regions on the basis of indicators of development and modernization. The analysis was based on forty variables selected for their availability, reliability, and relevance to human resource development, with a major emphasis on indicators of educational development, including indicators of stock, flow and expenditure on education.

The main interest in the study lies in the use of the taxonomic method (first developed by a group of Polish mathematicians in the 1950s, and developed by Hellwig [*1970*] for the UNESCO studies of human resource indicators) for ranking, classifying and comparing countries. Eight indices were constructed for seven components (economic, cultural, health, educational effort, high-level manpower (2), demographic) plus a composite index. Indicators were converted to a common scale by a process of standardization based on the mean and standard deviation of each indicator. Countries were classified into homogeneous groups by calculating the numerical distances on each variable. The 'pattern of development' for each country was measured by a ranking of differences on each variable from the 'ideal' country in each group. A 'measure of development' was obtained by calculating the percentage distribution from the ideal for each indicator. The method therefore is essentially classificatory, covering a relatively small but important area of development. No attempt has been made to reduce the number of variables through correlation analysis or factor analysis, and problems of representativeness and weighting are left on one side.

These four studies are all concerned with the quantitative analysis of relations between development indicators at different levels of development, drawing on cross-national data, but otherwise they are very different in approach, content and method of analysis, as well as in their purpose. The purpose of the UNRISD study, for example, is to construct a measure of socio-economic development, which will take into account social, economic, and structural aspects of development, and which provides a tool both for diagnosis and prediction, and the selection of indicators and the methodology used reflect this aim. The purpose of the Adelman and Morris study is to explore the interactions between institutional and other factors in the process of economic modernization, and this is reflected in their choice of indicators, and the use of factor analysis to examine the interdependence between variables.

There seems to be considerable agreement with the point made at the end of McGranahan's paper that in order to explore further the interrelation between economic and non-economic factors in development it is important to analyse time-series as well as cross-sectoral data, and still more, to go beyond national data to the analysis of interrelations at the regional and local level.[13] In the meantime, Adelman and Dalton [*1971*] have taken a big step in this direction with their recent quantitative analysis of modernization in Indian villages. In one of the contributions to this issue, Galtung has analysed the relation between education and economic growth in a number of countries, illustrating graphically the different shape of this relationship over time, and in different countries. In another paper Hechter has analysed the pattern of regional development in the

United Kingdom over the past hundred years, drawing on a number of development indicators to illustrate the divergent patterns of inter- and intra-regional growth.

DEVELOPMENT INDICATORS IN AN OPERATIONAL CONTEXT

The quantitative analysis of development indicators at the regional or local level suggests one avenue for exploring the interrelations between economic and non-economic aspects of development. Another is through the development of linkages between indicators in a policy-orientated context. We return in this final section to the distinction between theoretical analysis and policy-orientated analysis, between indicators needed for diagnosis and analysis of interrelations, and indicators needed for policy and planning. Most development programmes or sets of programmes have to be defined in terms of a number of variables drawn from sub-sets 'belonging' conventionally to different disciplinary approaches. A problem-orientated approach draws extensively on the current emphasis on system analysis, theories of decision-making and organization theory. The delimitation of boundaries and sub-systems, the relation between resources, activities, and functions or outcomes, and the relations between different sub-systems, provides a generalized framework through which it may become possible to integrate the different dimensions of development in a number of policy-orientated models.

Such a policy-orientated approach involves a number of steps: defining major areas or themes of development policy: clarifying the concepts involved and the major dimensions of the problem; defining measures or operational indicators for these different dimensions; tracing the links between themes. This process of translating theoretical concepts into quantitative indicators is a crucial one, which is discussed in some of the papers in this issue. The definition of major areas or themes of development is essentially an empirical process reflecting urgent policy issues in the developing countries. This can be illustrated with reference to three interrelated development themes; equality or distribution, technological change, and institutional change, particularly political participation. These are all complex concepts which need further clarification if adequate indicators are to be developed. They are all themes which are only partially covered by national accounting, or conventional economic indicators of development. They are all themes which cut across the sub-systems of variables discussed earlier.

Distribution and minimum income levels

Indicators reflecting aspects of equality, particularly distribution of income and minimum income levels are dealt with in a number of the papers in this issue, and will only be touched on briefly here.

Dudley Seers, in the article which follows this, has defined three closely related themes (poverty [minimum income levels], employment, and distribution of income [equality]) as major economic criteria of development, and discusses the development of operational measures and indicators in relation to each of these three dimensions. A distinction is made between indicators of distribution and indicators of poverty or minimum income levels, the latter introducing the concept of the income needed to meet

B

basic physical requirements relating to food, clothing, footwear, shelter, etc. Seers discusses problems of defining and measuring minimum standards. or requirements, in relation to income, while Tabbarah, in his paper on 'The Adequacy of Income', puts the determination of minimum requirements (or poverty line) within the context of a generalized concept of adequacy of income, which takes into account the level of needs (as revealed in family budget data) of different socio-economic groups.

Charles Elliott goes further into the theoretical discussion of distribution of income in relation to economic development, and makes a strong case for measures which reflect differentials in income and availability of social services between relevant socio-economic groups, illustrating this by means of a simple matrix incorporating data for Zambia.

Both Seers and Elliott stress the links between distribution of income (and assets), and other forms of social and political inequality. The development of indicators to reflect these different dimensions of equality involves drawing on relevant variables from the different subsets discussed earlier, again within a particular operational context.

Technological change[14]

Technological change provides a second illustration of a complex issue which calls for the development of a wider range of indicators. The ability to apply science and technology lies at the heart of economic modernization and social change. Conventional indicators of economic growth or of investment throw little light on the process involved. Investment does not necessarily reflect technological innovation. It is necessary first to elucidate the concept and to break it down into manageable parts. In its broadest sense technologies are bodies of skills, knowledge and procedures for making, using and doing useful things. To the economist 'technological progress consists of all better methods and improvement of organisation that improve the efficiency (i.e. the utilization) of both old capital and new and result in an upward shift of the production function' [Bell, 1968, p. 178]. There are a number of different concepts involved here, as Solow, Denison, and many others have pointed out in the continued discussion of the factors in economic growth and their empirical measurement. First, scientific knowledge, which has to be distinguished from technological change. Bell defines knowledge as that which is objectively known, an intellectual property which is part of social overhead investment, measured by such indicators as the number of scientific journals and learned papers, by expenditure on R and D, and the stock of high-level scientists. Second, technological progress, which has been defined above, including not only new methods embodied in new equipment and machinery, measured by such indicators as rate of output per man-hour of labour, use of mechanical power, use of irrigation and fertilizers, but also better organization (enterprise, administrative efficiency), better information about available technologies, better communication, and better education and skills in terms of professional and technical personnel, numbers of scientists and engineers, and more 'development-relevant' education (to borrow Galtung's term).

In the developing countries these general concepts have to be adapted to the major concern with the development of indigenous technology.[15] Knowledge becomes knowledge which is relevant to the problems of the developing countries. Technological progress and innovation involves the adaptation of existing techniques as well as the introduction of new techniques. Information about available technologies and sources of supply plays an important role. Organization, information and education and skills are essential parts of the process of technological change. As G. Jones [*1971*] has recently reminded us, technological transfer and diffusion has to be seen as a cultural, social and political process, involving institutionalized channels of action.

The further clarification of these different dimensions of technological change would lead to the selection of variables which would cut across the various disciplinary sub-sets defined earlier, and drawing their meaning from the particular operational context.

Institutional change and political participation

The significance of institutional change as a characteristic of development has been stressed in the opening paragraphs of this paper, but this is an area where clarification of relevant phenomena within an operational context is only just beginning. From an operational point of view, for example, a distinction has to be made between organizational changes such as the strengthening of public administration, or improvement in the efficiency of tax administration, and institutional change which is more closely bound up with the structure of property and power, and with social organization and social stratification. The analysis of institutional change involves elaborating and clarifying complex issues such as the concentration of economic power, the degree of social cohesion, and the degree of political participation.

The relevant economic institutions in this latter sense are those relating to the concentration of property and wealth. The critical relation is that between the property structure and such conditions of development as technological innovation and utilization of resources. National accounting measures of wealth and income from wealth are of limited use in developing countries. More has been done in developing measures relating to the structure of land tenure, the degree of concentration of land holdings, and the degree of indebtedness of farmers. (Such indicators are suggested in the system of indicators proposed for evaluating progress in the second development decade.) Parallel indicators of industrial concentration are less developed. Relevant indicators will vary according to the level and kind of development. For example, in one situation development may be related to the break-up of tribal control of communally held land, in another to a decrease in the inequality of land-holding, in another to a loosening of the power of the money-lender in the villages.

Similarly with regard to social institutions there are a number of different dimensions involved which call for much further clarification. Social stratification, social cohesion, social mobility, all affect social relations and attitudes, and are related to the capacity of society to respond to and to integrate the demands of different social groups. Again, relevant indicators will vary according to particular situations; social constraints may relate for example to the caste system, to relations between ethnic groups, or to family and tribal structure.

The degree of political participation is a further dimension of institutional change which is discussed in detail by Adelman and Morris in their contribution to this issue and there is no need to elaborate further here. They trace the steps by which they arrived at a redefinition of the concept of political participation in terms of basic components by a process of testing *a priori* concepts against actual country situations and show how the final selection of indicators was related to these basic components.

The development of a system of indicators representing dimensions of the three themes discussed briefly here, equality and distribution, technological change, participation would draw from the different subsets of variables, and would be closely linked with each other, for example, the kind of technological change would affect employment and the distribution of income, and would be affected by the degree of political participation. Different patterns of relations between indicators would represent clearly defined development 'styles', with a capital-intensive technology dominated by foreign investment, relatively greater inequality, relatively lower degree of political participation contrasted with a more indigenous type of technological development, relatively greater equality and relatively higher level of participation. The two contrasting 'styles' would be further reflected in different patterns of international relations.

CONCLUSION

This brings the discussion back to the initial definition of development as concerned with structural change as well as output, and with relations between countries as well as within countries.

The aim of this introductory paper has been to provide a general review and framework for the articles which follow. The scope is necessarily broad. Discussion about development indicators reflects current discussion about development theory and development planning, and different approaches are reflected in different ideas about the nature and scope of indicators and the relations between them.

A number of strongly held, sometimes conflicting, points of view are expressed in the papers. Two distinctions in particular stand out. The first is the distinction between those who would integrate indicators representing different conditions of development (different subsets of variables) within an economic framework, however broadly defined, and those who are looking towards a broader system approach. The second distinction, not unrelated to the first, is between those who see indicators primarily within an operational and planning context, and those who see them primarily within an analytical context.

I have suggested in this paper that further work on indicators is likely to proceed in three rather different (but related) directions. The first is through the sharpening of theoretical models, or partial models, within particular disciplines, particularly those where interest in operational model-building is relatively recent. The second is through the quantitative analysis of interrelations between different subsets of variables, particularly at the local level. The third is through the specification of relevant variables within an operational and problem-orientated context. Development indicators are currently at the same stage that national accounting indicators were some forty or fifty years ago, and it is still too early to force them into any particular mould.

NOTES

1. The methodology of indicators is discussed in a number of the papers in this issue, particularly in those by McGranahan, Adelman and Morris, and Drewnowski. Much of the literature on the methodology of social indicators is equally relevant to development indicators. See, for example, Olson [*1969*].

2. The two Compendia of Social Statistics put out by the United Nations (1963 and 1968) included data on Population and Vital Statistics, Health Conditions, Food Consumption and Nutrition, Housing, Education and Cultural Activities, Labour Force and Conditions of Employment, Social Security and Income and Expenditure. The development of a system of demographic, manpower, and social statistics series has now been given high priority in the programme of the United Nations Statistical Office and the Conference of European Statisticians.

3. Amongst the better known of these collections are Banks and Textor [*1964*], which as its name indicates focuses on political data, and Russett *et al.* [*1964*], which includes cross-national data on Human Resources, Government and Politics, Communications, Wealth, Health, Education, Family and Social Relations, Distribution of Wealth and Income, Religion. The Banks' collection has now been expanded to include time-series going back to 1815 [*Banks, 1971*], and a second edition of the Russett collection with time-series going back to 1950 is to be published shortly [*Taylor and Hudson, 1972*]. Additional references are given in Taylor's paper in this issue.

4. The same point has been well made by Pye [*1968*], where he writes: 'Our feeling was that it might be all too tempting to rely excessively upon available socio-economic data, which are customarily collected not with an eye to their relevance for comparative political analysis, and thus not to establish the essential political categories for which data should be gathered.'

5. See the discussion of the interdependence of sub-systems of variables handled by different disciplines in Lipton [*1970*].

6. Indicators which have long since become accepted tools of development analysis, thanks to the pioneering work of Colin Clark, Simon Kuznets, and others.

7. The literature on international comparisons of real income is not reviewed here. A brief review can be found in Beckerman [*1966*]. Other references are given in Tabbarah's paper in this issue.

8. This approach is reflected in the UNRISD system of indicators [*UNRISD, 1970*].

9. This short reference does not do justice to the extent and wealth of literature on social indicators which has appeared in the last few years. See, for example, Bauer [*1966*], U.S. Department of Health, Education and Welfare [*1969*], Gross [*1969*], Delors [*1970*], U.K. Central Statistical Office [*1970*], United Nations [*1971c*]. Additional references are given in the paper by Drewnowski in this issue.

10. See the critical evaluation of modernization theories in Bernstein [*1971*].

11. See Myrdal [*1968, Vol. III, Appendix 2*]. The categories of conditions in Myrdal's system include (1) output and incomes, (2) conditions of production, (3) levels of living, (4) attitudes towards life and work, (5) institutions, and (6) policies. Myrdal adds that this structure of categories represents the conditions in a country viewed from an 'eceonomic' angle.

12. For further details, see McGranahan [*1971*].

13. Both the Institute of Development Studies and the U.N. Research Institute for Social Development, for example, are now emphasizing projects concerned with village level studies and with the analysis of development indicators at the local level. See the reference to the I.D.S. village studies in Lipton [*1970*].

14. It was unfortunately not possible to include a paper on indicators of technological development in this issue, as had been hoped.

15. Some of these issues have recently been discussed by Singer [*1971*].

REFERENCES

Adelman, I., and Dalton, G., 1971, 'A Factor Analysis of Modernisation in Village India', *Economic Journal*, Vol. 81, September.
Adelman, I., and Morris, C. T., 1967, *Society, Politics and Economic Develpoment*, Baltimore: The Johns Hopkins Press.
Adelman, I., and Morris, C. T., 1971, 'Analysis-of-Variance Techniques for the Study of Economic Development', *Journal of Development Studies*, Vol. 8, No. 1.
Almond, G. A., 1965, 'A Developmental Approach to Political Systems', *World Politics*, Vol. 17, January.

Almond, G. A., and Coleman, J. S., eds., 1960, *The Politics of the Developing Areas*, Princeton: Princeton University Press.

Banks, Arthur, and Textor, Robert, 1964, *A Cross Polity Survey*, Cambridge, Mass.: M.I.T. Press.

Banks, Arthur, 1971, *Cross Polity Time Series Data*, Cambridge, Mass.: M.I.T. Press.

Bauer, R. A., 1966, *Social Indicators*, Cambridge, Mass.: M.I.T. Press.

Beckerman, W., 1966, *International Comparisons of Real Incomes*, Paris: OECD Development Centre.

Beckerman, W., and Bacon, R., 1966, 'International Comparisons of Income Levels: a Suggested New Measure', *Economic Journal*, Vol. 76.

Bell, D., 1968, 'The Measurement of Knowledge and Technology', in E. Sheldon and W. B. Moore, eds., *Indicators of Social Change: Concepts and Measurement*, New York: Russell Sage Foundation.

Bernstein, H., 1971, 'Modernization Theory and the Sociological Study of Development', *Journal of Development Studies*, Vol. 7, No. 2, January.

Delors, Jacques, ed., 1970, *Les Indicateurs Sociaux*, Paris: S.E.D.E.I.S.

Deutsch, K. W., 1961, 'Social Mobilization and Political Development', *American Political Science Review*, Vol. 55, September.

Gross, Bertram, ed., 1969, *Social Intelligence for America's Future*, Boston: Allyn.

Harbison, F. H., Maruhnic, J., and Resnick, J. R., 1970, *Quantitative Analysis of Modernization and Development*, Industrial Relations Section, Princeton University.

Hellwig, Z., 1970, 'Procedure for Evaluating High-level Manpower Data and Typology of Countries by means of the Taxonomic Method', UNESCO working paper, mimeo.

Jones, Graham, 1971, *The Role of Science and Technology in Developing Countries*, London: Oxford University Press.

Lipton, Michael, 1970, 'Interdisciplinary Studies in the Less Developed Countries', *Journal of Development Studies*, Vol. 7, October.

McGranahan, D. V., 1971, 'The Interrelation between Social and Economic Development', *Social Science Information*, 9 (6).

Myrdal, Gunnar, 1968, *Asian Drama*, 3 vols., New York: Pantheon.

Nisbet, R. A., 1969, *Social Change and History: Aspects of the Western Theory of Development*, London: Oxford University Press.

Olson, M., Jr., 1969, 'Social Indicators and Social Accounts', *Socio-economic Planning Sciences*, Vol. 2.

Organski, A. F. K., 1965, *The Stages of Political Development*, New York: Alfred A. Knopf.

Pye, L. W., 1968, 'Political Systems and Political Development', in S. Rokkan, ed., *Comparative Research across Cultures and Nations*, Paris: Mouton.

Rosenstein-Rodan, P. N., 1969, 'Criteria for Evaluation of National Development Effort', *Journal of Development Planning*, No. 1, New York: United Nations.

Russett, Bruce, M., *et al.*, 1964, *World Handbook of Political and Social Indicators*, New Haven, Conn.: Yale University Press.

Sametz, A. W., 1968, 'Production of Goods and Services: the Measurement of Economic Growth', in E. Sheldon and W. B. Moore, eds., *Indicators of Social Change: Concepts and Measurements*, New York: Russel Sage Foundation.

Singer, H. W., 1971, 'The Technology Gap and the Developing Countries', mimeo, paper presented to the British Association Meeting at Swansea, September.

Taylor, Charles Lewis, and Hudson, Michael C., 1972, *World Handbook of Political and Social Indicators* (Second Edition), New Haven: Yale University Press.

United Kingdom, Central Statistical Office, 1970, *Social Trends*, No. 1, London: H.M.S.O.

United Nations, 1954, *Report on International Definition and Measurement of Standards and Levels of Living*, New York: United Nations.

United Nations, 1961, *International Definition and Measurement of Levels of Living: An Interim Guide*, New York: United Nations.

United Nations, 1963, *Compendium of Social Statistics*, New York: United Nations:

United Nations, 1968, *Compendium of Social Statistics*, New York: United Nations.

United Nations, 1971a, 'A System of Over-all Review and Appraisal of the Objectives and Policies of the International Development Strategy', E/5040, 28 May, mimeo.

United Nations, 1971b, *International Development Strategy*, New York: United Nations.

United Nations, 1971c, 'French Experience in Respect of Social Indicators', in *Long Term Planning*, Geneva: United Nations.

United States, Department of Health, Education and Welfare, 1969, *Toward a Social Report*, Washington, D.C.

UNRISD, 1970, *Contents and Measurement of Socio-Economic Development* Report No 70. 10, Geneva: United Nations Research Institute for Social Development.

What are we Trying to Measure?

By Dudley Seers*

SUMMARY

Development means creating the conditions for the realization of human personality. Its evaluation must therefore take into account three linked economic criteria: whether there has been a reduction in (i) poverty; (ii) unemployment; (iii) inequality. G.N.P. can grow rapidly without any improvement on these criteria; so development must be measured more directly. The conceptual and practical problems of a number of indicators are discussed and also the inplications for planning, both national and international.

Why do we confuse development with economic growth? Surely one could hardly say that the situation depicted by a set of projections was preferable to that shown by another set simply because the former implied higher *per capita* income. After all, in what sense is South Africa more developed than Ghana, or Kuwait than the U.A.R., or the United States than Sweden?

One explanation is that the national income is a very convenient indicator. Politicians find a single comprehensive measure useful, especially one that is at least a year out of date. Economists are provided with a variable which can be quantified and movements in which can be analysed into changes in sectoral output, factor shares or categories of expenditure, making model-building feasible.

We can, of course, fall back on the supposition that increases in national income, if they are sufficiently fast, sooner or later lead to the solution of social and political problems. But the experience of the past decade makes this belief look rather naïve. Social crises and political upheavals have emerged in countries at all stages of development. Moreover, we can see that these afflict countries with rapidly rising *per capita* incomes, as well as those with stagnant economies. In fact it looks as if economic growth not merely may fail to solve social and political difficulties; certain types of growth can actually cause them.

Now that the complexity of development problems is becoming increasingly obvious, this continued addiction to the use of a single aggregative

* Director of the Institute of Development Studies at the University of Sussex. The first third of this paper is derived from 'The meaning of development' published in the *International Development Review* (Vol. 11, No. 4, 1969), and republished in I.D.S. Communications Series, No. 44; *Revista Brasileira de Economia,* (Vol. 24, No. 3); *Internationale Spectator,* (Vol. XXIV, No. 21); *Ekistics,* 1970; *Sociological Abstracts,* U.S.A., 1970; *The Political Economy of Development* (ed. Ilchman and Uphoff) 1971; and *INSIGHT,* July 1971. I am grateful for comments from Hans Singer on a draft of this part, which was also discussed at seminars at the Universities of Boston and Toronto, and formed the basis of a lunch talk at the 11th World Conference of the Society for International Development (New Delhi, November 1969). The remainder was written specially for this collection.

indicator, in the face of the evidence, takes on a rather different appearance. It begins to look like a preference for avoiding the real problems of development.

THE DEFINITION OF DEVELOPMENT

In discussing the challenges we now face, we have to dispel the fog around the word 'development' and decide more precisely what we mean by it. Only then will we be able to devise meaningful targets or indicators, and thus to help improve policy, national or international.

The starting-point is that we cannot avoid what the positivists disparagingly refer to as 'value judgements'. 'Development' is inevitably a normative concept, almost a synonym for improvement. To pretend otherwise is just to hide one's value judgements.

But from where are these judgements to come? The conventional answer, which Tingerben accepts for his system of economic planning, is to draw our values from governments. But governments have necessarily a rather short-term view, in some cases discounting the future at a very high rate. More seriously, some governments are themselves the main obstacles to development, on any plausible definition, and once this is conceded, where is one to obtain the yardsticks by which government objectives are to be judged? Even supposing that governments represented faithfully, in some sense, popular attitudes, these are endogenous to the development process and therefore cannot provide a means of assessing it.

Another approach is to copy the development paths of other countries, which implicitly means aiming at thir present state as the goal. This is what model-builders, for example, are really doing when coefficients are taken from an international cross-section analysis, or from functions that fit the experience of an industrial country. Yet few if any of the rich countries now appear to the outside world as really desirable models. Some aspects, such as their consumption levels, seem enviable, but these are associated, perhaps inseparably, with evils such as urban sprawl, advertising pressures, air pollution and chronic tension. Besides it is by no means obvious or even likely that the rest of the world could trace the history of the industrial countries even if they wanted to.

If values are not to be found in politics or history, does this mean that we are each left to adopt our own personal set of values? This is fortunately not necessary. Surely the values we need are staring us in the face, as soon as we ask ourselves: what are the necessary conditions for a universally acceptable aim, the realization of the potential of human personality?

If we ask what is an *absolute* necessity for this, one answer is obvious— enough food. Below certain levels of nutrition, a man lacks not merely bodily energy and good health but even interest in much besides food. He cannot rise significantly above an animal existence. If anyone has any doubt on the primacy of food, they should reflect on the implications of recent research [*Scrimshaw and Gordon, 1968*] showing that if young children are not properly nourished the result may well be lasting impairment not merely of the body, but also of the mind.

Since foodstuffs have prices, in any country the criterion can be expressed in terms of income levels. This enables it to take account also of certain other minimum requirements. People never spend all their money (or energy) on food, however poor they are. To be enough to feed a man, his income has also to cover basic needs of clothing, footwear and shelter.

But I am not talking about consumption needs in general; I am talking about the capacity to buy physical necessities.

Peter Townsend and others who support a 'relative' concept of poverty describe those in any society as poor if they are unable to 'participate in the activities and have the living conditions and amenities which are customary in that society. These activities and customs have to be described empirically. In addition to food and clothing customs, they include, for example, in the United Kingdom, such things as birthday parties for children, summer holidays and evenings out' [*Townsend, 1970, p. 42*]. This concept of poverty as social deprivation implies that the poverty standard would rise as living conditions improve, and indeed that poverty could *never* be eliminated, except perhaps by making the distribution of income very equal. But to see one's child doomed by malnutrition to life-long physical and mental inferiority or to be unable to buy a blood transfusion to save one's wife's life is surely a different sort of poverty from being unable to afford the cakes for a children's party or to take one's wife out to the pictures.

What I am asserting is that below the level at which a man can in some sense provide 'enough' food for his family, the marginal utility of income is much greater than it is above that level. This is of course an old-fashioned view, and it raises many problems of concepts and measurement to which I return later. But wherever there is serious poverty, a normative approach to development, which I have argued to be inevitable, implies a utility function of this general shape.

Another basic necessity, in the sense of something without which personality cannot develop, is *a job*. This does not necessarily mean paid employment: it can include studying, working on a family farm or keeping house. But to play none of these accepted roles, i.e. to be chronically dependent on another person's productive capacity, even for food, is incompatible with self-respect for a non-senile adult, especially somebody who has been spending years at school, perhaps at university, preparing for an economically active life.

It is true, of course, that both poverty and unemployment are associated in various ways with income. But even a fast increase in *per capita* income is in itself far from enough, as the experience of many economies shows, to reduce either poverty or unemployment. In fact, certain processes of growth can easily be accompanied by, and in a sense cause, growing unemployment.[1]

The direct link between *per capita* income and the numbers living in poverty is *income distribution*. It is a truism that poverty will be eliminated much more rapidly if any given rate of economic growth is accompanied by a declining concentration of incomes. Equality should, however, in my belief, be considered an objective in its own right, the third element in development. Inequalities to be found today, especially in the Third World where there is massive poverty, are objectionable by any religious or ethical standards. The social barriers and inhibitions of an unequal society distort the personalities of those with high incomes no less than of those who are poor. Trivial differences of accent, language, dress, customs, etc., acquire an absurd importance and contempt is engendered for those who lack social graces, especially country dwellers. Since race is usually highly correlated with income, economic inequality lies at the heart of racial tensions. More seriously, inequality of income is associated with other inequalities, especially in education and political power, which reinforce it.

The questions to ask about a country's development are therefore: What has been happening to poverty? What has been happening to unemployment? What has been happening to inequality? If all three of these have become less severe, then beyond doubt this has been a period of development for the country concerned. If one or two of these central problems have been growing worse, especially if all three have, it would be strange to call the result 'development', even if *per capita* income had soared. This applies, of course, to the future too. A 'plan' which conveys no targets for reducing poverty, unemployment and inequality can hardly be considered a 'development plan'.[2]

Of course, the true fulfilment of human potential requires much that cannot be specified in these terms. I cannot spell out all the other requirements, but this paper would be very unbalanced if I did not mention them at all. They include adequate educational levels (especially literacy), participation in government and belonging to a nation that is truly independent, both economically and politically, in the sense that the views of other governments do not largely predetermine one's own government's decisions.[3]

As undernourishment, unemployment and inequality dwindle, these educational and political aims become increasingly important objectives of development. Later still, freedom from repressive sexual codes, from noise and pollution, become major aims.[4] But these would not override the basic economic priorities, at least for really poor countries, with large numbers of undernourished children. A government could hardly claim to be 'developing' a country *just because* its educational system was being expanded or political order was being established, or limits set on engine noise, if hunger, unemployment and inequality were significant and growing, or even if they were not diminishing. Indeed, one would doubt the viability of political order in these circumstances, if one didn't consider the claim *prima facie* somewhat suspect; on the other hand, certain political patterns may well be incompatible with development.

Before leaving this issue I must make it clear that the national income is not totally meaningless, just because it is an inappropriate indicator of development. It has some significance as a measure of development *potential*. Suppose that two countries start a decade with the same *per capita* income and one grows faster than the other over ten years, but that the increase in income in the former goes entirely to the rich, and that, because growth has been due to highly capital-intensive techniques, unemployment rates remain unchanged, while in the latter growth has been slower but has meant lower unemployment and thus benefited the poorest class. Then, although the country with faster growth has, on my criteria, developed least—in fact not developed at all—it has achieved greater potential for developing later.

In the first place, the fiscal system could bring about development more rapidly the greater the income available for transfer to the poor. Moreover, a fast growth rate implies a greater savings capacity, which could more easily mean true development in the future. Indeed the faster-growing country may well already have a higher level of investment *per capita*;

if this investment is in agricultural projects which will raise food production and provide more rural employment, or in rural schools, genuine development could already be foreshadowed for the future.[5]

From a long-term viewpoint, economic growth is for a poor country a necessary condition of reducing poverty. But it is not a sufficient condition. To release the development potential of a high rate of economic growth depends on policy. A country where economic growth is slow or negligible may be busy reshaping its political institutions so that, when growth comes, it will mean development; such a country could develop faster in the long run than one at present enjoying fast growth but with political power remaining very firmly in the hands of a rich minority. It will be interesting to compare, for example, what happens in Cuba and Brazil in the remainder of this century.

PRIORITIES IN THE SOCIAL SCIENCES

It may help us to withstand the strong intellectual attraction of the national income as a yardstick of development if we look back a little.

By about 1950 the great economic problems had been brought largely under control in the industrial countries. Unemployment had been reduced to historically very low levels; absolute poverty in the sense I use the word had been largely eliminated; taxation and educational advances had reduced economic inequalities, and, though a good deal of what remained was associated with race, this was not a source of great political at that time, and it was largely overlooked by the social scientists, especially the economists.

We could say that these countries had managed in various ways to meet, in some degree at least, the challenges they had faced in the 19th century. One reason, of course, was that they benefited from world economic leadership and political power—to this I'll return later. But another was that social scientists such as Booth, Towntree, Boyd-Orr, the Webbs, Keynes, Beveridge and Tawney focused attention sharply on poverty, unemployment and inequality in the first half of this century. (I hope I am not being excessively nationalistic in choosing British examples: the names *are* rather significant.) Most economists, even Pigou, took greater equality as an obviously desirable objective.

With the easing of the big problems, however, economists turned their attention to innovations in professional techniques. In as far as they retained interest in current affairs, it was mainly in the progress of the nation conceived as a whole. The national income seemed ideal for comparing growth rates of a country during different periods, or for constructing an international league table. Moreover, it has maintained its role as a predictor of the level of employment—if the economy is diversified and the labour force is mobile, big short term changes in the national income are closely associated with changes in employment.[6]

We now see that even in the industrial countries basic economic problems had not really been cured. Their social scientists, notably in the United States, have been rediscovering their own poverty. Moreover, unemployment has recently grown, and inequality may well have done so too.

But the fundamental problems have never even started to disappear from sight in the Third World. In Africa, Asia or Latin America, development had been very limited on any of the three economic criteria until

1950. Since then, there has certainly been some reduction in the proportion, even if not in absolute numbers, living in poverty. But it has recently
been estimated by Francis Keppel that seven out of every ten children
in the entire world are 'affected by the apathy typical of chronic protein
deficiency, an apathy which translates into diminished learning potential'
[*Scrimshaw and Gordon, 1968*]; the fraction among many countries of the
Third World, such as India, must of course be higher. Unemployment
seems to have grown, judging from the countries for which data are available. It is probable, though data are extremely poor, that in most countries inequality has not been reduced; in many, it may well have increased.
A paper by A. J. Jaffe [*1969*] on five Latin American countries for which
comparable studies over time are available concludes that all showed increasing inequalities, with the possible exception of Mexico. It is even
possible that, were the data available, we would find economic growth
to be directly associated with growing unemployment and increasing inequality. If that has indeed been the case, there has been a negative correlation between growth and development. Even if that were not so, it is
clear that the connection between them is not at all as straightforward
as was once believed.

CONCEPTUAL AND MEASUREMENT PROBLEMS

One defence of the *national income* is that it is an objective, value-free
indicator, Yet it is in fact heavily value-loaded: every type of product and
service is assigned its own particular weight (many being zero). This
weight is mainly determined by market forces, which reflect the country's
income distribution. A familiar question in economics—how adequately
income measures demand when its distribution is unequal—gets additional point when the distribution is as highly concentrated as it is in the
countries of the Third World. Another question—how objective demand
is when it is partially determined by salesmanship—appears even more
cogent when tastes are to some extent imported from abroad. But, in addition, official policies, e.g. fostering import substitution by controls, often
increase the prices of luxuries much more than of necessities. There are
often egalitarian reasons for such policies, but the outcome is paradoxi-
cally that increases in production of luxuries count very much more highly
in the estimation of rates of economic growth than they do in industrial
countries.[7] While prices of staple foods and clothing may be comparable
between poor countries and rich, perhaps lower in the former, prices of
cars, refrigerators, etc., are several times as high. The absurd consequence
may be that in a country where there is serious poverty, a car counts for
more than ten tons of rice.

To estimate or use the national income also implies a set of judgements
about what activities it should cover—what are the 'final' products, as
against 'intermediate' products which are not considered intrinsically
valuable and only produced because they make possible the products of
other, more desirable, products. This raises the basic question: what
activities are we trying to maximize?—a question once posed by Kuznets
and now revived by Sametz [*1968*].[8] The issue of distribution can be raised
in these terms too—are the luxuries of the professional classes a 'necessary cost' of raising the incomes of the poor, the real maximand?

It has also been argued on behalf of national income as a development indicator that it could at least be quantified. But what are all the voluminous tables of national income accounts really worth? So far as the Third World is concerned, much of what they ought to cover is virtually outside the scope of official statistics. This applies above all to output of domestic foodstuffs, even the staples, let alone subsidiary crops which come under the general heading of 'market gardening' (American 'truck farming'), not to speak of fish, forest products, etc. Extremely rough methods of estimation are often used, much of the output being assumed to rise in proportion to the increase in rural population, an increase which is in turn assumed to be some constant arbitrary rate in the absence of registration of births and deaths, or data on migration.[9] Secondly, we know very little about construction in the countryside by the farming community itself; this apparently amounts to a good deal if one takes account not only of building houses, but also clearing land, digging wells and ditches, constructing fences and hedges, etc. Thirdly, there are practically no basic data on domestic service and other personal services, even those which are remunerated.

We should ask national income estimators conceptual questions such as: which of the activities a farm family does for itself without payment, such as haircutting for example, have you included in the national income? And why? And practical questions such as: how many fishes were caught in Province A in the years concerned? How many huts were constructed in Province B? How many barbers worked in Province C? And how do you know?

We should also ask those who quote the national income, for example in a planning office or a university, how much time they have spent with the estimators? It is unsafe and therefore unprofessional to use national income data until one has personally satisfied oneself on how such questions have been handled.

I have examined the worksheets in about twenty countries; the blunt truth of the matter is that when one takes into account the difficulties of allowing for inventory changes and depreciation, and of deflating current-price data, the published national income series for a large number of countries have very little relevance to economic reality.[10] In many countries, any reasonably competent statistician could produce from the meagre basic data series showing the real *per capita* income either rising or falling. Decimal places are fantasy. Some series are in fact in a way more misleading than sets of random numbers would be, because they *appear* to have a significance. It would, of course, be very convenient if the national income data published in such quantities had objective meaning, but unfortunately this does not make them meaningful.

It might be argued that some numbers called national income series are at least available, whereas data on poverty, unemployment and inequality are very scrappy. This is, however, the result not so much of basic differences in estimation possibilities as of attitudes to development. The type of data collected reflects priorities. What work is done by a statistical office depends in practice partly on what its own government demands, partly on the advice it receives from various U.N. agencies, especially the U.N. Statistical Office. As a realization of the importance of social problems spreads, statistical offices will put less weight on national income estimation, more on preparing appropriate social indicators.[11]

I do not deny that there are conceptual problems with development

indicators too. The difficulties in assessing *poverty* standards, or even minimum nutritional standards, are well known.[12] For a household these
should reflect the ages and also the physical activities of its members.[13]
Moreover, many households which can afford to exceed the nutritional
minimum expenditure will not in fact do so, because they spend their money in a sense unwisely (whether because of conventional expenditures on
non-essentials, lack of information or personal taste).[14] The recognition
of this is indeed implicit in the official U.S. poverty line which allows
$750 a head, of which about $250 is for food.

But we need not give up. When as in India, an official poverty line
has been established, the resultant estimates of the proportion with incomes
below a specified poverty line are not without meaning.[15] However rough,
they have some significance as a yardstick for measuring development
over time—certainly such comparisons convey more than changes in the
per capita national income.

There are other well-known measures of poverty which I can only mention briefly here. One is the infant mortality rate (though this reflects in
particular the effectiveness of health services, as well as diet, housing, etc.).
Data on protein consumption and the incidence of diseases of undernourishment, such as rickets, are further clues on development, as are the
height and weight of children.[16] However, they are only clues, and may
well be misleading if used to compare nations of very different genetic
stock, dietary habits, etc.

Unemployment is, of course, notoriously difficult to define in non-
industrial societies. An urban unemployed person can be roughly identified by the usual test questions designed to reveal the last occasion when
work was sought (though this means excluding from the unemployed
those who would only look for a job if they thought there was any chance
of finding it, and on the other hand including those who would in fact
only accept particular types of work). In addition there is involuntary
short time working, and people are more or less idle, at least for most of
the day, in jobs which are more or less fictional (from superfluous posts in
government to shining shoes). The volume of this is hard to measure; so is
disguised rural under-employment because of seasonal variations in
activity. One needs much more detail by sector, by region, by sex, by age,
by educational qualification, to throw light on the nature of unemployment and underemployment in any country and on the attitudes of people
to work.[17]

Inequality can be measured in many ways—by size, race, region, or by
factor shares. All have their uses for different purposes, and they are of
course all interconnected. They are also all limited in one important respect, namely that there are other sources of inequality than income. One's
standard of living may be affected by access to free cars, for example. (An
ambassador may well have a higher level of living than somebody with ten
times his salary.) It also depends on access to public services such as health
(especially important in urban-rural comparisons). More fundamentally,
political power may greatly influence the inequality of people in terms of
their ability to develop their personality, even to speak their minds.

Even concentration of income by size can be measured in many ways.
If one wants a single measure, the Gini coefficient, derived from the Lorenz
curve (showing cumulative proportions of income received by cumulative
proportions of recipients), is probably still the most useful, for either in-

come or wealth. But, if we are mainly concerned with inequality as a cause of poverty, a more meaningful measure may be to express (say) the lowest decile as a fraction of the median (following the general approach in a recent study by Harold Lydall [*1968*].[18] We are after all not greatly interested in changes *within* the top half of the income ladder.

Of course, all these measures of distribution raise the same conceptual problems as national income measurement—for example, where to draw the boundary between activities which are marketed and those which are not. In addition, such measures take no account of the price structure, which may well affect the concentration of *real* income—an important point in, e.g., countries where the burden of protection is borne mainly by the rich.

All in all, however, the conceptual problems of these indicators do not seem to be more formidable than those of the national income—we have just grown accustomed to ignoring the latter. And many of the practical problems are the same as those that face the national income estimators. But indicators of any of the elements of development I have mentioned also require supplementary information. Thus to measure the proportion of the population above a poverty line one needs to know how many people share each household income (and whether they are males or females, adults or children). To measure unemployment meaningfully, one needs to know what jobs people would be prepared to take (and at what income), and what hours they work. To measure distribution in any of its dimensions, one needs to know more than the national estimator about who receives various types of income.

But again we must not be diverted by such technical problems from attempting the assessment which really matters. There is one possible source for all of these measures, surveys of households designed to provide them; these can yield the necessary cross-classifications by region, race, income, etc. The systematic development of the information required to study trends in poverty, unemployment and income distribution in any country requires pilot surveys in depth to clarify the conceptual issues in their local context and guide the construction of indicators. This is best achieved if a permanent sampling organization, such as India has in its National Sample Survey, is established to collect the necessary information professionally, systematically and regularly.

I can only mention briefly indicators for the educational and political dimensions of development. In as far as education is provided by the formal educational system (which is very much open to argument) the main source is, of course, inputs and outputs of various levels of education. A technique for combining these in a diagram showing trends over time has been developed by Richard Jolly [*1969*].

Measurement of the extent to which the political aims have been achieved is of course much more difficult; possible clues include the number of prisoners held for political or quasi-political reasons, and the social and racial composition of parliaments, business boards, senior public administrative grades, etc., and also of those enjoying secondary and university education.

More general indicators of welfare, reflecting political and other influences, include the rates per million people of crimes of violence, suicide, alcoholism and other types of drug addiction. Here the main problem is to cope with the consequences of different standards of reporting, stemming from differences in definition (what is an alcoholic?) and in coverage (e.g. comprehensiveness of police records, death registers, etc.). Interpretation raises further problems. Thus is rural violence to be treated as a reflection of intolerable living conditions or of envy—or is it to be considered a necessary cost of a desirable social change?

Clues on the degree of national independence include the proportion of capital inflows in exchange receipts, the proportion of the supply of capital goods (or intermediates) which is imported, the proportion of assets, especially subsoil assets, owned by foreigners, and the extent to which one trading partner dominates the patterns of aid and trade. But there are also qualitative indicators such as the existence of foreign military bases and overflying rights, and the extent to which the country follows the lead of one of the great powers in the United Nations.

THE COMPATIBILITY OF INDICATORS

This section raises the problem of weighing and comparing different indicators, a major indicator problem. It is, of course, impossible to explore all its aspects here, but it may be useful to indicate some major possibilities of inconsistency and how serious these seem to be.

On the face of it, there is a strong causal interrelation between the three leading indicators. Development on any of them implies, or helps bring about, or may even be a necessary condition for, development on one or more of the others. To reduce unemployment is to remove one of the main causes of poverty and inequality. A reduction in inequality will of course reduce poverty, *ceteris paribus*.

But are other things equal? Does lowering the concentration of income imply a slower rate of economic growth—and growth is, as we have seen, in the long run a necessary condition for eliminating poverty. And would slower growth impair employment prospects? There is a well-known, indeed classical, argument that inequality generates savings and incentives and thus promotes economic growth and employment.

I find the argument that the need for savings justifies inequality unconvincing in the Third World today. Savings propensities are after all very low precisely in countries with highly unequal distributions; the industrial countries with less concentration of income have, by contrast, much higher savings propensities. Savings are, of course, also affected by the absolute level of incomes, but the explanation of this paradox must in part lie in the high consumption standards of an unequal society.

Moreover, the rich in most countries tend to have extremely high propensities, not merely to spend, but to spend on goods and services with a high foreign exchange content, and, for countries suffering from an acute foreign exchange bottleneck, this is a major obstacle to development.[19] It is true that import demand can be held in check by administrative controls, but this leads to the elaboration of a bureaucratic apparatus which is expensive, especially in terms of valuable organizing ability, and which in some countries becomes riddled with corruption. In fact, the result of import control is often to create a protected and highly profitable local industry, which itself depends heavily on imports of intermediate products and capital goods, and remits abroad a large flow of money in profits, interest, royalties, licence fees and service charges of various sorts.[20] In any case, in a highly unequal society, personal savings often flow abroad or go into luxury housing and other investment projects of low or zero priority for development, or even for growth.

The argument that only inequality can provide the incentives that are necessary is also obviously of limited validity in a country where there are barriers of race or class or caste to advancement. Still, we cannot dismiss it out of hand. The needs for private entrepreneurial talent vary according to the circumstances of different economies, but there are very few where this need is small. Countries relying on growing exports of manufactures, as many do, depend heavily on the emergence of businessmen with the drive to penetrate foreign markets. All countries depend in some degree on the appearance of progressive farmers. Will these emerge without financial rewards on a scale that will make nonsense of an egalitarian policy? Are rising profits of companies, especially foreign companies, an inevitable feature of growth in many countries? Or are we exaggerating the importance of financial incentives? Can other non-financial rewards partially take their place?[21] Can social incentives be developed to a point where people will take on such tasks with little or no individual reward (as the governments of China and Cuba are trying to procure)?

The compatibility of growing equality and rising output and employment has recently become doubtful for an additional set of reasons. Can the people who are professionally necessary be kept in the country if they earn only a small fraction of which they could earn elsewhere? How much unemployment will their departure involve, because their labour is complementary to that of the rest of the labour force? Yet what are the costs in terms of human welfare and even efficiency if they are prevented from leaving?[22]

On the other hand, there are also very serious reasons for questioning the compatibility of *in*equality and the growth of income and employment. One is implied by the discussion of the composition of consumption above. Can a manufacturing industry be created to correspond to the structure of demand that arises in a highly inequitable society (leaving aside the question of whether it *should* be created)? Will production rise rapidly if the proportion of the labour force which is too badly nourished for full manual and mental work is only sinking slowly? Can the government obtain the co-operation of the population in wage restraint, and in many other ways that are necessary for development, if there is visible evidence of great wealth which is being transmitted from generation to generation, so that the wage earner sees his children and his children's children doomed indefinitely to subordinate positions? Or if there is little prospect of reducing unemployment? Can political leaders under such circumstances mobilize the energies of the population and break down social customs which obstruct development, especially in rural areas?

I do not pretend to know the answers to this complex of questions, which point to a set of 'internal contradictions' in the development processes more severe than those to which Marx drew attention. Any answer must in any case be specific to the country concerned. All I would say is that such questions have usually been ignored in the past, leading to a failure to appreciate the damaging consequences of inequality.

Yet another set of questions arises out of the potential inconsistency between employment in the short-run and employment in the longer term—which is often formulated as a conflict between employment and growth. There has recently been much discussion of this [*Stewart and*

C

Streeten, 1971]. All I would say is that here too the conflict has been exaggerated. It would after all be surprising if the mobilization of all the above labour in a typical economy caused anything but a big rise in output.

My original paper, to which I referred in the first footnote, went on to discuss the consistency between these economic objectives and those mentioned above, in the political and social planes—political order and liberty, independence and education. I will not go over this ground here—it would take us rather far from the subject of development indicators (the interested reader can turn to the references given in that paper—though this is not to deny that political and economic dimensions of development are connected, certain political systems are incompatible with progress towards equality, because of the relationship between the distribution of income and political power.

IMPLICATIONS FOR PLANNING

The most important use of development indicators is to provide the targets for planning. The realization that the national income is in itself an inadequate yardstick of development implies a recognition that national income targets are not very relevant. We need instead targets for poverty, employment and income distribution, specifying some of the dimensions of the structure of society at which we are aiming.

The difference in approach is more profound than it seems. Formerly the basic technique consisted in extrapolating past trends and choosing investment patterns that would produce an acceptable increase in national income in a five-year period, tacitly assuming many constraints as given—thus consumption patterns were projected in a way that assumed little or no change in income distribution or in tastes or attitudes. Now we must try to envisage what might be a satisfactory pattern at some time in the future, in terms not only of production and employment structures, but of the patterns of income distribution, consumer demand and jobs, and then work backwards, to see if there is any plausible path for getting there.

The econometrician searches for planning models with multiple objectives, in response to this challenge. But perhaps the task is much simpler: to lift every family above a poverty line, based on food requirements, bare minimum though it may be. To achieve this must imply the elimination of poverty and unemployment and (especially if the time span is short) a reduction in inequality. It implies setting target incomes for various sizes of families and working out what measures would be needed to achieve these (the measures may include not only employment creation, but also welfare schemes such as special food programmes for children, pensions, etc.). The final step is to estimate what measures need to be taken in policy areas such as taxation and incomes.

This approach raises statistical problems. In the first place, sufficiently detailed income and expenditure studies are rarely available; even if they were, there would be problems of relating poverty lines to household composition, referred to above. Further, it would be hard to incorporate complicated indicators in development models and one might have to settle for something as crude as a minimum household income. Converting targets into policies raises further problems because of the many different influences on the income of the poor and because typically there is no machinery for straightforward fiscal redistribution. But the approach is nevertheless worth pursuing—its difficulties are no excuse for persisting with inappropriate, even dangerously misleading, planning models designed to maximize economic growth.

To concentrate on the elimination of poverty implies that increased income for the rest of the population is irrelevant so long as there is undernourishment, especially of children. So be it. We must however, recognize the risk that some redistributive strategies *may* in some circumstances hamper economic growth and thus the more fundamental long-term solution of the problem of poverty.

INTERNATIONAL DEVELOPMENT

The criteria suggested above can in principle be applied to any unit—a village, a province, a nation, a continent or the world. Let me in closing refer briefly to indicators of world development. Basically the same concepts of poverty and employment apply, but in the case of inequality we are now primarily concerned with comparisons between incomes of different nations, as a guide to the policy tasks which face the rich countries if they are to contribute to the development of the poor.

There has been progress, especially since the 1930s, on the poverty criterion; the proportion of the whole human population living below any subsistence line must have fallen. But total overt world unemployment must have grown, since the emergence of unemployment in the Third World must numerically outweigh the decline of unemployment in the industrial countries. In recent years, in any case, unemployment has risen in the latter too, so there can be no doubt of the world trend (though it is not very meaningful to add together national statistics for something like unemployment which takes so many forms). Moreover, since the middle of the last century enormous gaps have opened between rich countries and poor: inequality on the present scale is an entirely new phenomenon, as papers by Simon Kuznets [*1971, pp. 27ff.; 1966, pp. 390–400*] and Surendra Patel [*1964*] have brought out.

Economic inequality between nations, like inequality within them means differences in status and power, poisoning the attitudes of men towards each other. This, again as on the national level, means growing tensions between races, broadly in this case (as also inside many countries) between the whites and the remainder. Moreover, the incompatibility of inequality with the elimination of poverty is clearer for development on the international than on the national plane. The seepage, through many channels, of the consumption habits of rich countries has contributed to unemployment in poorer countries (see above), and probably also meant slower economic growth. The transfer of technologies designed for rich countries has had similar effects; available technologies are becoming increasingly inappropriate for the worlds needs. The growing difference in *per capita* incomes also stimulates the 'brain drain' and exerts an upward pull on professional salaries in poor countries. Thus national and international inequality are linked.[23]

When we consider the world scene, it is wrong to talk about 'development', on the criteria suggested above. One cannot really say that there has been development for the world as a whole, when the benefits of technical progress have accrued to minorities which were already relatively rich. To me, this word is particularly misleading for the period since the war, especially the 'development decade' when the growth of economic inequality and unemployment may have actually accelerated. (The prospect of a 'second development decade' is daunting: a repetition of the 1960s with unemployment and inequality rising still further, would be socially, economically and politically disastrous whatever the pace of economic growth!)

The measurement of international inequality raises its own set of conceptual problems. Egalitarians like myself face a theoretical paradox. If we argue that the national income is an inappropriate measure of a nation's development, we weaken the significance of a growing *per capita* income 'gap' between rich nations and poor. However, there is really no alternative—a world income distribution by size, showing the magnitude of absolute poverty, would be immensely difficult to construct.

There are, moreover, special conceptual difficulties about international comparisons of income. Comparisons of incomes have limited significance when life styles are so different (affecting among other things the proportion of activity covered by cash transactions and thus included in 'income'), and when there are differences in climate.

A familiar measurement problem is the inapplicability of exchange rates as means of converting incomes in different currencies to a standard of comparison (such as the U.S. dollar). Attempts have been made to prepare exchange rates more appropriate for measuring the true purchasing power of different currencies, but these run up against well-known problems of weighting.[24]

Still, we must not fall into the familiar trap of criticizing statistics to the point where we deny them any meaning. Despite all its limitations (including the additional one of defining a 'rich' country) the statement that during the first 'development decade' the ratio between the average income of rich countries and poor has increased from about 12:1 to about 15:1 is not entirely lacking in content, either morally or analytically. It illustrates the widespread impact on poor countries of increasingly inappropriate salaries, consumption patterns and technologies, aggravating their own intractable problems of inequality and unemployment.

One thing this critique suggests the need for the continued worldwide development of subsidiary indicators mentioned above, such as infant mortality rates, calorie and protein consumption, and the incidence of diseases of poverty and under-nourishment.

There are of course political dimensions to international as to national development. A big step was taken in the first post-war decade with the creation of a whole system—the United Nations and its agencies. But since then progress has been very gradual, due basically to the unwillingness of the rich countries to limit their sovereignty and accept the authority of international organizations. The continued eruption of wars is an eloquent indicator of a lack of political progress which goes far to explain the negative development of the world as a whole.

NOTES

1. Thus in Trinidad the growth in *per capita* income averaged more than 5 per cent a year during the whole period 1953–68, while overt unemployment showed a steady increase to more than 10 per cent of the labour force.

2. Suppose, for example, that a perspective plan specified that *per capita* income of Brazil doubled in the next thirty years, but assumed no change in distribution or in the proportion unemployed. Then at the turn of the century, a big landowner in the Matto

Grosso could run four cars, instead of two, and a peasant in the North-East could eat two kilogrammes of meat a year instead of one. His son might well be still out of work. Could we really call that 'development'?

3. These dimensions are discussed in Mrs Baster's introduction.

4. Even for countries at a high level of development in any sense, the use of national income as an indicator is being widely challenged, e.g. by Mishan [*1967*], on the grounds that the environmental costs are ignored.

5. In an interesting paper Divatia and Bhatt [*1969*] put forward a different index of development potential, based on fundamental factor inputs such as capital and skills (though it is misleadingly described as a measure of the 'pace of development'). Movements in such an index could foreshadow what the future pace of economic growth could be. The index for India, for example, is encouraging because it shows a rate of increase twice as fast as the real national income. But, of course, it does not follow that growth potential *will* be released, let alone that development will take place.

6. This use of the national income had been developed by Colin Clark [*1937*]. In fact the great spurt forward in national income statistics in the 1930s and 1940s was due largely to the unemployment problem, although also to the need to quantify alternative wartime policies.

7. In addition, indirect taxes of various kinds on luxuries are relatively heavy, so such biases are particularly severe when market prices are used as weights.

8. For example, is a journey to work really an end product, as national estimators assume (especially a journey on a metropolitan underground railway!)? Additional issues are now being posed in industrial countries by the failure of national income to allow for the costs of environmental destruction, i.e. to be a sufficiently 'net' concept in that sense.

9. Every so often a researcher tries to draw conclusions about trends in *per capita* food consumption, which of course simply means revealing the implications of assumptions made by official statisticians.

10. There is an upward bias as well. The share of output covered by official statistics, and included in the national income, tends to rise, partly because a growing proportion of output passes through the hands of organized business, which is more adequately covered by official statistics, but also partly because of the general improvement in data collection.

11. The U.N. Statistical Office's 'A Complementary system of Statistics of the Distribution of Income, Expenditure and Wealth' is a useful starting-point.

12. Various poverty lines in India, where there has been much work on this question, are discussed by Fonseca [*1970*].

13. See papers by Abel-Smith, Bagley, Rein and Townsend in Townsend [*1970*].

14. This problem was first recognized by Rowntree [*1901*] in his classic enquiry in York, leading him to distinguish between 'primary' and 'secondary' poverty—the latter referring to the poverty of those who could afford the nutritional minimum but do not in fact attain it.

15. See, however, an interesting pair of articles by Minhas [*1970*] and Bardhan [*1970*], which show that even using the same criterion of poverty (one proposed in 1962 by a distinguished group of economists to the Planning Mission) very different conclusions can be reached on trends in the proportions lying below the poverty line through using different sources of consumption data, different allowances for price changes and different interpolation procedures.

16. Several indicators can be combined to give us an indicative profile of the prevalence of poverty in a nation, such as the U.N. Research Institute for Social Development has been experimenting with in Geneva. In fact they have taken a step further and produced a tentative 'development indicator', a weighted average of various series. The Institute's investigations of multiple associations are interesting and worth while, but we should not fall into the trap (as we could, although the Institute's Director warns us against it) of treating this indicator as 'normative'. It simply measures the extent to which a country has advanced along a path indicated by data from countries at different states of progress; see UNRISD [*1969*].

17. See I.L.O. [*1970*]. The point is made there that the measurement of unemployment depends very much on the dimension of the problem that concerns one—unemployment as a cause of personal frustration, low income or loss of output.

18. The Pareto coefficient, on the other hand, which long had its advocates, is expressly limited to measuring distribution among higher incomes.

19. To draw the conclusion that the income distributions should be changed, one

has to assume that Engel curves are non-linear, but this seems not to need specifying. Consumption of such luxuries is zero over a considerable income range.

20. See I.L.O. [*1970*] for a discussion of the compatibility of a high concentration of income with full employment. Unfortunately most theoretical texts concentrate on the relation between income distribution, savings and growth, ignoring the more important effects via the composition of consumption.

21. Though, of course, these imply inequalities of other types, even if only of social prestige.

22. I have dealt with these issues elsewhere [*Seers, 1971*].

23. See Seers [*1971*] and Jolly and Seers [*1970*].

24. Although this problem takes the form of finding the right expenditure weights for a price deflator, what we are actually doing is obtaining price weights for quantity comparisons, and this is extremely hard when price structures vary so much (see above). Analogous difficulties arise whenever comparisons are made between regions of a country (due to geographical variations in prices and consumption patterns) but much less severely.

REFERENCES

Bardhan, Pranab K., 1970, 'On the Minimum Level of Living and the Rural Poor', *Indian Economic Review*, Vol. 5, April.

Clark, Colin, 1937, *National Income and Outlay*, London: Macmillan.

Divatia, V. V., and Bhatt, V. V., 1969, 'On Measuring the Pace of Development', *Quarterly Review*, Banco Nazionale del Lavoro, No. 89, June.

Fonseca, A. J., 1970, 'The need-based Wage in India: A Computerized Estimate', reprinted from *Wage Policy and Wage Distribution in India*, Bombay: University of Bombay.

I.L.O., 1970, *Towards Full Employment*, Geneva: International Labour Office.

Jaffe, A. J., 1969, 'Notes on Family Income Distribution in Developing Countries in Relation to Population and Economic Changes'; paper given at meeting of International Association for Research in Income and Wealth, August; to be published in *Estadistica*, Inter-American Statistical Institute, No. 104.

Jolly, Richard, 1969, *Planning Education for African Development*, Nariobi: East Africa Publishing House.

Jolly, Richard, and Seers, Dudley, 1970, 'The Brain Drain and the Development Process', proceedings of the International Economic Association Conference to be published in E. A. G. Robinson (ed.), *The Gap Between the Rich and the Poor Countries*, London: Macmillan.

Kuznets, Simon, 1966, *Modern Economic Growth*, Studies in Comparative Economics No. 7, New Haven: Yale University Press.

Kuznets, Simon, 1971, *Economic Growth of Nations: Total Output and Production Structure*, Cambridge, Mass.: Belknap.

Lydall, Harold, 1968, *The Structure of Earnings*, Oxford: Clarendon Press.

Minhas, B.S., 1970, 'Rural Poverty, Land Redistribution and Development', *Indian Economic Review*, Vol. 5, April.

Mishan, E. J., 1967, *The Costs of Economic Growth*, London: Staples Press.

Patel, Surrendra, 1964, 'The Economic Distance Between Nations', *Economic Journal*, Vol. 74, March.

Rowntree, B. Seebohm, 1901, *Poverty: A Study of Town Life*, London: Macmillan.

Sametz, A. W., 1968, 'Production of Goods and Services: The Measurement of Economic Growth' in E. Sheldon and W. B. Moore (eds.), *Indicators of Social Change: Concepts and Measurements*, New York: Russell Sage Foundation.

Scrimshaw, N. S., and Gordon, J. E. (ed.), 1968, *Malnutrition, Learning and Behaviour*, Cambridge, Mass.: M.I.T. Press.

Seers, Dudley, 1971, 'The Transmission of Inequality' in Robert K. A. Gardiner (ed.), *Africa and the World*, London: Oxford University Press.

Stewart, Frances, and Streeten, Paul, 1971, 'Conflicts between Output and Employment Objectives' in Ronald Robinson and Peter Johnston (eds.), *Prospects for Employment Opportunities in the Nineteen Seventies*, London: Her Majesty's Stationery Office.

Townsend, Peter (ed.), 1970, *The Concept of Poverty*, London: Heinemann.

UNRISD, 1969, *Research Notes No. 2*, July, Geneva: United Nations Research Institute for Social Development.

Income Distribution and Social Stratification: Some Notes on Theory and Practice

By Charles Elliott*

SUMMARY

This paper starts with a brief statement of the assumption that income distribution improves as income per head rises and that one way in which this is achieved is the 'trickle-down' of expenditures (and therefore incomes) to the lowest income groups. Some conditions are defined for this assumption and subjected to some theoretical criticism. More particularly, a plea is entered for a more attentive hearing of the structuralist case that social and political forces need to be taken into account in any description or analysis of income distribution. Still couched in very general terms, a brief review of some development strategies show that typically two popular strategies are likely to be attended by increases in the inequality of income distribution. The second part of the paper looks at some of the problems of definition of indicators and measurements of income distribution with regard to the familiar constraints of lack of data availability and the need to take account of the structuralist demand mentioned above. Rejecting as inadequate a regional approach, the paper ends by proposing a somewhat unusual form of tabulation and applies this technique to Zambian data for 1970.

INTRODUCTION

A number of reasons ranging from an exclusive obsession with growth to problems with interpersonal welfare comparisons under all but the most restrictive assumptions combined in the past to ensure that distributional problems were under-explored intellectually and largely ignored in policy formulation. Further, as Dudley Seers emphasizes in this volume, cultural transfer has blinded economists not only to problems that loom large in developing countries but also to the inapplicability of some of their own concepts and analytical tools. For example, saving interpreted in a pure Keynesian sense has been a fetish which has seemed to justify inequality of distribution. Presenting a case for the opposition then the approach of this paper is acknowledgedly partisan. The intention is to make a case for a much more thoroughgoing consideration of income distribution in the early stages of economic development and to enter a plea for a more conscious treatment by professional economists, whether they be analysts or practitioners, of the 'marginados' and the very poor. We shall argue that the justification of the neglect of income distribution by appeal to the assumption of 'trickle-down' is no longer tenable; and that both development strategies and analytical tools are loaded against the poor. In the

* Member of the Overseas Development Group, University of East Anglia.

second part we make an incomplete suggestion about how this deloading could be begun.

SOME THEORETICAL CONSIDERATIONS

We must begin with a statement of what we take the assumption of trickle-down to be. Starting from a purely traditional economy, the development of a 'modern' sector, characterized by higher productivity and wages higher than the subsistence income of the traditional sector, skews income distribution.[1] But thereafter two processes are set in train. First, urban demand for rural products (food and raw materials) rises and thus gives rise to increasing productivity in the rural sector—and hence higher rural incomes. Second, the urban, high productivity sector itself grows and generates employment opportunities for an increasing flow of migrants. Thus in the Lewis/Ranis-Fei equilibrium models, the processes are looped and rural productivity rises as the urban sector grows [*Lewis, 1954, ff. 139–92; Fei and Ranis, 1964*]. In this sense, the benefits of higher urban productivity and income 'trickle down' to the rural areas through increased demand for rural goods and services. This process may be accentuated by deliberate redistributional policies; e.g. the taxation of urban incomes to provide rural services (health, education, transport, electrification) which the tax receipts from the rural areas would not justify. Furthermore, voluntary redistribution may take place through kinship bonds that ensure that the relatively wealthy urban income-receivers pass some of their earnings to rural relatives.[2]

These processes, it is assumed, would inevitably take time and therefore income distribution would become more regressive in the early phases, but as employment expanded, agricultural productivity rose and redistributive policies were adopted (or became effective) this deterioration would give way to a reverse process whereby the poor 'caught up' with the relatively affluent and income distribution became more equal. Income distribution could thus be related to growth of G.N.P. or income per head. In the early stages of the growth process, distribution would deteriorate but, after some critical point,[3] the process of growth itself would ensure that labour productivity in all sectors was equated and thus a more equitable income distribution was achieved.[4] Seen in this light, it was understandable that economists should believe that distributional problems were largely self-correcting and could therefore be safely ignored. The best remedy for maldistribution was growth; and to try to interfere with distribution would certainly be to jeopardize growth. Thus Professor Harry Johnson:

> The remedies for the main fault which can be found with the use of the market mechanism, its undesirable social effects, are luxuries which underdeveloped countries cannot afford to indulge in if they are really serious about attaining a high rate of development. In particular, there is likely to be a conflict between rapid growth and an equitable distribution of income; and a poor country anxious to develop would probably be well advised not to worry too much about the distribution of income [*Johnson, 1958*].[5]

Put in that general form with all the crucial parameters unspecified, the assumption is open to serious challenge. What precisely is meant by an improvement in income distribution? A statistical definition would be a fall in the Gini index of concentration, but that is theoretically consistent with deepening poverty of the lowest decile or even lowest two deciles. This possibility formally depends upon the relative size of the population of the income deciles and the dispersion of incomes in the remaining deciles. Broadly, the smaller the proportion of the whole population in the lowest income decile and the lower the dispersion of income in the three upper deciles, the more possible it is that a given improvement in the distribution of income, as measured for instance by a fall in the Gini index of concentration, is consistent with a deterioration in the income accruing to the lowest decile. Now it is true that these conditions are rarely fulfilled. The size of the lowest income deciles is usually very large: indeed the lowest quartile of income can be received by as high a proportion as 85 per cent of the whole population. Similarly the dispersion of incomes amongst the rest of the population tends to be marked.

Given these features, it will be required that the income of the lowest quartile and sometimes even the lowest decile rises relatively to other incomes to effect a fall in the Gini index. In that case we can accept a fall in the Gini index as an adequate representation of income redistribution. But it should be constantly borne in mind that as the conditions specified above are approached, this definition becomes unsatisfactory and one needs to refer more specifically to the income of the lowest deciles.

The critical point of inequality is reached in theory at the point at which the productivity gap is greatest. When the least productive group (e.g. urban unemployed or highly inefficient farmers) begins to increase its productivity and therefore income[6] at a rate that is faster than the rise in productivity and income of other groups, then income distribution, in the sense of the difference between the average income and that of the lowest decile, begins to improve.[7] But there is no means of telling when this extremely rigorous condition will be met. It assumes not only full employment (in the traditional sense) but a marked differential in productivity in favour of the most disadvantaged group. It may well be the case that workers are paid more than their marginal product, and hence that low marginal productivity is *per se* not an obstacle to redistribution. But labour is highly unlikely to be paid more than its average productivity over a prolonged period and, amongst the lowest income groups, average productivity is too low to offset regressive distribution.

Alternatively, we could postulate rigorous and effective redistributional policies which ensure that incomes rise irrespective of low productivity. But the conditions that must be satisfied for this hypothesis to be realistic are so rigorous—e.g. a relatively small lowest decile, substantial redistributable resources in the society, and political determination—that it is not surprising that Paukert found no empirical evidence suggesting that radical redistribution is usually associated with low *per capita* income [*Paukert, 1968, pp. 428 ff.*]. However, the point here is less that the required conditions are demanding than that, at the very least, the mechanisms by which maldistribution is corrected are unpredictable.[8]

This is clear from the most complete summary of income distribution data so far published.[9] Spearman rank correlation tests show that there is no clear relationship between income accruing to the lowest six deciles and the average level of income per head or average rate of growth of income per head.

TABLE 1

SPEARMAN RANK CORRELATION COEFFICIENTS

	Rate of growth of Y/hd (1960–65) N = 36	Average Y/hd N = 44
1. Income of lowest 20%	+0·12	−0·36
2. Income of lowest 60%	+0·02	−0·79

More sophisticated techniques would require more sophisticated and reliable data. But using these and similar data for the same countries, Adelman and Morris were unable to find a wholly satisfactory mathematical relationship between level of income and income distribution.[10]

This raises a second point. The cross-sectional evidence suggests an eventual improvement in income distribution. But such a trend is not inconsistent with a number of countries facing continuingly regressive income distributions at relatively high levels of average income. South Africa is an extreme example. Those economies heavily dominated by expatriate-controlled export industries are a less unusual case in point. In that situation, of course, *per capita* income is particularly meaningless. None the less, unless the government is able to enforce far-reaching redistributive policies (e.g. by using tax revenues imposed on the export sector to finance effective rural development policies) the usual experience is that a small urban élite, with relatively high incomes and advanced levels of living, contrasts with unrelieved poverty in the rural area. There is no automatic self-correcting mechanism here, particularly if one takes the view that political pressures on the government tend to favour the urban areas rather than the rural.

Third, it is worth repeating all the familiar caveats about generalizing from cross-sectional experience, particularly in the light of the effect of population growth on distribution. Given the fact that observed international experience is based on relatively low rates of growth of population during and after the process of industrialization, it is at least questionable how reliable a guide this experience is under modern demographic conditions. Only if it could be shown to be true that population growth rates fell uniformly across society at some (preferably early) point in the process would it be the case that high population growth rates could legitimately be ignored. In fact, of course, the evidence is too disparate to allow any such conclusion. In general, moreover, birth control permeates downwards with the result that the lower social groups, particularly those with high female illiteracy and unemployment, are the last to reduce the size of families. Even in the unlikely event of employment growth being adequate to ensure that these larger families are found jobs, one can safely assume under all normal conditions (i.e. explicitly excluding huge mineral wealth or freak technological progress) that the productivity of such labour is low and therefore that the distributional nadir is not reached. Historically, only when population growth has been such as to allow for the development of a chronic disequilibrium of under-supply in the labour market and (an included condition) when the poorest groups have ceased to breed away their scarcity value, has distribution become more equitable.

Fourth, it is worth emphasizing that the assumption of trickle-down assumes a process: indeed it could be written up in terms of another 'stage theory', with three roughly defined stages: increasing inequities as industrialization starts; a 'nadir period' in which distribution reaches its most inequitable; and an equalization period during which the amiserated catch up.[11] Put in such terms, it is evident that, like all stage theories, some self-propelling mechanism is assumed to carry the society through one stage to another. Growth of output is assumed to be that mechanism. But this begs the question. It misses the whole point of the last ten years of Latin American structuralist writing that repeatedly makes the point that there are sufficiently numerous and powerful jamming devices to ensure that the mechanism does not work.[12] These jamming devices are economic, social and political. It will be helpful to summarize some of the main structuralist arguments about each of these.

Even from a severely economic point of view, one must begin with the relationship between income distribution and the generation of social classes, or perhaps better, socio-economic interest groups. Problems of definition abound here and some recent work has confused the situation further [Arrighi, 1967; cf. Arrighi, 1970].[13] But for the basic point to be made some very simple propositions will suffice. The early stages of industrialization, whether they be carried out in colonial or post-colonial times, produce groups of beneficiaries. These beneficiaries acquire disproportionate economic and political power.[14] This power enables them to maintain, in part or in total, their absolute and relative position in the society. While this is not inconsistent with a gradual growth of the size of these beneficiary groups, it is inconsistent, given observed rates of growth of G.N.P. and average *per capita* incomes, with a rapid growth of the income of the very poor or with substantial redistribution. The rentier-beneficiaries protect their position by the use of their political power (e.g. to block land reform or effective taxation). The labour-beneficiaries and among them particularly public employees protect their position by using their economic power to entrench their privileges, e.g. most Latin American 'labour codes' and similar provisions for the labour-aristocracy of some West African and Asian countries.[15] Both groups have a common interest in preventing a major structural shift of income and wealth: they will tolerate redistribution only in the very restricted sense of accretion to their own class or interest group.

Further, the economic behaviour of both these groups is unlikely to ensure a rapid rate of accretion.[16] At this point the empirical evidence is weak, but some propositions seem fairly secure. The first is that the beneficiary groups have high average propensities to import. The effect of this is less important on the balance of payments than on the structure of domestic demand. For it follows that the creation of consumer industries on the small base provided by the purchases of the poor is rendered less practicable. This effect is much enhanced, if we assume with Land and Soligo (an assumption with more aprioristic appeal than empirical support) that the relatively rich tend to consume goods with a higher capital output ratio than the poor.[17] For with a capital constraint and Eckhausian factor proportion problems, the growth of domestic output and employment will be slowed. Further, such industries as are established are likely to have limited backward and forward linkage and thus the 'trigger effect' of domestic expenditures is reduced. The cumulative implications for employment and therefore for income distribution need no emphasis.

Secondly, this renders the controversy over the savings and investment habits of the beneficiary groups largely irrelevant. For if consumption habits distort the total structure of domestic demand, it follows that the investment pattern will be distorted if we assume 'normal' (Western capitalist) motivation and a free or relatively free enterprise economy.[18] Two possible exceptions are, first, exploitive industries based on export demand, and, less frequently, export-oriented manufacturing industries. In the former case, domestic capital tends to be associated less with the extractive industry than with small, low-linkage ancillary services [*Kessell, 1971*]: in the latter, high risk and quality premia tend to ensure increasing capital intensity. In either case associated 'trickle-down' is likely to be small and the effects on income-distribution and class structure proportionate.[19]

If a more democratic government, or a non-democratic populist government, tries to offset tendencies of the private sector, the trend towards increasing capital intensity in urban employment and a combination of political resistance and high cost (both of foreign exchange and skilled manpower) in rural development ensures that the rate of accretion is inevitably very slow.

This raises the question of the political obstacles to redistribution. We have already referred to the ability of the rentier groups to protect themselves from effective redistributional policies. The inverse is worth brief emphasis. Although the *marginalidad* school of sociology has recently been sharply challenged,[20] the challenge is more to the outworks of the theory (i.e. to the spatial expression of *marginalidad* and to the incohesiveness of the marginal groups themselves) than to the basic phenomena emphasized by the *marginalidad* writers. For the fact is surely undeniable that the very poor (e.g. the subsistence farmers, the urban unemployed) are also the very powerless. In democratic forms of government, they may have a political representative but almost by definition he does not serve their interests. Indeed he is likely to be largely ignorant of what their real interests are. He represents, more or less effectively, those who can bring pressure, particularly electoral pressure, on him. Since they are unorganized, inarticulate and inchoate, the very poor are incapable of delivering that kind of pressure and therefore their interests tend to be ignored. Indeed, it is not excessively cynical to observe that the political forces that in theory protect the marginal groups are precisely those that exploit them. Recent studies of Latin American squatments, for example, show that the worst injustices in the favellas and callumpas are perpetrated by those who have the political power to eradicate them [*Leeds, 1969*].

If reliance on trickle-down seems somewhat over-optimistic in the light of these considerations, it is worth emphasizing that some common strategies of development are in fact designed to minimize trickle-down. Let us take two illustrations. One popular strategy in the early stages of growth (i.e. during a period often associated with increasingly regressive income distribution) is import substitution. Normally this results in a highly monopolistic industrial structure, operating with some tariff protection. Two results follow. The first is that the prices of the relevant products tend to rise. Since it is safe to assume that import substitution starts with simple mass-consumption (i.e. necessary or quasi-necessary goods) this price rise is associated with a fall in the real income of a substantial proportion of the population. It is also clear that the proportionate fall in real income is higher for those who spend a larger proportion of their total income on these necessaries, i.e. the poorest groups. The *absolute* fall may be small for each household, but for the poorest groups the relative fall can be substantial.[21]

Second, there is some increase in employment at wage rates higher than the subsistence income and probably higher than marginal product. Either through social legislation on fringe benefits or through monopolistic labour practices or through 'beneficient employer' image-building, this tendency towards a high-wage enclave tends to be reinforced.[22]

One further result of great importance follows. The newly employed now buy foodstuffs from the agricultural sector. If the import substitution industry is local-resource based, there will be additionally the usually larger reverse flow of payments for the resource. Under certain conditions this reverse flow can offset the fall in real income suffered by the rural population as a result of the increase in the prices of necessary manufactured products. The question, however, is the *distribution* of this reverse flow. Typically, at least in the early stages of development, two factors combine to ensure that it is not widely disseminated. First, the higher incomes of the newly employed lead to a structural change in diet: 'inferior' foods are discarded and 'preferred' varieties are substituted. In so far as these are locally produced rather than imported, they are produced by those farmers who can adapt quickly and efficiently to changed market conditions and who are sufficiently technologically advanced to switch from traditional to improved crops. The same is *a fortiori* true of new cash crops for local processing.

Secondly, infrastructural development and particularly transport facilities impose a locational constraint. It is thus those farmers who are already relatively advanced who are likely to be the main beneficiaries of the increase in demand for agricultural products. Beyond that it is impossible to generalize. But Zambia in the post-Independence boom, the Kikuyu highlands of Kenya in the post-Swynnerton period, and the lower Nile farmers in Egypt in the late 'fifties are three African examples of the highly limited effect—in terms of space and numbers of farmers—of increased urban demand for agricultural products.

This leads immediately to the second example, that of rural development, or more specifically, extension policy. Here the problem is usually perceived, in Western classical terms, as that of maximizing returns to a given investment, usually in the short or medium term. Put like that, the distributional effects of extension policy are already prejudged. For the 'reinforcement of success' extension strategy is *aimed at* increasing disparities in wealth and income in the rural areas. That this can result in open conflict and a more rapid breakdown of social fabric is a fact ignored in the choice of strategy.[23]

GEOGRAPHICAL DISTRIBUTION AND CHOICE OF STRATEGY

What follows is an unhappy cross between a research plan and a theoretical approach to some, but only some, of these issues. As the research programme develops, it will hopefully become possible to test the approach against the exigencies of national data collection and policy-making requirements in a number of countries.

The basic objective is to develop an analytical framework which makes it possible to examine the effects of past and present policies on the whole society, disaggregated in such a way as will reveal not only the distribution of benefits according to class or income group, but also the generation and reinforcement of politico-economic structural obstacles. One possible approach would be to develop an income distribution framework to relate other benefits to income groups. In some ways this would be ideal since it would allow one to check the distribution of the consumption of other social goods (e.g. education and health services) against the distribution of income and thus build up a more adequate picture of the relative welfare of different sections of the whole community. But such an ideal is unattainable for well-known reasons—e.g. the scarcity of reliable income distribution figures and the impossibility (given current techniques of collecting income distribution data) of relating the consumption of other social goods to given income deciles. At least until such time as data are collected and interpreted in ways that are relevant to our interests here, indirect methods that correspond more closely to the realities of data availability must therefore be investigated. As will soon become evident, this is not to imply that the available data are adequate: if one is still obliged to make bricks without straw, mud bricks are better than no bricks.

In order to clarify some of the more important methodological problems that will occur later, we start with an examination of an approach that has been incorporated in many national plans. This is an analysis of the *geographical* distribution of income and social goods. It is well known that regional variations in income can be substantial. In *per caput* terms, the ratio between income of the poorest and richest provinces can vary from one-fiftieth (Kenya) to one-third (India). In the case of the consumption of social goods, Bugincourt has shown that the difference between Cinderella provinces and the urban areas can be even greater than in the case of income.[24] Further, there is some evidence that these gaps increase during the early stages of industrialization.[25]

Before questioning the validity of a spatial approach alone as a proxy for a more thorough-going distributional analysis, there are some points of estimation and interpretation that deserve brief mention. Particularly in Africa the cash income of the poorest provinces is estimated from known payments for government (and other) services and crops. Thus in Szereszewski's estimates of regional value added in Ghana, in the two poorest regions agriculture (including cocoa production in the case of Buong-Ahafo) and services accounted for around 80 per cent of gross value added [*Szereszewski, 1966*]. Similarly in the Northern Region of the Côte d' Ivoire, agriculture alone accounted for nearly 60 per cent of all income in 1965 [*Côte d'Ivoire, 1964*].

The problem, however, lies in assessing the multiplier effect of these inflows. Average and marginal propensities to import (into the region or Province) are directly related to income and education, and therefore tend to be low in the poorest and least educated regions. Savings propensities may well be higher than often assumed. A recent Zambian study, for instance, showed that subsistence farmers in the Eastern Province (not the poorest, it is true) saved 44 per cent of their *farm* income and 16 per cent of total income. Subsistence farmers in a more developed area of the Central Province saved 48 per cent of farm income and 36 per cent of total income [*UNZALPI, 1970*]. These figures are consistent with but higher

than figures quoted for a poorer province of Zambia by an earlier researcher, for India and other countries [*Kay, 1964*].[26] Further, the same data
reveal the relatively high proportion of income derived from 'intermediate'
activities. For each sub-group, cash gifts, usually from urban relatives,
are small:[27] it is through sources of non-farm income, particularly non-
agricultural part-time employment, and in the case of the more advanced
farmers the hire of oxen and/or equipment that can add as much as half
again to the farm income. This suggests that small-scale intra-regional
economic activity—construction, petty trading, beer brewing, transport
services—can easily be underestimated by the traditional approach of
estimating regional income from crop sales and government services.

A more knotty conceptual problem lies in the valuation of subsistence
income. The technical questions of the determination of consumption and
the prices to be applied are less important than the difference between the
subjective and objective valuation of subsistence income. For the fact is
that a proportion of the rural population has revealed a preference for
village life and near-subsistence income by, for example, returning from
paid employment in the urban areas to 'retire' to the village.[28]

Equally, the Zambian study referred to above found the distinction
between 'farmers' and 'villagers' analytically central. Such a distinction is
one of motivation and preference:

> Villagers have no real interest in making a cash income out of farm-
> ing. They may have retired to the village after employment elsewhere;
> or they may still have a paid job outside the village and be concerned
> more to retain their social position in the village than with making a
> cash profit; or they may not be sufficiently motivated to try to do more
> than provide the subsistence needs of their families. They are cultiva-
> tors because that is a way to live and because it is the way their fathers
> lived. They are much involved in village affairs and take the social de-
> mands of traditional village life seriously. They sell any surplus of pro-
> duction that may occur in a good year, and indeed, as a precaution,
> they may normally aim to produce slightly more than their subsistence
> needs, so that in a bad year they will not starve. But they do not view
> their farming activities as a source of income and are not anxious to ex-
> pand production. (. . .) By contrast, farmers endeavour to produce a
> surplus to generate income [*UNZALPI, 1970*].

If these differences are as crucial as the Zambian data suggest, interpersonal welfare comparisons are hazardous even within one region or
Province. *A fortiori*, they are extremely hazardous between the rural area
and the urban areas.[29]

But the problem of valuation is not confined to income: it applies no
less to social goods. Indeed, if the operational comparison between the
rural and urban areas is to be effective, it is not only necessary to establish
the distribution of such social goods, but also to establish the type and
quality of them required (i.e. felt to be needed) by the rural poor. It has
too often been assumed by planning departments that, since (allegedly)
the rural poor migrate to town to make use of the social facilities there,
what is required is reproductions of urban facilities in the rural areas.
In a sense this assumption has become self-justifying. For by consistently
presenting urban mores and structures as superior, the urban élites have
convinced the rural poor that urban standards are 'needed' in the rural

areas. The disastrous effects of the assumption are being increasingly challenged by those who see the provision of dysfunctional education and badly designed health services as one further form of oppression [*Bennett, 1970; Nyerere, 1968; Bryant, 1970*].

For example, the inappropriateness of traditional school curricula is an inverse function of the probability of the child graduating to a higher educational level.[30] But aggregative measures of educational services do not reveal this type of dysfunctionality. Further, it is generally true that the qualitative variations, also obscured by most indicators in these fields, are biased against the very poor. The quality of schools and hospitals tends to decline with distance from urban concentrations and with decreasing income per head.

These methodological problems aside, a spatial approach as a proxy for distribution of income and social goods falls foul of three serious objections.

First, by identifying the rural poverty problem with the problem of the Cinderella provinces, the approach ignores the fact that even in the comparatively well-developed areas there are groups that suffer real deprivation. The following table compares two regions in Zambia, one with an average income per head of K107, the other with an average income of K448:

TABLE 2

FAMILIES DISTRIBUTED BY INCOME GROUP: TWO ZAMBIAN RURAL AREAS

	Income group (kwacha)								
	0–10	11–50	51–100	101–200	201–300	301–400	401–500	501–750	751–1000	1000+
Mumbwa	5	18	25	20	15	19	9	10	5	9
Katete	8	53	14	13	8	5	1	1	–	1

Source: UNZALPI unpublished data.

It is evident that around three-quarters of the Mumbwa families have incomes of less than half the average income and about 43 per cent have incomes less than the median income in the poorer area. Indeed, 35 per cent earned less than K100, compared with 75 per cent in the poorer area. How far one can generalize from so small a base is problematic, but it is surely true that in very many countries a purely regional approach is likely to result in neglect of a significant proportion of the rural deprived.

Secondly, the regional approach tends to exclude the urban poor. Indeed, such an approach is biased *against* the urban poor. As the ILO report on Colombia has shown, the relative impact of poverty in urban areas can match that of the rural area. In Colombia, even the highly deficient data suggest that more than a third of the active urban labour force has around the same 'extreme poverty' income as about 40 per cent of agricultural producers [*ILO, 1970*]. In some ways, Colombia is doubtless an extreme case, but the point that poverty is not an exclusively rural problem must stand. As Sandra Berry [*1970*], writing on Africa, has put it: 'Part of the "traditional" sector of the economy is simply moving from the countryside into the cities.' Further, in the case of the consumption of social goods, there is some tentative evidence that the urban poor are reluctant to use such facilities as are available to them [e.g. *Zschock, 1970*]. To this

extent, they are less well-endowed than those sections of the rural population that are supplied with, and use, minimal facilities. Equally in the
case of housing, although Western modes of comparison are exceedingly
dangerous, it is surely true that in East and Central Africa, for instance,
village housing poses less of a health threat than Mathare Valley in Nairobi
or Kalingalinga in Lusaka.

Third, and most important, a regional or even purely income-distribu-
tional approach ignores the structuralist pleas for an approach that gives
due weight to the fact that socio-economic and political power is a key
determinant of income distribution and therefore of poverty. Even if one
were able to identify, quantify and frame policies for the relief of the
poverty of the urban and rural deprived, those policies would be ineffective
unless they took account of the defensive reactions of competing classes
and interest groups. In order to set up an adequate frame for examining
the implications of policy decisions for the poor, one needs to identify and
quantify the interest of those whose own welfare is threatened by an anti-
poverty strategy. To assess the distributional impact of policies and projects, progress as that alone would be, without examining their effects on
class-structure and power-distribution is to mistake the shadow for the
substance.

A TENTATIVE APPROACH TO SOCIAL DISTRIBUTION

Such an ambitious aim is beyond the reach of this paper. At this time,
we can only offer some suggestions about what such a method would look
like. What we require is a way of looking at the class structure of poverty
on a basis of existing statistical sources or reasonable guesstimates based
on them, with a view to being able to analyse the effects of major policies
on the poor. We need, therefore, to distinguish between those groups which
include the majority of the poor, the relatively prosperous in both rural and
urban environments, and certain key élite groups. We want to be able to
establish the average cash income of these groups, and check that against
the availability (or, better, use) of certain social goods. We *assume* that
the poor regard health facilities, education and housing as the most sensitive areas.[31] We can then draw up a matrix, with the relevant classes or
interest groups in the rows.[32] The illustration (Figure 1) might be applicable to an African country: it would obviously need modification for
application in Latin America or Asia.

Immediately it must be admitted that such a classification is unsophisticated. The 'classes' are crude and heterogeneous and perhaps defined too
much in economic terms. Further, the values of σ^2 could well be high,
thus indicating that the classification is a poor proxy for a normal income
distribution table.

Similarly, the choice of indicators of consumption of social goods runs
into all the familiar problems in this connection, some of which we have
indicated above. 'Housing' is practically meaningless in the rural areas;
and data on urban housing are notoriously deficient. Bearing in mind the
caveats that emerge from our earlier discussion, education could theoretically be measured in any of the conventional ways, and either in terms of
stock or flow. In practice, the supply of school places per 1000 children is
probably the most that can be attained. The same is true of health facilities.
Ambiguous and unsatisfactory as it is, a crude measure of the supply of

D

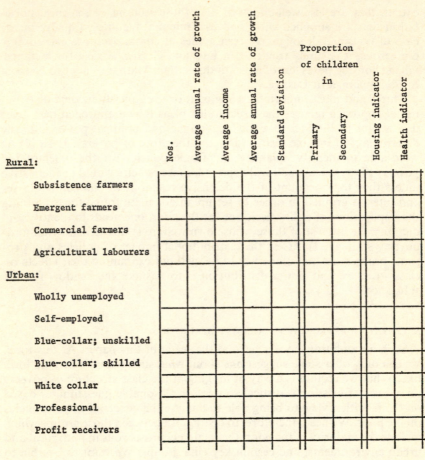

Figure 1

the service such as the number of beds available for each class, on a number of assumptions about the relationship between usage and proximity, must suffice. It is fundamental to this approach that the question 'for whom?' take precedence over the more traditional question of 'exactly what?'

Admitting all those weaknesses, however, let us attempt to complete such a matrix for a trial country. For this purpose, Zambia has been chosen.

At first sight this might seem an odd choice. A classic example of a dual economy, Zambia's regional problems have been aggravated both by the magnetism of the more highly developed but geographically limited line of rail and by a long tradition of labour export to South Africa and Rhodesia. However, natural resource wealth, extremely rapid development since 1964, government's alleged ideological bias against élitism and massive funds invested in rural development make it an interesting test-bed. Table III gives an indication of the size and rate of growth of the more important socio-economic groups.

Table III lays no claim to exactitude: it should be viewed purely as an attempt to lay out orders of magnitude and important relationships. The

TABLE III

INCOME BY SOCIO-ECONOMIC GROUPS, ZAMBIA, 1970

	Nos.		Average rate of growth of class (1)	Average income (K)	Standard deviation	Av. an. % incr. in real income
Rural						
Subsistence	500,000		<1	20[3]	fairly low	<3[2]
Emergent farmers	25,000		8		high	>10
Agric. labourers	34,500		nil	348	low	2
Commercial farmers	550		nil	>8,000	very high	—
Manual (non-agric.)						
skilled	7,000		5–10	800	fairly low	10–15
other	23,000		5–10	300	low	>5
Non-manual	18,000		<5	1,000	high	5–10
Employers, non-agric.	5,000		<5	1,000	high	—
	Afr.	*Eur.*				
Urban						
Manual workers						
skilled	40,000	5,000	8–10	1,200	fairly high	10–15
other	95,000		2–4	500	low	>5
Service						
domestic	38,000		nil	350	low	>5
non-domestic	50,000	1,000	14	750[1]	fairly high	5–10[1]
Clerical and sales	47,000	6,000	7	1,100 4,500	fairly low	10–15[1]
Admin. and managers	7,500	2,500	12	8,000	low	<5
Prof. and tech.	11,700	9,600	15	5,000	high	<5
Employers		8,000	5–10	?	very high	?
Unemployed	66,000		?	<100	low	—

Notes: [1] African employees only.   [2] Possibly negative in real terms.   [3] Per head of family.
Source: See text.

first two columns were compiled from three sources, all of which use different classificatory systems and none of which are wholly consistent with the others. The basic procedure was to derive the urban employed population from the Second Manpower Report and the 1969 Census and to allocate to the rural sector non-manual workers estimated from the teaching service and Government administration. The manual worker category was a residual worked back from the 'rural employee' figure in the CSO Employment Enquiry. This residual was then distributed between skilled and unskilled using a lower skill ratio than for urban employment.

Three particular anomalies in this process of estimation call for comment. The first is that the 1969 Census identified only 300,000 subsistence farmers. The report of the Census itself casts doubt on this breakdown and we have therefore raised it substantially. Second, there is a marked contrast between the Second Manpower Report and the Census in the enumeration of clerical and sales personnel, possibly because the latter included street-sellers and other underemployed 'salesmen' in this category. We have taken the lower (Manpower Report) figure but have not adjusted the Census figure for urban unemployed. If urban underemployed are included in this category, it should be nearer 100,000. Third, it is hard to reconcile the Second Manpower Report figures for unskilled manual workers with either the Census figure for 'production workers' or the industry breakdown of the CSO Employment enquiry. Our estimates are consistent with the Census figure, but may somewhat understate the level of skills in the urban areas.

Reference was made to the last published (Federal) income tax assessments for Zambia in 1963/64. This was interesting primarily for the highest income groups and, assuming no major structural changes since 1963, may suggest that our estimates for the professional/technical and administrative/managerial groups are too low.

The table speaks for itself, though, given the nature of its compilation, with a muted voice. The basic features are clear enough: the huge preponderance of the subsistence sector, and the fact that, after unskilled manual workers in the urban areas, the urban unemployed is the largest single group of the non-subsistence economy. But it is the growth rates that are most interesting. The three groups to which the ex-subsistence worker could hope to attach himself are agricultural labourers, unskilled rural (or, at a higher social, psychic and financial cost to himself, urban) unskilled workers, or, just possibly, domestic servants. Yet these are the three most slowly growing groups of all: employment growth rates in two of them are nil, and in the other the maximum growth rate now foreseeable is less than adequate to absorb the *growth* in the subsistence sector. If the low growth-rate of the latter is realized, therefore (i.e. if urban migration continues at over 2 per cent of the subsistence population per year) it can only result in increased urban unemployment. For even if all new skilled posts are filled by recruits from unskilled (but employed) labour, so that around 8,000 unskilled urban jobs become available each year, the natural growth of the urban population delivers around 16,000 *male* job seekers to the market.[33] Hence the outlook for a reduction in the total number in the subsistence and urban unemployed categories is grim indeed. Rather, with a rate of increase of employment of less than one-fifth of the natural rate of increase of *urban* population, there is every prospect that they will increase. The effects upon distribution are self-evident.[34]

It would be folly to suggest that the data as currently analysed allow us to fill in the columns for health, housing and education. By examining the regional data available for each social good[35] and such few micro-studies as are available, we can, however, make some observations about the distribution of these goods.

First it is becoming increasingly clear that the single most important determinant of the distribution of the consumption of health and educational services is availability. Although the migratory tradition for work was adapted relatively easily to enable children to move to an area comparatively well endowed with schools, those that did migrate were, of course, only a tiny percentage of the whole unschooled child population. The same is true of health. Of course, the sick travelled great distances for treatment (or better treatment) but those that did so were a small proportion of the total who would have used facilities had they been available. Work in Uganda, less rigorously corroborated by Zambian material, suggests that the effective radius of a clinic is under ten miles [*King, 1965*].[35] That of a primary school is almost certainly less. It is thus surprising to find that in the First National Development Plan aggregate *per capita* investment in the education and health sectors in the two poorest Provinces was only 40 per cent of that for the two richest.

The central significance of availability naturally puts at a premium government locational policies, both in the rural and urban areas. In Zambia there has been an irregular development of policy in this respect marked by two major discontinuities—Independence, and government acceptance of responsibility for social services in the large and rapidly growing 'illegal townships' (i.e. slums) in 1968/69.

Inspection of data on primary school places by Province and relevant demographic data suggests that there is no maldistribution so obvious that it is revealed by this crude (but inevitable) technique. The only two major conclusions are first that the Central Province looks badly under-provided and secondly that the Provinces with very sparse, scattered populations do not have ratios sufficiently high to compensate for this disadvantageous low density. Together these observations imply that the two groups that are disproportionately deprived are the very distant, very poor subsistence producers who are unwilling or unable to 'farm out' their children to urban relatives and those urban dwellers (particularly in Kabwe and Lusaka) who live neither in the major townships and compounds nor in the more densely settled rural areas of the Central Province but in those twilight settlements, the periurban squatments. These have not yet achieved the proportions of a political threat and are therefore largely ignored. While the inadequacies of the data are at this point almost wholly unrelieved, those who know well these areas report that they contain a large proportion of either wholly unemployed or technically under-employed. They tend to act as transit camps for those who are arriving in or being forced out of the towns. Inevitably therefore they contain an unusually large proportion of economically deprived.

However, it is when we look at the regional distribution of secondary school places that the difference between rural and urban becomes most marked, with the former having less than half the places of the latter. This is testimony both of the lower *quality* of primary education in the rural areas and of the administrative difficulty of building and staffing secondary schools in the remoter areas. But the fact that only one primary school graduate in fifteen is likely to go to a secondary school in the Western Province (compared with one in ten on the Copperbelt) points up the question of *content* more forcibly. For a primary education in the Western Province achieves little more than the acceleration of deculturation—a process which urban society can adapt to much better than rural. The statistical injustice is thus only the tip of an iceberg: the larger mass of alienation and frustration is submerged.

The statistics on the distribution of health facilities are again only available on a province-by-province basis. Interestingly, the same broad picture emerges. The sparsely populated Provinces with poor communications are disproportionately poorly served statistically. But this disadvantage is compounded by the difficulties of communication and the dispersion of the villages. Equally, the underprovision in the periurban areas is marked in the urban Provinces. Those who can afford transport (i.e. those who have a reasonable income from regular employment) make use of the urban facilities. For the great majority of the population of these twilight areas, health care is virtually non-existent.[37]

CONCLUSION

This suggests at the very least that some means must be found of introducing distributional questions into both strategic and tactical thinking on policy formulation. In general, economists are not well equipped to do this at present. Even at the tactical level, there has been little conscious attempt to build distributional criteria into cost/benefit analysis. In this connection it is a pity that the latest and seemingly highly influential handbook on cost/benefit analysis in developing countries dismisses such a procedure in three pages [*O.E.C.D., 1969*]; and that a recent collection of case studies does not include one mention of distributional criteria.[38] The technique itself should not pose a problem, the only major difficulty being the choice of discounts to apply to incomes received by non-marginal groups. This is ultimately a political decision and therefore runs into the kind of problem of political pusillanimity that we have already encountered. This is precisely the problem. Either one can agree with Little and Mirlees that relocation can only be a marginal activity: or one can risk running counter to the interests of the political powers. Perhaps the rule of thumb that most nearly reconciles the irreconcilable is to choose the highest rate of discount that one thinks one can get away with in the existing political climate. Such a procedure is at least to challenge the politicians to reveal their own preferences. And that is as far as even a partisan economist can go until very much more work has been done in this whole field.

NOTES

1. The precise form of this statement, whether classical or neo-classical, makes no practical difference to the rest of the argument. See Dixit [*1970, pp. 229 ff.*].

2. There is evidence that as detribalization accelerates, these eleemosynary transfers become much smaller than sometimes represented. See Baldwin [*1966, pp. 133–37*].

3. In the Ranis-Fei model, this is 'phase three', when 'it is . . . to the advantage of the landlord to bid actively for labour; . . . the institutional wage is abandoned and competitive market forces yield the commonly accepted equilibrium conditions' [*Ranis and Fei, 1961, p. 537*].

4. This may appear to imply a belief in marginal value product pricing of labour. We show below that so restrictive an assumption is not in fact neccessary.

5. It is sometimes forgotten, too, that in his model Lewis assumes that investment is a function of income distribution and that only profit receivers save.

6. Here and throughout, unless otherwise stated, we refer to real income only.

7. Strictly, we are assuming that the lowest decile and the (former) least productive group are coterminous. This is purely for ease of expression.

8. Further, even the 'weak' hypothesis of the second turning-point of the Ranis-Fei model (which does not, of itself, lead to an *improvement* in distribution but only to the end of deterioration) is a very advanced development historically—e.g. as late as the 1960s for Japan. See Reynolds [*1969, pp. 97–8*].

9. The best collection of income distribution data will be published in Adelman and Morris [forthcoming 1972, excerpted in *USAID Development Digest*, Oct. 1971]. I am most grateful to the authors for allowing me to see an early draft of their paper and for their continuing co-operation.

10. 'The relationship between the share of income at the lowest 20 per cent and economic development varies with the level of development. Economic development is associated with increases in the share of the bottom 20 per cent only after relatively high levels of socio-economic development have been attained.' Adelman and Morris [*1972*].

11. An interesting assumption is that the society starts from a position of relative equity. This, of course, is highly dubious since in many non-industrial societies wealth is concentrated in the hands of a ruling class.

12. Colombia is a good example of a country in which high rates of growth have failed to have any positive effect on distribution: indeed there is some evidence that they have had a negative effect. [*Bird, 1970, p. 522*]. If the argument is that this is still the 'early' stage, in 'nadir' period comes very late. See note 8.

13. This is important work, but Arrighi's unusual sociological morphology makes his analysis less general than it might otherwise be.

14. Much Latin American writing on these themes has already appeared. Perhaps the most persuasive is Cardoso [*1965*]. An interesting reinterpretation applied to Brazil is Fernandes [*1968, esp. pp. 523 ff.*]. For a recent critical application to Africa, see Berry [*1970, pp. 278 ff.*]; and for a rather less critical application, see Arrighi [*1970*].

15. For a revealing analysis in Latin America, see ILO [*1970, Chs. 13 and 14*]. For Africa, see Côte d'Ivoire [*1958, pp. 198–214*] for a detailed account of wage and salary fixing. For social security benefits of public employees, see Paukert [*1968*]. A notorious example relevant to the last part of this essay is that the Government of Zambia felt it necessary to provide housing for *all* government employees—even at a time when building capacity was a severe constraint on development.

16. It is easy to forget just how small some of the oligarchies are—though the last column of Adelman's table should serve as a reminder. One estimate of the economic oligarchy of Peru puts it at forty families. See Bravo Bresani [*1967, p. 40*].

17. Despite some rather restrictive assumptions and a formal stiffness, the Land–Soligo model is a most important contribution to the analysis of income distribution in a growth context (though the basic approach is comparative-static). See Land and Soligo [*1970*].

18. It is suggested by Berry [*1970*] that this condition is not in fact necessary since government is often unable, for reasons there suggested, to correct the distortions. But contrast the findings of Adelman and Morris [*1972*], where étatism appears as an important determinant of income distribution.

19. The Johnson thesis, recently given some empirical support by Morley and Smith [*1971*], that import substitution tends to attract foreign rather than domestic capital as a defensive reaction is likely to increase the regressive effect on income distribution and the élitist tendency of class structure. For his basic thesis see Johnson [*1965, p. 25*].

20. See, for instance, Singer [*1969*], and cf. Leeds [*1969, esp. pp. 47 ff.*].

21. The UNZALPI data suggest that richer farmers (average income K 669 p.a.) spend over 10 per cent of their total income on goods that are or are about to be produced by import substitutive industries.

22. This will have an immediate effect on the terms of trade of the rural sector if we assume some kind of full cost pricing in the import substitutive industry. The consequent effect on employment in the urban sector and total agricultural incomes is complex and depends upon cross elasticities of demand between the urban and rural sector products and the relative marginal propensities to consume 'imported' products in the two sectors; see Knight [*1971, p. 51*]. In so far as strategy skews objectives towards employment rather than output, this is achieved earlier, but the possibilities of such a skew are limited. See Stewart and Streeten [*1971*].

23. One of the side effects of the Green Revolution, particularly in India, has been to heighten awareness of these problems. See, for instance, Brown [*1970*].

24. See his path-breaking articles [*Bugincourt, 1970 and 1971*].

25. For example, in the period 1965–70, income *per head* in the north of Ivory Coast was estimated to grow at 2·1 per cent p.a. by contrast with 4·1 per cent in Abidjan. More striking, in Tanzania, *wage earners* in the poorest zone experienced only slightly higher rate of growth than those in the Dar es Salaam zone. But since the former *zone* includes a large number of subsistence and small peasant producers, total zonal income per head in Dar was clearly growing substantially faster than in the poor zone.

26. Kay's sample is very small and his conclusions must therefore be treated with even greater reserve than usual for a survey of this kind. For other countries see Firth and Yamey [*1964*].

27. It is very possible that these were underreported in the survey, though their diminishing volume is consistent with observed patterns of detribalization in the urban areas.

28. Baldwin [*1966*] estimated that about 15 per cent of the Zambian rural population were returned migrants.

29. We are, of course, abstracting from a host of sociological problems that enter in here. The effect of tribal differences is only one of many non-economic factors that make interpersonal welfare comparisons so awkward.

30. We assume that at post-secondary level traditional education becomes functional for it allows the student to enter competitively the modern sector.

31. This is, of course, a bold assumption. It ought to be checked against any attitudinal data that are available.

32. When this was written I had not seen the work by Riad on Egypt which is similar to, but less ambitious than, this scheme. His work is, however, most interesting in its own right and provides an illuminating contrast to what follows. See Riad [*1964, p. 41*] and, for a brief statement of the case for such a matrix, as well as a reproduction of Riad's matrix, Sachs, *La Découverte du Tiers Monde*, Flammarion, Paris [*1971, pp. 107–20*].

33. This assumes a 'normal' output of the educational system, i.e. bunching is smoothed.

34. Income of the unemployed is notoriously difficult to survey or estimate. The Urban African Demographic Survey of 1963, for instance, assumes all unemployed have no income, but this is not consistent with much micro data. See, for instance, Bettison and Rigby [*1970*]; cf. Pfefferman [*1968*].

35. I am grateful to Dr Stein of the Statistical Department of the Ministry of Health, Lusaka, and to the Planning Department of the Ministry of Education for supplying me with such data as they have.

36. UNZALPI [*1970*] data for Zambian rural areas. Forthcoming work by Felix Savage for two Lusaka townships. Dr Savage suggests that availability may determine what kind of treatment a patient selects—'traditional' or Western.

37. Further, traditional medicine is not easily practised in these areas. The 'witch doctors' have profitable practices in town; the older female relations who act as medical advisers tend to remain in the village until the family is better established and the man of the household may be prevented from (or certainly discouraged from) the often time-consuming business of collecting herbs from the bush by the need to search for a job.

38. Kendall [*1971*]. J.-F. Boss of France does discuss regional considerations, but only in the context of developed countries.

REFERENCES

Adelman, I., and Morris, C. T., 1972, 'An Anatomy of Patterns of Income Distribution in Developing Nations', *American Economic Review*, forthcoming excerpted in USAID, *Development Digest*, October 1971.

Arrighi, G., 1967, *The Political Economy of Rhodesia*, The Hague: Institute of Social Studies.

Arrighi, G., 1970, 'Labour Supplies in Historical Perspective: A Study of the Proletarianization of the African Peasantry in Rhodesia', *Journal of Development Studies*, Vol. 6, No. 3.

Baldwin, R. E., 1966, *Economic Development and Export Growth: A Study of Northern Rhodesia, 1920–60*, Berkeley: University of California Press.

Bennett, N., 1970, 'Primary Education in Rural Communities—an Investment in Ignorance?' *Journal of Development Studies*, Vol. 6, No. 4.

Berry, S. S., 1970, 'Economic Development with Surplus Labour: Further Complications suggested by Contemporary African Experience', *Oxford Economic Papers*, 22: 2.

Bettison, D. G., and Rigby, P. J., 1970, *Patterns of Income and Expenditure; Blantyre, Limbe, Nyasaland*, Rhodes-Livingstone Communication No. 20, University of Zambia Institute of Social Research.

Bird, R. M., 1970, 'Income Distribution and Tax Policy in Colombia', *Economic Development and Cultural Change*, 18: 4 Part 1.

Bravo Bresani, J., 1967, *Mito y Realidad de la Oligarquía Peruana*, Lima: Instituto de Estudios Peruanos.

Brown, L. R., 1970, *Seeds of Change: The Green Revolution and Development in the 1970s*, New York and London: Praeger.

Bryant, J., 1969, *Health and the Developing World*, Ithaca: Cornell University Press.

Bugincourt, J., 1970 and 1971, 'Conjonction, correlations et contiguité des disparités régionales en Afrique', *Cultures et Développement*, II: 3–4 and III: 1.

Cardoso, Fernando Henriques, 1965, *El Proceso del Desarrollo en América Latina, Hipótesis para una Interpretación Sociológica*, Santiago: CEPAL.

Côte d'Ivoire, 1958, *Inventaire Economique et Social de la Côte d'Ivoire, 1947–58*, Abidjan: Ministère des Finances.

Côte d'Ivoire, 1964, *Plan Quinquennal de Développement Economique, 1965–70*, Abidjan: Ministère des Finances, des Affaires Economiques et du Plan.

Dixit, Avinash, 1970, 'Growth Patterns in a Dual Economy', *Oxford Economic Papers* 22 (2).

Fei, J. C. H., and Ranis, G., 1964, *Development of the Labour Surplus Economy*, Homewood: Irwin.

Fernandes, F., 1968, 'Société de Classes et sous-développement au Brésil', *Cultures et Développement*, 1: 3.

Firth, R., and Yamey, B., 1964, *Capital, Saving and Credit in Peasant Societies*, London: Allen & Unwin.

I.L.O., 1970, *Towards Full Employment*, Geneva: International Labour Office.

Johnson, H. G., 1958, 'Planning and the Market in Economic Development', *Pakistan Economic Journal* 8: 2.

Johnson, H. G., 1964, 'Tariffs and Economic Development: Some Theoretical Issues', *Journal of Development Studies*, Vol. 1, No. 1.

Kay, G., 1964, *Chief Kalaba's Village*, Manchester: Manchester University Press for Rhodes-Livingstone Institute.

Kendall, M. G., 1971, *Cost-benefit Analysis*, London: English Universities Press.

Kessell, N., 1971, 'Mining and the Factors Constraining Economic Development' in C. Elliott (ed.), *Constraints on Zambia's Economic Development*, Nairobi: O.U.P.

King, M., (ed.), 1965, *Medical Care in Developing Countries*, London: Oxford University Press.

Knight, J. B., 1971, 'Wages and Employment in Developed and Underdeveloped Economies', *Oxford Economic Papers*, 23: 1.

Land, J. W., and Soligo, Ronald, 1970, 'Income Distribution, Employment and Growth in Labour Redundant Economies', paper read to Southern Economics Association, Atlanta, Georgia, November.

Leeds, A., 1969, *The Significant Variables determining the Character of Squatter Settlements*, I.L.A.S. Offprint No. 105, University of Texas.

Lewis, W. A., 1954, 'Economic Development with Unlimited Supplies of Labour', *Manchester School*, 22.

Morley, S. A. and Smith, G. W., 1971, 'Import Substitution and Foreign Investment in Brazil', *Oxford Economic Papers*, 23: 1.

Nyerere, J., 1968, 'Education for Self-Reliance' in *Ujamaa: Essays on Socialism*, Dar es Salaam.

O.E.C.D., 1969, *Manual of Industrial Project Analysis*, Development Centre Studies, Paris: Organization for Economic Co-operation and Development.

Paukert, Felix, 1968, 'Social Security and Income Distribution: A Comparative Study', *International Labour Review*, 98: 5.

Pfefferman, G., 1968, *Industrial Labour in the Republic of Senegal*, New York: Praeger.

Ranis, G., and Fei, J. C. H., 1961, 'A Theory of Economic Development', *American Economic Review*, 51, September.

Reynolds, L. G., 1969, 'Economic Development with Surplus Labour: Some Implications', *Oxford Economic Papers*, 21: 1.

Riad, H., 1964, *L'Égypte Nassérienne*, Paris: Les Editions de Minuit.

Sachs, I., 1971, *La Découverte du Tiers Monde*, Paris: Flammarion.

Singer, Paulo, 1969, *Crescimento Económico e Evolução Urbana*, Rio de Janeiro: Companhia Editôra Nacional, Editôra da Universidade.

Stewart, F., and Streeten, P. P., 1971, 'Conflicts between Output and Employment Objectives in Developing Countries', *Oxford Economic Papers*, 23: 2.

Szereszewski, R., 1966, 'Regional Aspects of the Structure of the Economy' in W. Birmingham, I. Neustadt and E. N. Omaboe, *A Study of Contemporary Ghana*, London: Allen & Unwin.

UNZALPI, 1970, 'Report to the Government of Zambia' (unpublished), Lusaka: Universities of Nottingham and Zambia Agricultural Labour Productivity Investigation.

Zschock, D. K., 1970, 'Health Planning in Latin America: Review and Evaluation', *Latin American Research Review*, University of Texas, 5: 3.

The Adequacy of Income:
A Social Dimension in Economic Development

By Riad B. Tabbarah*

SUMMARY

The adequacy of income of a household may be defined as the ratio of its income to the income level required to achieve the conventional standard of living in the socio-economic group to which the household belongs. This concept has greater relevance than that of income for the study of consumer behaviour (e.g. propensity to save) and other social behaviour and pathologies. Income and need for income in a country do not necessarily rise proportionately over time, thus resulting in periods of declining, as well as periods of rising, income adequacy. Furthermore, in spite of the international demonstration effect, the need for income in developing countries is significantly lower than in developed countries resulting in a much smaller gap between income adequacies than between incomes.

The national accounts concepts of income (national, personal or disposable), whether total or *per capita*, are admittedly inadequate for the study of consumer behaviour (e.g. with regard to the propensity to save) and for the understanding of other social phenomena that are affected by welfare considerations (e.g. poverty). A major reason for this is that the need for income varies among individuals so that the same level of income may reflect totally different levels of income adequacy among them; as a result, their welfare-related behaviour tends to be significantly different from one another. Thus, in a given community, for example, the head of a household containing six dependents may be considered in abject poverty at an income level that is quite adequate for a two-person household. On the other hand, for the same *per capita* income the larger household tends to be better off. Consequently, the proportion of income saved by the two households may be quite different although their incomes may be virtually the same.

A number of alternative concepts which take the need for income into account have been developed. As will be seen, however, most of these concepts were devised for the purpose of explaining or analyzing a specific social or economic phenomenon (e.g. poverty) and are, therefore, of limited applicability. The purpose of this article is to present a general view of income adequacy, by presenting a measurable income adequacy

* The author is a staff member of the United Nations. This article is part of research supported by a grant from the United States National Institute of Child Health and Human Development to International Population and Urban Research, Institute for International Studies, University of California, where this research was undertaken. I am deeply grateful to Thomas Espenshade and David Goddard for a thorough reading of an earlier draft and their valuable comments, I am also grateful to Eduardo Arriaga for many useful suggestions.

concept that explicitly relates income to the need for income. Certain potential uses of this concept, as well as its relationship to other concepts relating means to needs, will also be discussed. It must be emphasized, however, that the ideas presented here are aimed more at illustrating a potentially useful line of enquiry than at drawing definitive conclusions from it.

POVERTY

Historically, but particularly during the past decade, studies of the relationship between income and the need for income have been largely conducted in conjunction with efforts to determine the extent and nature of poverty. The income–need relationship was found particularly useful for the identification of the poor. First, for any group of households of a given size and type it was necessary to determine the income level at and below which the household should be considered 'needy' or 'poor' (i.e. the poverty line) and hence qualified for anti-poverty, relief or other assistance programmes. Second, since needs of households for income vary not only with prevailing price levels but also with size and age structure (i.e. type) of households, a different poverty income level had to be determined for these different size-type households. Once these poverty lines have been determined, a household of a given size and type was considered poor if its income was equal to, or less than, its corresponding poverty line. In other words, if for the kth household, i denotes the size, j the type, Y income and N need, an index of poverty would be:

$$W = \frac{Y_{k(ij)}}{N_{ij}} \qquad (1)$$

and poor households would be defined as those for which $W \leqslant 1$.

Morgan et al. [1962] called the ratio in equation (1) the 'welfare ratio' and classified the families in a sample by welfare ratio intervals 0–0.4, 0.5–0.6 . . . 2.1 and over; they then proceeded to study the characteristics of families in intervals below 1.0; in general, the farther down is the interval the more abject is the poverty level at which the families live.[1]

INCOME ADEQUACY

The study of poverty may be viewed as a specialized aspect of the study of income adequacy. The adequacy standard described by the poverty line does not necessarily reflect that of families *as viewed by themselves*; it is, in a sense, the minimum level of adequacy that *society* is willing to tolerate before vigorous and co-ordinated collective action is deemed necessary. Therefore, while the poverty level of need is quite relevant for the formulation of programmes of the anti-poverty type, it is not very relevant to the study of social behaviour related to the adequacy of income. It is obvious that, if incomes of all households in England or the United States were to become equal to their corresponding poverty lines, social disintegration and upheaval would ensue. In fact, major social dysfunctions (e.g. rise in suicide rates) among the now more privileged groups would probably appear much before that level is reached.[2] In other words, the need for income varies not only because of the size and age structure of the household (and prevailing prices) but also because of its 'socio-economic status'. While status beyond the poverty level may not be directly relevant to anti-poverty policy, it is quite relevant for more comprehensive studies of income adequacy in society. To say that a physician whose income has fallen to the poverty level enjoys the same income adequacy as a slum dweller whose income has risen to that level does not obviously correspond to these two participants' views of reality and hence tends to conceal causes of their differential behaviour. Just as the poverty line in India is not relevant to the study of poverty in the United States, the poverty line in the United States is not relevant to the study of income adequacy of, say, the professional class in that country.

THE NEED FOR INCOME

A few elementary notions relating to the sociological concept of human needs may be briefly stated at this point: first, 'need' (i.e. human need) may be defined as '[a] state of tension or dissatisfaction felt by an individual that impels him to action toward a goal he believes will satisfy the impulse' [*Theodorson and Theodorson, 1969, p. 272*]. From the negative side, it may be said that an individual may be denied the satisfaction of a need 'only at the cost of an intra-personal conflict' [*Etzioni, 1969, p. 871*]. It follows, therefore, that the nature of needs in a society and the degree to which that society permits their satisfaction may be an essential prerequisite for investigating certain attitudes in it as well as certain of its major dysfunctions.

Furthermore, human needs may be 'physiological', that is deriving from the biological nature of man, or they may be 'social', that is learned by the individual through social interaction and internalization (or legally imposed[3]). Needless to say, physiological needs are those that man largely shares with other animals while social needs are essentially peculiar to man.[4] However, even the most physiological needs of man become socialized in that they tend to contain an element peculiar to the society in which the man in question happens to live. Thus, while the need for food is universal, the type of diet through which this need is satisfied differs significantly among different societies.[5]

Finally, human needs are obviously varied and the means for satisfying them—i.e. the 'answers' to them—are also varied. Furthermore, 'There is no one-to-one connection between any specific need and any specific "answer"; on the contrary, the needs can be satisfied in a very large variety of ways' [*Etzioni, p. 871*]. Nevertheless, it is by and large true that, given the type of society in question, there are groups of needs that are generally most readily satisfied through a specific means. For example, in Western societies (and in others), the need for clothing is generally satisfied through the expenditure of money—obtained, as a rule, in a socially determined manner (by productive activity or by inheritance, social assistance or other such transfer payments)—while the need for affection or socialization in childhood is generally answered by the nuclear family. The means are, of course, often related,[6] as is almost everything else in a social system, but may nevertheless be separated for analytical purposes.

'Need for income', therefore, refers here to a set of needs that are generally satisfied by income (cash or imputed). It is, hence, an aspect (though partial or 'specialized') of the concept of human need and by that fact is subject to basically the same principles: need for income is mainly social (or socialized) and the failure of an individual or a group to satisfy that need may result in certain specific responses among that group. What this imples is, first, that the best measure of this need in a group would have to rely heavily, if not solely, on the true preception of the group of it and any projection of this need would have to constitute a projection of that perception (though not necessarily through an enquiry from the group itself). Furthermore, since needs are largely socialized (even if after a lag), they may differ considerably among groups even within the same country. The degree of satisfaction of these needs (income adequacy) would therefore have to be determined at different levels of needs for different groups. It is basically for this reason that, as was said earlier, the poverty line is not relevant to the study of the income adequacy and related behaviour of the more privileged classes. This is not to say, of course, that existing privileges should be maintained but only that they should be taken into account in the study of income adequacy and the social phenomena affected by it.

THE MEASUREMENT OF NEED FOR INCOME

Perhaps the most widely used measure of need for income is the standard family budget (SFB).[7] Generally speaking, the construction of SFBs is made in at least three major steps: first, for a given size-type household (e.g. family of four including two children in two given age brackets) 'quantities' are determined for all consumption categories (food, housing, clothing, etc.) in a way as to reflect a predetermined standard or way of living (e.g. at the poverty line). Second, all quantities are priced, generally, in a 'realistic' way, that is, in a way that reflects the actual prices that would be paid by these households. Finally, a process of translating the SFB of this particular size-type family to other size-type families is undertaken (e.g. to families of different sizes and age composition).[8]

In general, for categories of consumption (particularly food and shelter) for which 'scientific' standards are available, quantities required are set according to these standards. For the remaining consumption categories, attempts are often made at setting quantities on the basis of the consumers' revealed tastes.[9]

The standard family budget could well form one of the basic tools for the study of income adequacy. However, at least two major modifications should be made from its present usage. First, budgets should be constructed not only for a single standard as is generally done presently, but for different standards corresponding to different socio-economic groups in the population.[10] These groups would have to be chosen because they differ significantly from each other in terms of their revealed tastes while relative homogeneity exists within them in this regard.[11] Their needs for income may therefore differ from one another because of differences in average income levels, their respective degrees of integration in society and of exposure to higher standards, the relative extent of their (and society's) awareness of egalitarian 'rights', their ethnic and cultural backgrounds, their rural or urban way of life and other such factors that may, upon investigation, prove to be relevant in the particular situation under review. In existing budgets, the real need of households is made to vary mainly with their size and age distribution (i.e. size and type); for general income adequacy purposes they would be made to vary, in addition, with their 'socio-economic status'. In this fashion the need for income becomes also a function of the existing social structure and dynamics.

Furthermore, calculations of the standard family budget would have to rely more heavily on the revealed tastes of the population. Comparison of scientific requirements for calories and proteins with the actual intake of the population is of course quite useful (e.g. to health officials) but is not particularly relevant in itself to the general study of income adequacy. According to the present definition of the problem, income may very well be considered 'adequate' by a family which has a deficient diet. What is required here is a comparison between what the family believes is adequate —that is, in practice, the 'conventional standard' for the relevant group— and what it is able to obtain with its income. These two approaches therefore have two very different purposes: the first may be useful for investigating such phenomena as undernourishment and the second, for example, alienation.

Another method of determining need for income is through the use of public opinion surveys of the Gallup type. A series of questions may thus be asked to determine—for a family of a given size, type and social status— the quantities or values of the different consumption categories that together are deemed to constitute a standard family budget at a clearly indicated adequacy level. If quantities only are indicated independent pricing should be undertaken to estimate the cost of the budget. A global question (or questions) could also be asked to obtain the respondent's estimate of what *total* income would satisfy the indicated level of adequacy. This could then constitute a 'check' on the results of the more elaborate set of questions. As will be seen, this latter type of question has been asked, at different times and in different countries, by the Gallup Organization[12] but no data relating to the more detailed type of enquiry are available.

INCOME

Ideally, the measure of income to be used in conjunction with a standard family budget would have to depend on the method used in calculating the budget. Thus, if the value of the SFB includes personal taxes, that of income should also include such taxes. On the other hand, if education is free and so considered in the SFB, its value should not be imputed to income. This is, of course, true whether the SFB is calculated from consumption data or from Gallup-type enquiry. In practice, complete coincidence between the concepts of SFB and income is not always possible to insure since, so far, the methodologies of budgets and incomes in a given country are not likely to have been co-ordinated.

More important perhaps is the fact that the income of a household in a given year may not be totally representative of the cash flow to the household during that year. Dissavings may constitute a significant part of a household's income particularly among the unemployed and the aged. While an estimate of dissavings should be added to income, at least for these groups, it is important for social analysis to indicate groups for which this constitutes a significant part of income.[13]

Finally, the net worth of an individual may be thought to have, often, a significant effect on his income adequacy level. The difficulty in combining income and net worth is well known and arises from the fact that income is a flow and net worth is a stock. Nevertheless, attempts at combining them may be found in recent welfare literature.[14] However, such expanded concepts of income are not essential in the present context since the main interest here is in the adequacy of realized, and not potential, income. Knowledge of potential income among different socio-economic groups, however, is important additional information for social analysis.

The above list of issues to be considered in the choice of the income concept is of course not exhaustive, it is only illustrative. It must be noted however, that the difficulties are by no means insurmountable and good approximations of the 'ideal' income concept are not more difficult to find than most economic statistics. The greater need for information is obviously with regard to the need for income of the different socio-economic groups.

INDICES OF INCOME ADEQUACY

As was already mentioned, the adequacy ratio for a given household differs from the welfare ratio given in equation (1) in two major ways: first, the need for income reflects not a 'scientific' (or partially scientific) standard but that of the socio-economic group in which the household falls. Obviously, a certain degree of homogeneity with regard to need is assumed to exist within the group. Second, the level of need for income is a function not only of the size (i) and type (j) of household but also of the household's socio-economic status (m). The adequacy ratio of the kth household therefore may be stated as follows:

$$A_{k(ijm)} = \frac{Y_{k(ijm)}}{N'_{ijm}} \qquad (2)$$

where N' is the average need for income calculated according to revealed tastes. The average adequacy index for the n_{ijm} households of a given size, type and socio-economic status (e.g. families of four persons with head of household aged 30–35 years and who has a professional occupation) is therefore:

$$\bar{G}_{ijm} = \frac{\sum\limits_{k=1}^{n_{ijm}} Y_{k(ijm)}}{N'_{ijm}} \div n_{ijm} \qquad (3)$$

The General Income Adequacy Index of society is the average of all these indices weighted by the proportion (H_{ijm}) of total households in each group; it may therefore be stated as follows:[15]

$$\bar{G} = \sum_{ijm} \bar{G}_{ijm} . H_{ijm} \qquad (4)$$

There are as many possible uses for these indices of income adequacy as have properly been made of the concept of household income itself. Equations (2) and (3), for example, may be used to identify households and groups of households by the adequacy of their income. They would, therefore, permit comparisons of income adequacy among, say, different socio-economic groups or different size-type households within a given socio-economic group. They would also permit the study of association between income adequacy and certain relevant indices of social behaviour with a view to improving our understanding of the latter.

Within such intra-societal analyses, the two indices in equations (2) and

(3) permit inter-temporal comparisons of the income adequacy of given household groups (e.g. black families in the United States). It may be found, for example, that while incomes of these groups have been rising, their adequacy standards have been rising more rapidly (because of such factors as greater degree of urbanization, integration and social awareness), resulting in a decline in income adequacy. Such a situation may result in certain specific social responses on the part of the group that cannot obviously be explained by the upward trend in their income. Furthermore, these two indices permit international comparisons of the income adequacy of, say, given social status groups, as for example physicians or civil servants in different countries.

The General Income Adequacy Index ($\bar{G}$) may also be used for inter-temporal and international comparisons. Such comparisons have interesting implications particularly to the study of development. Since, as was already mentioned, data for estimating $\bar{G}$ in different countries and over time are not totally reliable, some of these implications can be illustrated only through the use of rough approximations of the trend of $\bar{G}$ over time, or partial data relating to its comparative international level. In the following two sections, such data will be used to illustrate the application of adequacy analysis to the inter-temporal and international study of development.

INCOME ADEQUACY AND ECONOMIC DEVELOPMENT

Economic development, in the sense of a long-term growth in *per capita* income, is generally accompanied by a number of structural and social changes which, on balance, increase the need for income. There is, first, the traditional decline in fertility levels which results in a higher median age of the population. Since the need for income of an adult tends to be greater than that of a child, the growth in *per capita* income tends to exaggerate the growth in income adequacy. Second, these basic demographic changes, together with the increased prominence of the nuclear family (partly because of increased internal migration), result in a smaller average size of household and hence a reduction in the 'economies of scale' associated with household size. Third, economic development is generally accompanied by increased urbanization which tends to increase needs in general and particularly of certain recently urbanized groups because of their greater interaction with other more privileged groups and the demonstration effect associated with such interaction. Fourth, economic development is generally accompanied by an 'upgrading' of the labour force, through better education and training, and of the population in general, and hence by greater social awareness on the part of the less privileged groups as well as a general shift in the social structure in favour of groups with higher needs. Finally, and most important, economic development permits the ever-increasing consumption of goods and services which, through the process of internalization, tend continuously to become part of human needs. This latter point, in a sense, overshadows all the rest because it implies that, once physiological needs are met, income and need for income tend to rise together and, perhaps also, in a proportionate way to each other.

The question may legitimately be asked, therefore, is not the whole argument of this paper a spurious one, at least on the basis of a socialized

E

view of man? If income and need for income have parallel trends, then adequacy levels remain fairly constant over time and are, therefore, not useful for the study of social behaviour. This, however, is not the case and this for several reasons:

First, there are the demographic and social variables just mentioned (age distribution of the population, average size of households, urbanization and education) which tend to affect need independently of income and hence to disturb the proportionality between them.

Second, as was mentioned earlier, the need of a lower status group may increase independently of income because of the greater 'integration' of this group with the rest of society (and greater social awareness among its members). Thus, for example, the increased exposure of the lower status group to the consumption habits of other groups tends to place a social strain on its income through an increased demonstration effect.

Third, the process of internalization of new consumption habits is not a simple or 'unique' process. For one thing, it is generally completed only after a lag (especially when new consumption habits conflict with 'prior socialization') so that a changing rate of growth of income tends to result in a changing income adequacy ratio over time. This tendency is accentuated by the fact that a decline in income does not necessarily result, in the short term at least, in a decline in need for income; in other words, internalization of higher levels of living is likely to be effected much faster (and with less intra-personal conflict) than that of a declining level.

The fact that income and need for income may change at different rates may be illustrated with the use of the U.S. data in Table 1. In column 2 of that table, the *per capita* values of the SFB for an urban family of four (net of direct taxes, dues, etc.) at the 'moderate' level are given for the years 1929, 1949 and 1969. Since *per capita* need changes with size of household, an adjustment was made to take into account the different 'average number of persons per household' in these three years (column 3). In column 4 the adjusted data are expressed in 1958 prices and in column 6 *per capita* disposable income is also stated in 1958 prices. The respective rates of growth in these two variables for the periods 1929–49 and 1949–69 are indicated in columns 5 and 7.

Accordingly, for the period 1949–69, both *per capita* need for income and *per capita* disposable income seem to have risen by the same yearly rate (2.5 per cent). For the period 1929–49, however, apparently because of the intervening depression, the rate of increase in need for income was of the order of 1.8 per cent while the corresponding rate of increase of *per capita* disposable income was 1.1 per cent.

These findings are confirmed and supplemented by a parallel analysis undertaken with the use of Gallup data (Table II). For the post-war period as a whole (1947–70) the rates of increase in *per capita* need and *per capita* disposable income were fairly equal. However, for the decade of slow economic growth (1950–60) within that period need increased substantially faster than income while for the decade of relatively more rapid economic growth (1960–70), the opposite seems to have been the case.

It must finally be noted that the relationship between income and need for income tends to be even less strict in other, less developed countries than the United States, because of the *international* demonstration effect. The intensity of this demonstration effect may be much greater on certain groups within the country than on others with the possible result that higher income groups which are exposed to foreign influences may experience greater inadequacy of income than the relatively isolated lower income groups. Similarly, for the country as a whole, the extent of the international demonstration effect will not only depend on the relative position of that country on the international or regional development scale but also on its degree of exposure to outside influences. Thus, it is to be expected that the adequacy standards of the Albanian population, for example, would be less affected by the higher levels of living in western Europe and North America than the adequacy standards of more open countries in the region such as Italy, Lebanon or Greece. There is little doubt, furthermore, that the policy of an 'iron curtain', as in the U.S.S.R., has helped restrain the rise in adequacy standards (i.e. need for income) in the periods when the growth in personal incomes was deliberately kept in check in order to permit high rates of investment (which resulted in a spectaular rate of economic growth). It may not be totally coincidental, furthermore, that the recent relative relaxation in the iron curtain policy of the Soviet Union was accompanied by relatively greater emphasis on the production of consumer goods in the country.[16]

It is interesting to note, therefore, that the problems of income inadequacy and poverty in the developing countries are becoming increasingly less dependent on the internal distribution of income and hence outside the power of the respective governments to solve them (short of closing the country to outside influences). It is becoming increasingly true that to redistribute the income equally in these countries would make everyone poor, even in the long-run, since needs are partly determined outside the national borders and since the upward pressures of the international demonstration effect will continue to be felt. On the other hand, in a country like the United States where consumption levels are high relative to the rest of the world, the relationship between income and need for income is by and large determined internally and the solution to income inadequacy and poverty is basically a redistributional one. Furthermore, a slowdown in the rate of economic growth in this country (e.g. as a result of devoting a larger share of investment to social 'non-productive' ends) is not likely to have a major negative effect on income adequacy levels; it may only ease the pressure on those levels in the rest of the world.

INCOME ADEQUACY AND INTERNATIONAL COMPARISONS

One of the central problems involved in making international income comparisons relates to the setting of 'a purchasing power equivalent' with which to express the value of income (or GNP) in a country in terms of the currency of another[17]. The most common device for doing this is the rate of exchange, but the shortcomings of this procedure makes the resulting comparisons extremely rough and hence of somewhat limited usefulness [*Gilbert and Kravis, 1954, pp. 14–17*].

A variety of alternative methods of calculating purchasing power equivalents have been devised.[18] The purpose of this section is not to summarize these methods but only to compare the more conventional approach with that based on income adequacy.[19] This analysis is intended to show that there are more than one legitimate purchasing power equivalent depending on the purpose of the income comparison; it will also help to indicate the type of questions that may be answered by each of these two approaches. For the sake of clarity, the conversion ratios obtained by the income adequacy approach will be referred to as 'adequacy equivalents'.

Consider, then, the simplified example of two countries, A and B, whose respective gross national products are described by two sets of quantities (Q_a and Q_b) and prices (P_a and P_b). The GNP of A in A prices (say, dollars) is, therefore,

$$GNP_{a,a} = \Sigma Q_a P_a \tag{5}$$

and that of B in B prices (say, pounds) is,

$$GNP_{b,b} = \Sigma Q_b P_b \tag{6}$$

One method of obtaining a purchasing power equivalent consists of computing the value of the GNP of A in terms of the prices of A and B separately and then calculating the purchasing power equivalent as the ratio of these two values; thus:

$$PPE_1 = \frac{\Sigma Q_a P_a}{\Sigma Q_a P_b} \tag{7}$$

What this means is that since the same basket of goods, Q_a, fetches $\Sigma Q_a P_a$ dollars in A and $\Sigma Q_a P_b$ pounds in B, then the amount of dollars indicated has an equivalent purchasing power as the amounts of pounds.[20] One can also, therefore, price the quantities in the GNP of B in the prices of A and B respectively and obtain an alternative purchasing power equivalent; thus:

$$PPE_2 = \frac{\Sigma Q_b P_a}{\Sigma Q_b P_b} \tag{8}$$

It may then be argued that, since PPE_1 and PPE_2 are the purchasing power equivalents according to the 'tastes' or conditions in A and B respectively, then the average of the two (e.g. 'Fisher's ideal index'), though admittedly somewhat ambiguous in its economic meaning, may nevertheless be considered superior, for the purpose of overall comparisons, to either extreme [*Gilbert and Kravis, 1954, p. 26*]. Thus:

$$PPE_3 = \sqrt[2]{PPE_1 . PPE_2} \tag{9}$$

This method of 'binary comparison', therefore, is usually used for comparing the value of output—the 'economic strength' [*Gilbert and Kravis, 1954, p. 26*] as it were—of different countries; the same approach may also be used for comparative analyses in such related areas as productivity.

The binary comparison technique, however, is not intended for welfare type comparisons. It does not, for example, take into account the fact that needs vary among countries. These variations may come from at least two major sources: demographic differences arising mainly from differences in age structure and average size of household and social differences arising from variations in consumption habits, conventional standards of living (that may be affected by the international demonstration effect) and social structure.

The fact that international variations in need for income from these two sources may be quite significant is not too difficult to document. For example, Kleiman presented estimates of the effect of the demographic factor on need for income in a group of developed and developing countries [*Kleiman, 1966*]. He 'adjusted' *per capita* income in these countries by factors reflecting need variations due to differences in age distribution and size of household to obtain 'income per consumer unit'. A comparison between this and *per capita* income revealed that the 'relative divergence' between them differs significantly among countries. Furthermore, although no strict correlation between the relative divergence and *per capita* income was found, it was obvious that income per consumer unit was generally more favourable to developing countries (relative to developed countries) than *per capita* income [*Kleiman, 1966, pp. 50–51*]. This is, of course, not surprising since, mainly because of generally higher fertility rates and lower geographic mobility, developing countries tend to have younger populations and larger average households.

Gleason, on the other hand, made a comparison between incomes in the United States and in Japan with the use of standard family budgets [*Gleason, 1961*]. For the United States, he used the 1951 SFB for an urban family of four at the modest but adequate level. For Japan he constructed a similar budget using, in essence, the maximum elasticities method used in the U.S. budget. Since the Japanese budget was made to refer also to a family of four, the resulting comparison did not take into account differences in need for income arising from the demographic factor. It may be taken however, as indicative of the relative effect of the social factor on income adequacy in the two countries. The purchasing power equivalent resulting from Gleason's calculations was 63 yens to one U.S. dollar which was about one-sixth of the foreign exchange rate of 360 yens to one U.S. dollar. Here again, the 'gap' between incomes (measured with the use of exchange rates) seems to be wider than that between income adequacies.[21] This is again not surprising since, even in the presence of the international demonstration effect, social standards and need for income are likely to be lower in lower income, than in higher income, countries.

Finally, the significance of the combined effect of the demographic and social factors is clearly indicated by the data in Table III. In this table, need for income is determined by the Gallup poll data for Greece, the Netherlands, the United States, the United Kingdom and West Germany. Column 5 of the table gives *per capita* private consumption in local currency in 1969. These values were than converted to U.S. dollars with the use of the official exchange rates (column 4) and the adequacy equivalents (column 3) respectively. For each set of data obtained, the percentage that each country's *per capita* consumption is of that of the United States was obtained and the results were listed in columns 6 and 7. Estimates of the corresponding percentages (for 1960) which would be obtained by using purchasing power equivalents are given in the last column of the table.[22]

For the present purpose, the most interesting comparison is between the relative levels of consumption as indicated in the last two columns. Here again the gap between the consumption levels of the different countries and the United States as measured by purchasing power equivalents seems to be wider than that measured by adequacy equivalents. As expected, this is most clearly so with regard to Greece, the least developed of the five countries. Thus, roughly speaking, while the average Greek can purchase only less than one-sixth of the goods and services of an average American, his consumption is more than half as adequate as that of the American.[23] For the United Kingdom and West Germany, on the other hand, the difference between these two measures is, again as expected, not as substantial.[24]

The income adequacy method of obtaining purchasing power equivalents requires, then, the calculation, for each country, of standard family budgets for each size-type-socio-economic status (i.e. N'_{ijm}) and to obtain from this the weighted average for all households. Thus, for country A, for example,

$$\overline{N}'_{a,a} = \underset{ijm}{\Sigma} N'_{ijm} . H_{ijm} \tag{10}$$

The adequacy equivalent may then be stated as follows:[25]

$$A = \frac{\overline{N}'_{a,a}}{\overline{N}'_{b,b}} \tag{11}$$

The 'income adequacy' method of comparison, therefore, is based on the relative values not of the same basket of goods but of two different baskets, which are 'comparable' because they reflect the average adequacy standards in the two countries. This method may hence be used to determine the relative degree of effectiveness of different economies in meeting the adequacy requirements of their respective populations. It may also be used for the comparative study of economic and social phenomena (e.g. personal savings rates, reproductive behaviour) as well as the comparative study of certain social pathologies which may be affected by income adequacy.

It is clear, therefore, that these two approaches to international comparisons (through purchasing power equivalents and through adequacy equivalents) are not mutually exclusive, but are complementary; the insight into comparative development obtained from the one is only extended by the other. In general, while the binary approach is particularly useful for comparative economic analysis, the adequacy approach is more useful for the understanding of comparative social phenomena.

CLOSING REMARKS

As a tool of development analysis, the national accounts concept of income (GNP, personal income, etc.) has proven to be quite useful for certain purposes. These uses include the estimation of tax returns, the analysis of structural changes in production, the study of productivity, that is, by and large, the study of economic phenomena directly related to production. The usefulness of the national accounts concept of income for explaining consumer behaviour (e.g. with regard to consumption and savings levels) and other social phenomena which are affected by welfare considerations (e.g. poverty), is certainly more restricted, and often so inadequate as to lead to serious errors in judgement. The concept of income adequacy is an attempt at expanding the usefulness of the income concept into these areas of socio-economic analysis by relating it to the idea of need for income.

There is clearly a good deal of similarity between the present line of reasoning and that underlying Duesenberry's relative income hypothesis [*Dusenberry, 1949*]. A basic tenet of this hypothesis, it will be recalled, is that an individual's consumption level is significantly enhanced by his exposure to 'superior goods' consumed by others with whom he comes frequently in contact [*Dusenberry, 1949, esp. p. 27*]. As a result of this 'demonstration effect', the individual's ratio of savings to income, that is, his propensity to save (which in the present context may be considered a rough indicator of his relative need for income) is highly correlated (negatively of course) with his relative position on the income scale in society.

An obvious similarity between the two approaches, therefore, is that, in both cases, an attempt is made to formulate a concept which would relate the concept of income to that of need for income. Furthermore, both formulations accept a similar (socialized) view of man[26] which, *inter alia*, relates an individual's need for income to the realized needs of others (that is, both formulations accept the idea of 'interdependent preferences').

Nevertheless, there are still major differences between income adequacy and relative income, both in approach and in their respective scopes of application. For example, relative income does not readily or adequately take into account differences in need for income arising from the age distribution within the household or from the economies of scale associated with its size. In general, however, the basic difference between the two approaches arises largely from the fact that income adequacy involves methodologically the reverse process of reasoning underlying relative income. Thus, in the latter approach, the actual relationship between income and need for income (as reflected in the propensity to save) is explained by a certain view of the interrelation among the consumption levels of individuals in society, while in the present approach the actual relationship between income and need for income (as indicated by the income adequacy ratios) is, itself, used to explain the interrelation among the consumption levels of different individuals or groups. In other words, the propensity to save is not intended as a tool for investigating income adequacy and related social behaviour, while income adequacy ratios are specifically designed for that purpose.[27] On the basis of these ratios, the adequacy of income of a given group may be found to be affected not only by the relative position of the group on the income scale and the intensity of its contact with other groups in the population but, perhaps also, with its degree of contact with higher levels of living abroad, the relative awareness of its members of egalitarian rights, its ethnic and cultural background and style of life or, in fact, with any other factor that may become obvious on further analysis of the particular situation. In this sense, the income adequacy approach allows for a more elaborate and flexible view of man and of consumer expenditure.

Another closely related difference between the two approaches arises from the fact that the relative income approach does not indicate, quantitatively, the level of need for income of an individual or group of individuals as does the income adequacy approach. As a result, the relative income approach has a more restricted applicability for inter-temporal and international comparisons of income adequacy than the present approach. For example, adequacy equivalents which are a natural extension of income adequacy analysis cannot be readily obtained from the comparative analysis of relative incomes.

The income adequacy approach bears also some similarity to Cantril's attempt at measuring people's aspirations with the use of the 'Self-Anchoring Striving Scale' [*Cantril, 1965*]. According to this method, '[a] person is asked to define on the basis of *his own* assumptions, perceptions, goals, and values the two extremes or anchoring points of the spectrum on which some scale measurement is desired—for example, he may be asked to define the "top" and "bottom", the "good" and "bad", the "best" and the "worst". . . Then, utilizing a nonverbal ladder device [from 0 to 10], . . . he is asked where he thinks he stands on the ladder today, with the top being the best life *as he has defined it*, the bottom the worst life, *as he has defined it*.' [*Cantril, 1965, p. 22*]. For the purpose of inter-temporal comparisons, '[he] is also asked where he thinks he stands in the past and where he thinks he will stand in the future.' [*Ibid*]. A 'mean rating' for a community or country, with reference to each of the three periods, is then obtained as the arithmetic average of all responses.

The similarity in this instance is largely due to the fact that, in both cases, means and needs are being related and the relationship is determined on the basis of the opinions or attitudes of the persons in question. The differences however are quite obvious. Suffice it to mention that, while Cantril attempted to relate, in a way, all means to all needs, the income adequacy approach attempts to relate a specific means (income) to the needs that are most readily satisfied by it. The concept of income adequacy, therefore, is 'specialized' or 'partial' in relation to that of Cantril. It is, by that fact, however, likely to be more 'stable' (in the economic sense) and the results of its application to be less ambiguous and more easily interpreted. At any rate, a comparison between the results of the two concepts may, in itself, prove to be quite revealing.[28]

The concept of income adequacy, although it may be considered in the family or welfare concepts, is not presented as a goal of development—i.e. as a variable that must be maximized by development policy. The fact that, according to this concept, an individual who has a car now may have the same income adequacy level than one who had a mule a hundred years ago would imply that the intervening development process was not justifiable (whether or not it was, involves a more complicated decision). Furthermore, since, as was already mentioned, the general income adequacy index is partially determined by the existing distribution of the population by socio-economic status, its maximization as a goal may tend to perpetuate existing privileges (whether or not this is desirable again involves a more complicated decision).

It must finally be noted that, because the income adequacy concept is partial in terms of the means and needs to which it refers, its use as a major development goal suffers—though to a lesser degree—from similar defects as those encountered in the use of income: a number of 'externalities' to income, or 'social costs', which are important from the welfare point of view, are also externalities to income adequacy. Consider the simple example of two individuals with the same real income, living in two different areas. Assume everything else to be the same except that in the first area the air is polluted and in the other it is not. If pollution requires the first man to visit the physician more frequently than the second, then his need for income will be higher. To that extent the income adequacy concept would take into account externalities to income. However, assume that the first man's life expectation is reduced by, say, two years. This will not appear in his standard family budget (as need for income) and therefore will remain an externality. It must be noted, however, that externalities are inherent to every partial measure of welfare; they can be taken into account in policies aimed at optimum allocation only as a result of less rigorous analysis than presently found in allocative economic literature [*Mishan, 1969, pp. 79–81*].

TABLE I

PER CAPITA NEED FOR INCOME IN STANDARD FAMILY BUDGETS
AND PER CAPITA PERSONAL DISPOSABLE INCOME, UNITED STATES
1929, 1949 AND 1969

Year[1]	Per capita SFB (net) (current prices)[2]	Per capita S.F.B. adjusted for household size in current prices[5]	Per capita S.F.B. adjusted for household size (1958 prices)[6] % increase from Value previous date		Per capita personal disposable income in 1958 prices[7] % increase from Value previous date	
(1)	(2)	(3)	(4)	(5)	(6)	(7)
1929	408[3]	404	682	—	1,236	—
1949	836[4]	875	1,054	1·8	1,547	1·1
1969	1,955	2,131	1,681	2·5	2,535	2·5

1. Equidistant years were chosen since S.F.B.s are stated to represent standards of the respective decades.

2. U.S. Department of Labor, 1959, *How American Buying Habits Change*, Washington, D.C.: U.S. Government Printing Office, p. 237; Phyllis Groom, 1967 'A New City Worker's Family Budget', *Monthly Labor Review*, Vol 90, no. 11 (November), p. 2; and 'Spring 1969 Cost Estimates for Urban Family Budgets', *Monthly Labor Review* Vol. 93, no. 4 (April 1970), p. 63.

3. Wage earners only; figure also refers to only one city, San Francisco, but is nevertheless believed to be comparable to later data because San Francisco's S.F.B. has subsequently shown to be always very close to the average of the cities for which budgets were constructed. The figure used for 1929 was adjusted from 5-person to 4-person family by use of the equivalence scale (100/114) from 'Budget Levels for Families of Different Sizes', *BLS Bulletin no. 927*, Washington, D.C., 1948, p. 51, last column of table.

4. The 1949 figure was obtained by averaging data for 1947 and 1951.

5. Adjustment made on the basis of the increase in *per capita* need for income implied in the equivalence scale of note 3 above.

6. Using Consumer Price Index in U.S. Department of Labor, Bureau of Labor Statistics, 1970, *Handbook of Labor Statistics, 1970*, Washington, D.C.: U.S. Government Printing Office, p. 285.

7. U.S. Department of Commerce, Office of Business Economics, 1971, *Survey of Current Business*, Vol. 51, no. 7, part 1 (July), p. 42.

TABLE II

PER CAPITA MINIMUM NEED FOR INCOME IN GALLUP POLLS
AND PER CAPITA PERSONAL DISPOSABLE INCOME (BOTH IN 1958 PRICES) UNITED STATES,
SELECTED YEARS 1947–1970

	Year and Level				*Period and Rate of Growth*		
	1947	1950	1960	1970	1950–60	1960–70	1947–70
Income	1,513	1,646	1,883	2,595	1·3	3·2	2·3
Need[1]	750	810	1,100	1,340	3·0	2·0	2·5

1. Data obtained by correspondence with the Gallup Organization. Levels were adjusted for size of household (see footnote 5 of Table I). Slight discrepancies between the stated rates and those implied by the stated levels are due to rounding.

TABLE III

INTERNATIONAL COMPARISONS OF INCOME BY ALTERNATIVE METHODS

Country and Currency	Per capita need/year in local currency (1969)[1]	Adequacy equivalents ($1.00 =)[2]	Official exchange rates 1969[3]	Per capita private consumption, local currency 1969 ($1.00 =)[3]	Per capita consumption index (US = 100) according to		
					Official exchange rate 1969[5]	Adequacy equiv. 1969[5]	Purchasing power equiv. 1960[6]
(1)	(2)	(3)	(4)	(5)	(6)	(7)	(8)
Greece (Drachma)	20,530[7]	12·5	30·0	18,971	22·1	53·2	15·0
Netherlands (Guilder)	2,315	1·4	3·6	4,426	43·1	110·8	52·1
United Kingdom (£)	371	0·23	0·42	515	43·0	78·5	71·4
United States ($)	1,638	1·0	1·0	2,854	100·0	100·0	100·0
W. Germany (Mark)	4,457	2·7	4·0	5,683	53·8	73·8	61·4

1. From data in *The Gallup Opinion Index*, report no. 67 (January 1971), p. 6; these data were reconverted to local currency with the use of exchange rates in column 4; they were also converted to *per capita* per year form and adjusted for size of household (U.S. = 100).
2. Obtained by dividing each country's figure by that of the U.S.
3. From United Nations, *Statistical Yearbook 1970*, Table 186.
4. Total consumption data for all countries except Greece were obtained from worksheets in United Nations' files made in preparation of the forthcoming (i.e. 1970) edition of the *Yearbook of National Accounts Statistics*. Corresponding figure for Greece obtained by geometric extrapolation of 1967 and 1968 data in *Yearbook of National Accounts Statistics, 1969*. Population data for all countries were obtained from United Nations, *Demographic Yearbook, 1969*, Table 4.
5. Obtained by expressing column 5 in U.S. dollars with the use of indicated equivalence and then obtaining the percentage each country is of U.S. figure.
6. From Wilfred Beckerman and Robert Bacon, 1966, 'International Comparisons of Income Levels: A suggested New Measure', *The Economic Journal*, vol. 76, no. 303 (September), p. 533.
7. Athens only.

NOTES

1. A somwhat similar and earlier use of welfare ratios may be found in David [*1959*].

2. It may be noted that there is empirical evidence pointing to the existence, at least within certain communities in the United States, of correlation between a couple's view of the adequacy of their incomes and their desired number of children. See, for example, Freedman and Coombs [*1966*].

3. Thus, an individual in the city may feel biologically (or even socially) adequate in sub-standard housing (e.g. a tent) but may not live in such housing because of city ordinances.

4. Physiological or primary needs must be differentiated from *basic* human needs. The latter needs, while also presumably universal, do not have a biological foundation. For a defence of their existence, see Etzioni [*1968, pp. 871 and 873*] and for a list of basic human needs, see Davies [*1963*].

5. The view implicit in this paragraph and in the present essay may be labelled the 'social but not entirely socialized' conception of man. See Wrong [*1968, esp. pp. 129–32*].

6. For example, a certain level of income may be a prerequisite for the proper functioning of the family.

7. For methods of identifying the poor without the use of standard family budgets, see Miller *et al.* 1967, pp. 20–22] and Orshansky [*1965*].

8. For a description of methods of constructing standard family budgets, see United Nations [*1969a, pp. 57–70*] and references therein. It must be mentioned that some of the ideas in the present article may be found in the background paper referred to in the above document. This is due to the fact that the present author was the United Nations staff member responsible for the preparation of that document.

9. One method of doing this which has recently gained wide recognition is that initially used more than two decades ago by the U.S. Bureau of Labor Statistics in determining the 1947 SFB for city workers at the 'modest but adequate' level (a level distinctly higher than that of poverty). According to this method, the empirical relationship between consumption and income for families of the budget type is examined for each category of consumption and the point and maximum elasticity (the inflection point) taken as the quantity for that consumption category (e.g. clothing) reflecting the 'modest but adequate'—or 'moderate'—standard. 'The inflection point has been interpreted as the income level at which families stop buying "more and more" of a category of goods and services and begin buying other goods or items of higher quality' [*Brackett, 1969, p. 5*],

10. Recently, the U.S. Bureau of Labor Statistics began publishing three separate standards. The moderate standard is obtained through the method described above. The lower and higher standards correspond to 'the income classes immediately below and above the class containing the point of maximum elasticity'. These latter standards, therefore, do not reflect the needs of identifiable socio-economic groups.

11. The breakdown by socio-economic categories will also depend on availability of relevant data.

12. The question asked, however, is not free of ambiguity: 'What is the SMALLEST amount of money a family of four (husband, wife and two children) needs each week to get along in this community?' For example, it is not clear what the ages of the children are, nor whether the income needed is before or after direct taxation [*Gallup Opinion Index, 1971, p. 5*].

13. In fact, the source of income is an important consideration in the study of welfare in that, for example, a person who works twice as hard, or as long, as another but receives the same income is likely to enjoy a lower level of welfare. An attempt at combining a measure of leisure into the welfare ratio was made by Morgan and Smith [*1969*].

14. A recent attempt tries to combine them 'by converting net worth into an annuity value, which is added to current income' [*Weisbrod and Hansen, 1968, p. 1315*].

15. Under certain conditions, $\overline{G}$ may be roughly approximated by the G_{ijm} for the size-type-socio-economic-status household most commonly found in the population in question (e.g. the four-person urban worker's family in the United States).

16. It should perhaps be noted at this point that the concept of income adequacy does not support the idea of the 'happy native': that since culturally secluded groups are happy because of their ignorance of better ways of life they should be left alone to enjoy this state as long as possible. On the contrary, it may rightly be argued that since exposure to higher standards is admittedly inevitable in the long run, development

efforts should be made as early as possible; otherwise, when hitherto stagnant need begin eventually to rise rapidly, income will be found to lag hopelessly behind.

17. There has been a number of attempts at devising non-monetary indicators for level of living comparisons but these will not be dealt with here. For a description of some of these, see Beckerman [*1965, pp. 16–21*].

18. For a summary of many of these methods, see Beckerman [*1965, pp. 1–15*]; also [*pp. 23–55*] for his alternative method.

19. With only minor modifications, the methods discussed may be used for inter-temporal, as well as international, comparisons. This section may therefore be viewed as an extension of the argument in the previous one.

20. This approach of obtaining purchasing power equivalents by pricing the same basket of goods in different countries is useful for certain particular purposes. With minor variations it is used, for example, by the United Nations for determining comparative salary levels of international civil servants in different countries [*United Nations, 1952*].

21. *Per capita* private consumption in Japan may be converted into U.S. dollars with the use of (1) official exchange rates, (2) purchasing power equivalents, and (3) adequacy equivalents. The percentage that the Japanese *per capita* consumption is of that of the United States according to these three methods is approximately 14, 33 and 81 per cent respectively (1960). For sources of data and methods of calculation, see Table III.

22. The data in column 8 are actually obtained by a method which presumably gives reasonable approximations of the purchasing power equivalents. For a criticism of this method, see Duggar [*1969*].

23. In fact, the adequacy of the Greek's income is even higher than this since the *per capita* need in column 2 relates to Athens only—an area likely to have higher needs for income than the rest of Greece.

24. It would, of course, be interesting to correlate personal savings rates of these countries with the corresponding values in columns 7 and 8 respectively to find whether or not a significantly higher correlation is obtained with the values of the former column (although results of simple correlations may not be easily interpreted). This, however, would not be appropriate, mainly because of the nature and size of the sample. Nevertheless, an interesting case is presented by the data of the Netherlands. The average Dutchman can purchase only about half the goods and services of the average American but his consumption is nevertheless some 11 per cent more adequate. At the same time, data not in the table show that the rate of personal savings has been consistently and substantially higher in the Netherlands than in the United States. In fact, the rate of personal savings in the Netherlands is the highest of all five countries listed in the table (see data on receipts and expenditures of households in United Nations [*1969b*].

25. A short-cut approximation is the one used by Gleason whereby the standard family budgets of the most common size-type socio-economic group of households in each country is used.

26. Compare, for example, the discussion in Duesenberry [*1949, pp. 25–32 and 85*] with the discussion on 'need for income' in the present article.

27. Note, for example, that an individual's need for income may be much higher than his income but his consumption more or less equal to his income because of his limited ability to borrow or dissave. In such cases, the propensity to save becomes a very poor indicator of income adequacy.

28. Some consistency in the relationship between the results obtained from using the two indices—the mean rating and the average income adequacy index—may be expected since the 'economic concerns' of people—as revealed by the more detailed questionnaire used by Cantril—seem to be extremely prominent in relation to other concerns in practically all countries studied [*Cantril, 1965, esp. ch. 8 and 9*].

REFERENCES

Beckerman, Wilfred, 1965, *International Comparisons of Real Incomes*, Paris: Organisation for Economic Co-operation and Development.

Brackett, Jean C., 1969, 'New BLS Budgets Provide Yardsticks for Measuring Family Living Costs', *Monthly Labour Review*, Vol. 92, No. 4.

Cantril, Hadley, 1965, *The Pattern of Human Concerns*, New Brunswick, New Jersey: Rutgers University Press.

David, Martin, 1959, 'Welfare, Income and Budget Needs', *Review of Economics and Statistics*, Vol. 41, No. 4.

Davies, James C., 1963, *Human Nature in Politics*, New York: Wiley.

Duesenberry, James S., 1949, *Income, Saving and the Theory of Consumer Behaviour*, Cambridge, Mass.: Harvard University Press.

Duggar, Jan Warren, 1969, 'International Comparisons of Income Needs: An Additional Measure', *Economic Journal*, Vol. 79 No. 313.

Etzioni, Amitai, 1968, 'Basic Human Needs, Alienation and Inauthenticity', *American Sociological Review*, Vol. 3 No. 6.

Freedman, Ronald, and Coombs, Lolagene, 1966, 'Economic Conditions in Family Growth Decisions', *Population Studies*, Vol. 22 No. 2.

Gallup Opinion Index, 1971, Report No. 67.

Gilbert, Milton, and Kravis, Irving B., 1954, *An International Comparison of National Products and the Purchasing Power of Currencies*, Paris: Organisation for European Economic Co-operation.

Gleason, Alan H., 1961, 'The Social Adequacy Method of International Level of Living Comparisons as Applied to Japan and the United States', *Journal of Economic Behaviour*, Vol. 1 No. 1.

Kleiman, E., 1966, 'Age Composition, Size of Households, and the Interpretation of Per Capita Income', *Economic Development and Cultural Change*, Vol. 15 No. 1.

Miller, S. M., Martin Rein, Pamela Roby and Bertram M. Gross, 1967, 'Poverty, Inequality and Conflict', *Annals of the American Academy of Political and Social Science*, Vol. 373.

Mishan, E. J., 1969, *Welfare Economics: An Assessment*, Amsterdam: North-Holland Publishing Company.

Morgan, James N., Martin H. David, Wilbur J. Cohen and Harvey E. Brazer, 1962, *Income and Welfare in the United States*, New York and London: McGraw-Hill.

Morgan, James N., and Smith, James D., 1969, 'Measures of Economic Well-Offness and their Correlates', *American Economic Review*, Vol. 59 No. 2.

Orshansky, Mollie, 1965, 'Counting the Poor: Another Look at the Poverty Profile', *Social Security Bulletin* (U.S. Department of Health, Education and Welfare, Social Security Administration), Vol. 28, No. 1.

Theodorson, George A., and Theodorson, Achilles G., 1969, *Modern Dictionary of Sociology*, New York: Thomas Y. Cromwell.

United Nations, 1952, *Retail Price Comparisons for International Salary Determination*, New York: United Nations.

United Nations, 1969a, *Social Policy and Distribution of Income in the Nation*. New York: United Nations.

United Nations, 1969b, *Yearbook of National Accounts Statistics*, New York: United Nations.

Weisbrod, B. A., and Hansen, W. L., 1968, 'Measuring Economic Welfare', *American Economic Review*, Vol. 58, No. 5, Part I.

Wrong, D. W., 1968, 'The Oversocialized Conception of Man in Modern Society' in S. G. McNall (ed.), *The Sociological Perspective*, Boston: Little, Brown and Co.

Social Indicators and Welfare Measurement: Remarks on Methodology

By Jan Drewnowski*

SUMMARY

The impossibility of measuring social conditions as one overall aggregate has to be recognized: it is only the three distinct 'aspects' of social conditions which can be considered conceptually measurable. They are: (1) demography (2) social relations and (3) welfare. Each of them must be measured in its own way. This paper is concerned with elaborating a methodology of measuring welfare by means of indicators and indices, based on observable and measurable facts. Welfare indices are supposed to serve not only for assessing the results of development but also as targets for development plans.

INTRODUCTION

The desirability of a quantitative approach to social problems has been generally recognized for some time. It has been realized that an adequate explanation of social situations and social change is not possible unless a quantitative approach is used. If this has been accepted to be the case in respect of *understanding* social problems it is even more evidently relevant for any deliberate *action* aimed at introducing social change or improving social conditions. Planning of any action is badly impaired if its aims and prospects cannot be given a quantitative expression.

The example of economics proves what spectacular progress can be achieved in both understanding and directing development through the application of quantification methods. The social scientists tended to look at economics with envy and were inclined to emulate its achievements in theoretical thinking and practical action. But they also looked at it with misgivings: it was felt that the economists were trespassing into the territory of social science and were influencing development in a biased and one-sided way.

As no possibility of measuring social conditions existed, economic variables such as G.N.P. and all its derivations were increasingly used to 'measure' social conditions and social progress. As development planning was introduced more and more widely these economic variables became criteria for determining the course of development. For quite a long time this state of affairs was endured, but by now it is generally recognized that traditional economic accounting variables cannot legitimately be used for measuring improvement in social conditions, nor can they be considered satisfactory as objectives for development planning.[1]

This attitude led to quite a considerable amount of work on 'social indicators'[2] which were supposed to provide the means of understanding

* Professor of Economic and Social Planning in the Institute of Social Studies in the Hague.

and influencing social processes. Lists of social indicators have been compiled and various analytical procedures applied to them.[3] Not only individual researchers but high-powered official bodies have been engaged on that exercise.[4]

Although a number of interesting proposals have been put forward and ingenious procedures suggested, meaningful and durable results of this activity have so far been rather meagre. The day when the traditional economic indicators will come to be replaced by social indicators in measuring the progress of development is still far off. It is not yet clear which of the many suggested social indicators are fit to serve that purpose.

And no wonder. What has been created so far is an incoherent maze of variables, the definitions of which are muddled, quantification procedures questionable, and practical uses, if any, extremely doubtful. There is no doubt that many of them may prove quite useful, but they are lost among others which are useless. What is badly needed is the establishment of some ordering principles which would make possible a selection of useful indicators, and rejection of the ill-conceived and inapplicable ones. Suggestions to this effect are the subject of the present paper.

'MEASURABLE ASPECTS' OF SOCIAL CONDITIONS

When indicators are selected with a view to measuring social conditions it must be made clear which aspect of these conditions is to be measured. It is essential to realize that the position in this respect is the opposite to the position in economics. Practically all the main aggregate variables commonly used in economics are expressed in monetary units. Their numerical values are derived from prices, which in turn reflect market conditions which existed at some place at some time. Serious limitations are implied in this method of quantification; but it certainly has one merit: there is no ambiguity about what is being measured and the procedures for quantification are relatively straightforward. This was possible because it was unequivocally assumed that the most important question about the elements of the economic situations related to the monetary value of this or that. Within the framework of traditional economic thinking this was a natural question to ask and it was also natural that the answer given was accepted as satisfactory, again within the narrow economic approach prevailing at present.[5]

Such a procedure is, however, unacceptable if we take a broader view of social problems. Not one, but several questions have to be asked if a meaningful quantification of the social situation is to be obtained. These questions will be concerned with various aspects of social conditions. The answer to each question will call for a different quantification methodology.

A simple example may help to explain this. Measurement is certainly practicable in astronomy, but even there we must know what it is that we want to measure. Measurement can be attempted only on something which is conceptually quantifiable. Before we proceed to measurement we must make clear exactly what we are trying to measure and then make sure that it is a measurable concept. We must not attempt to measure a planet, as a planet as such is not conceptually measurable. On the other hand, a number of 'conceptually measurable' aspects of a planet can be measured, namely its mass, volume, density, temperature, speed of its various move-ments, etc. The measurements are expressed in different units specific to each of these aspects.

In the same way 'social conditions' are not 'conceptually measurable' and it does not make sense to try to measure them as such. But certainly there are some aspects of 'social conditions' which are 'conceptually measurable'. The first task is therefore to discover what they are; then procedures for measuring them may be devised. They will have to be different, of course, for each of the 'aspects'.

Unfortunately the determination of the 'aspects' of social conditions is not as straightforward and uncontroversial as a similar exercise in nat-ural sciences. However difficult and questionable it may be, it has to be undertaken as it is a necessary precondition for the solution of the difficult problems of measurement of social variables.

The demographic characteristics of a population are an essential ele-ment of the social conditions of that population. Demography may there-fore be taken to be the first 'aspect' of social conditions in the taxonomy of 'aspects' which it is necessary to establish. The quantitative methods of demography are well known and so there is no need to justify or explain them. We note the 'demographic aspect' of social conditions, and leave it at that.

The second 'aspect' of social conditions may be called the 'social rela-tions aspect'. It covers what is called social stratification, social groups and relations between them, problems of authority and dependency on all levels (family, class, state, empire), problems of social cohesion, of stability and change, and of war and peace. Probably these phenomena have enough in common to be classified as one 'aspect', which means that the quantification of these relations can be based on a similar methodology; but this is not certain. Perhaps it might be possible to find criteria for divid-ing this 'aspect' into two or three distinct entities, but the test of this will come only when quantification is seriously attempted, and we do not propose to do so here. What has been done so far to quantify social re-lations cannot be discussed here either, as it is still too early to summarize this work, while any detailed discussion of it falls outside the scope of this paper.

The third 'aspect' of social conditions may be called the 'welfare aspect'. It is concerned with the satisfaction of human needs. The possibility of measuring this aspect of social conditions has a practical significance for assessing the progress of development and for setting development plan-ning targets. This results from the prevailing conviction that the main task of development is to provide for the satisfaction of human needs, that is, to increase the welfare of the people.

As the three 'aspects' of social conditions have to be measured by different means calling for three separate sets of indicators, it seems advisable to abandon the use of the term 'social indicators', and to introduce instead three separate terms distinguishing the three aspects of social conditions. They would be: demographic indicators, social relations indicators and welfare indicators.[6]

The remainder of this paper is concerned with the methodology of de-vising 'welfare indicators' and with their applications.

F

WELFARE INDICATORS

Welfare indicators are observable and measurable phenomena which contain information about the degree of satisfaction of human needs. A judiciously-selected set of indicators may provide that information for a good part of the spectrum of human needs, and may therefore be considered as a means for measuring the level of satisfaction of the needs or welfare of an individual or a population.

It is necessary to use this method of measurement because welfare is not directly measurable, but we must be aware of the inherent imperfection of these 'indirect' methods. The indicators selected could never comprehensively cover all the components of welfare. On the other hand, even such an imperfect way of measuring welfare is superior to not measuring it at all or to measuring it in terms of misleading national accounting variables.

Welfare indicators have to be distinguished from other social indicators (that is demographic and social relations indicators) and from indicators which cannot be called social at all.

It is the traditional national accounting and economic variables that are in danger of being confused with welfare indicators. This is because they have been used, in the absence of social indicators proper, for measuring the prosperity of the population. We realize now that this is not a valid practice.[7] Such variables as G.N.P. or consumption per head do not measure the satisfaction of needs but the market values of the means that could be (but not necessarily are) used for satisfaction of these needs. They express the results of intermediate changes of economic activity which constitute the costs of generating the ultimate outcome of that activity, that is, welfare. Similarly, such variables as employment or income cannot be considered social indicators. They refer to even earlier stages of the productive process: employment is only the opportunity to earn income, and income only the opportunity to acquire goods. This is still very far from the actual satisfaction of needs.[8]

The distinction between demographic and welfare indicators is relatively clear. It might be noted that demographic indicators can sometimes become substitutes for welfare indicators proper. Infant mortality, for instance, which is obviously a demographic variable, may substitute for an indicator of health. Whereas this is permissible, we should always be aware of the category to which each indicator really belongs.

Social relations indicators have not so far been elaborated in any systematic way. It is difficult therefore to draw an *a priori* delimitation line between them and the welfare indicators. The more detailed analysis of the characteristics of welfare indicators which will be undertaken below should also make clear the distinction between them and other kinds of indicators, including the social relations ones.

THE DIMENSIONS OF WELFARE INDICATORS

'Social indicators' as at present conceived do not only refer to various 'aspects' of social conditions but are also expressed in all kind of units. This is the case even when they are meant to refer to one 'aspect' only.[9] Thus we find indicators expressed in monetary and in physical units (real terms), in absolute and in percentage values, as levels and as increments, in units measured at an instant of time and in units measured per unit of time; as single variables and as ratios of two variables, those that can be interpreted as scalars and those that can be interpreted as vectors.[10] This heterogeneity of expression makes interpretation of the indicators difficult, if not impossible. A systematic approach to the problem is needed.

Among these many indicators it is possible to find some which have something in common, that is, they are either additive (directly or after some transformation) or at least aggregative (it is the conceptual possibility of aggregation which is meant here; procedures will be discussed later). Such indicators may be said to belong to one 'dimension'. Several such dimensions may be conceived, each with a set of indicators 'belonging' to it. Each 'dimension' would be distinguished by the kind of units specific to that dimension in which the relevant indicators would be expressed.

We are interested in selecting indicators in terms of which welfare could be measured. Before doing that, it is necessary to establish whether welfare is measurable in one or more dimensions, and what these dimensions are. We have to start our reasoning from commonsense concepts of welfare, of which there seems to be two.

The first concerns the question of how well the needs of an individual or of a population are satisfied as they manifest themselves from day to day, week to week and year to year. People need food every day, they have to spend their lives in some sort of housing, medical attention should be readily available, schools are needed to educate their children. The degree to which such needs are satisfied would constitute the welfare which that population receives. It may therefore be called the *flow of welfare*. If we try to find a numerical expression for such welfare we shall have to use indicators expressed in their specific units per unit of time. Such as: calorie intake per day, floor space occupied in dwellings per year, medical attention received per year, children in school per year and so on.

The flow of welfare may be accepted as one of the 'dimensions' of the 'welfare aspect' of social conditions.

It is possible, however, to have a different conception of what constitutes welfare. If the question is asked: 'How well-off is this population at this very instant of time?' the answer will have to be set in terms of units expressing the state of the population at this particular moment. It is evident that the indicators which will express the state of welfare of the population will have to be different from those that were used to express the flow of welfare. They will also be expressed in different kinds of units namely in specific units for each indicator in absolute figures, and *not* per unit of time. Such units might be numerical units of physiological tests assessing 'nutritional status', numbers of population free from endemic diseases, literacy rate number of graduates, etc. This concept of welfare which refers to the state in which the population finds itself at one particular time may be called the *state of welfare*. It will constitute another 'dimension' of the 'welfare aspect' of social conditions.

It is important to stress that these two ways of looking at welfare can be conceived independently of any measurement attempt. It is only after we have realized that the flow and the state of welfare are conceptually distinct that we may try to measure each of them, by selecting sets of indicators which would be adequate for measuring the 'flow' and the 'state' respectively.[11] The difference between the units in which these two concepts of welfare can be measured leads to their being regarded as two different 'dimensions'.

What we call the flow of welfare corresponds roughly to what is generally termed the level of living. We may therefore use these two terms synonymously. In doing this we give the term 'level of living' a meaning more precise than that which it normally has, and at the same time create the possibility of measuring it through the set of 'flow of welfare indicators' mentioned above.[12]

There is no term in common use which would correspond to what has been called above, the 'state of welfare'; we must therefore adopt it as a new term.[13]

It is worth noting that the idea of having two separate welfare concepts, 'flow' and 'state', has a parallel in the economic field, the national product or income (flow of products) corresponding to level of living (flow of welfare) and national wealth or capital corresponding to state of welfare. There is also the analogy between the flow of welfare as an agent in the state-of-welfare formation and the contribution of income to capital formation.

These symmetries are relevant, as many social problems can be stated more clearly and more precisely if we present them in terms of relations existing between the new welfare variables (level of living and state of welfare) and the traditional national accounting variables.

These relations can be expressed by two further classes of welfare indicators, which would correspond to additional dimensions of the 'welfare aspect'. These dimensions will not, however, express the magnitude of welfare itself, but its relation to economic magnitudes.

The national product, or more precisely that part of it which is consumed, is supposed to generate welfare. But it is common knowledge that the welfare it generates varies according to a number of circumstances.[12] The ratios between the level of living or state of welfare indicators and national product variables constitute a new class of indicators, which would give numerical expression to welfare generation, that is, measure the welfare effect of economic growth. Several *welfare effect indicators* can be conceived. They will always be ratios in which the welfare variable will be in the numerator and the economic variable in the denominator. They may take various forms, such as the ratio of absolute numerical values to the variables in question, or their increments or their relative (percentage) increments. Different degrees of aggregation of these variables are also possible, from single welfare indicators and corresponding sectoral economic variables, to the overall level of living or state of welfare (expressed in comprehensive indices) and the aggregate consumption or natural product.

The relation between welfare indicators and economic variables is not limited to the 'welfare effect'. Increase in welfare raises the productivity of labour and boosts production. This may be called the productivity effect of welfare and can be measured by the ratios between economic variables and welfare variables. Such ratios will constitute *productivity effect indicators*. They again can refer to absolute values or movements or relative increments and to indicators in varying degrees of aggregations.

Once we have the welfare effect and productivity effect indicators it is possible to proceed to the construction and computation of what could be called the 'welfare generation functions' and 'production functions containing social factors'. These are concepts modelled on the familiar production functions and could be computed in a similar way. The welfare generation function will have some welfare indicator as the dependent variable and economic factors as independent variables. The welfare effect indicators will be reflected in the parameters of the function. The 'social' production function will be more like the familiar production function with the difference that a welfare indicator will appear in it as one of the independent variables (and not be relegated to the residual as is the common practice). This is not the place, however, to enlarge upon these possibilities.[15]

To sum up, we have distinguished in this section four kinds of welfare indicators, namely (1) flow of welfare (level of living) indicators, (2) state of welfare indicators, (3) welfare effect indicators, (4) productivity effect indicators. (1) and (2) constitute clearly two separate dimensions of welfare; (3) and (4) constitute at least two more dimensions, and probably more as ratios of absolute quantities, ratios of increments and ratios of relative increments must be considered as belonging to different dimensions.

SPECIFIC FEATURES REQUIRED FROM WELFARE INDICATORS

Apart from the general characteristics of welfare indicators which have been discussed in the previous section there are some special features which an indicator must possess to be fit for measuring welfare.

First the welfare indicators should have the same *direction* as welfare. That means that an upward movement of an indicator's numerical values must correspond to the improvement in the satisfaction of needs,[16] for example, an increase in the daily intake of calories improves the satisfaction of the need for food and consequently increases the flow of welfare. Calorie intake is therefore an appropriate indicator for measuring welfare. The number of children per family, however, is not, for although changes in the numerical value of that indicator do influence welfare in some way, the influence may go in either direction (increasing or decreasing welfare) depending on the circumstances. Consequently the number of children per family (which is an important indicator in the demographic aspect of social condition) cannot be accepted as an indicator for measuring welfare. The same would be true of indicators which might be devised for measuring social relations (for example, mobility indicators). Their relation to welfare may be ambivalent, and therefore they cannot be used for measuring it.

Welfare indicators can assume various numerical values. While the direction of change of these values must conform to the direction of change of the magnitude of welfare (expressed as flow or as state as the case may be) which is supposed to be measured, this is not enough. To obtain a meaningful measure of welfare it is necessary to have not only the numerical value of the indicator but also points of reference against which the value of the indicator can be assessed.

The amount of calorie intake per day is not very illuminating if we do not know the minimum intake necessary for the population to survive and also the intake which in the conditions of that population could be considered as minimal for normal life and work. The same refers *mutatis mutandis* to education and health; school enrolment must be referred to the number of children of school-going age and the adequacy of medical services will depend on the conditions prevailing among the population in question.

It is therefore necessary for every indicator to be *scaled*; a minimum level of satisfaction of human needs has to be established in terms of a numerical value of each indicator. This value will constitute a 'critical point' on the indicator and it will serve as a point of reference for assessing the meaning of observed values of the indicators. We shall refer to that point as 'M point' (for Minimum human conditions).

Apart from the M critical point we may consider also another point for the indicator values: this will be the point marking the beginning from which the values of the indicator are measured. We may call it the zero point or 'O point'. In most cases this would mean that the indicator actually takes the value equal to zero (such as no education whatever, no medical services, etc.) but in some cases, the 'O point' would represent 'a survival point' or a destitution point where the indicator does not actually take value 'O', but below which human conditions cannot descend. For example, the zero point for calorie intake cannot be fixed at a point where calories intake is nil, as that would mean that everybody would be dead within a few days, but it is reasonable to fix it at a level of calorie intake which assures bare survival.

Once the O and M points for an indicator have been set, the distance between them may then be assumed to correspond to 100 units. It then becomes possible to express the values of that indicator in terms of these units, and so to transform the indicator expressed in physical units into an indicator index measured in units from O to 100. This last operation is not absolutely necessary, as welfare indicators in their original form, expressed in physical units, could also be used, but the transformation of indicators into indicator indices will be necessary when the aggregation of welfare indices is attempted.

The welfare indicators we have in mind can be used for assessing the level of living or the state of welfare of individual people, but this is not their prime purpose, which is to measure the welfare of populations. The welfare positions of individuals within a population are obviously unequal. The simple way of obtaining an indicator value valid for the whole population is to find an average value of that indicator per head of the population, which is how it is usually done, but this procedure ignores an important feature of the welfare problem. The welfare of the population depends not only on the average level of the satisfaction of needs, but also on the *distribution* of that satisfaction. Consequently the average-per-head values of indicators are inadequate to represent the welfare of the population. Unless it is assumed that some people are entitled to more welfare than others, a position of greater equality brings more welfare to the population (within given possibilities) than a position of inequality.

It is therefore necessary to take account of distribution in the procedures for measuring welfare. This can be done by multiplying the average-per-head value of each indicator by a distribution coefficient representing the distribution of the satisfaction of the need represented by that indicator. It would be most sensible for this distribution coefficient to take value 1 in the case of distribution being perfectly equal and to decrease in value as distribution becomes more and more unequal. This coefficient may be constructed in various ways, but the simplest is perhaps to make it the inverse of the concentration coefficient derived from Lorenz's curve.[17]

Various other ways of dealing with this problem are probably possible but it is not intended to discuss their various merits here: it is only necessary to stress that the problems must be tackled. Measuring welfare without taking a distribution into account can only produce very misleading results.

THE PLACE OF VALUE JUDGEMENTS IN WELFARE MEASUREMENT

The concept of human welfare cannot be free from value judgements. This is a problem which must be recognized: efforts at measuring welfare based on the assumption that it can be a 'value neutral' concept are misguided and futile, and carry the danger that, not being able to eliminate them, they will only conceal value judgements and confuse the issue even further.

Value judgements must be given their proper place in the system devised for welfare measurement: it is also desirable that the value judgements included in the system are such as would meet with fairly general approval. This is in itself a controversial question, but it is possible to keep the controversial element to a minimum.

Value judgements would have to enter the system at various stages. The very selection of indicators is not value-neutral. The system of needs which we have in mind when selecting indicators is of course culture-determined; in the list of indicators which have been suggested so far[18] it is possible to recognize European-culture-derived system of values. This system is, however, generally recognized (explicitly or implicitly) in all discussions of development, and we probably have no option but to accept it.[19]

In scaling indicators we also express a value judgement. To some extent it is possible to be guided by expert information about objective fact (e.g. what calories intake is necessary to perform some kind of work efficiently), but the extent of value judgement is quite considerable in most indicators, for example, in determining the minimum level of education or of health services or of housing conditions. This must be taken as unavoidable, all we can do is to try to ensure that the critical points of indicators reflect at least some consensus on what are the minimal human requirements. This is not an impossible task as a considerable degree of consensus has been already achieved on a number of questions. In various discussions within the United Nations such minimum requirements have been proposed and explicitly accepted.[20]

In introducing a distribution coefficient as explained above we make a value judgement considering equality superior to inequality. Again, this is a value judgement rooted in a very widespread egalitarian ideology.

The most controversial value judgements have to be made when we try to arrive at aggregate variables intended for measuring welfare, such as for instance a composite level-of-living index. To arrive at a composite index particular components of the level of living (such as nutrition, health, housing, education) have to be weighted one against another. It is obvious that a general consensus independent of time and space is not possible on that kind of problem. On the other hand it is important to realize that value judgements referring to such variables are not unusual or without precedent. Quite the contrary. Decisions involving political judgements on the relative importance of various level of living components are a matter of course when policies are determined and development plans formulated. Those decisions constitute objective facts which may be significant in establishing procedures for constructing aggregate level-of-living and state-of-welfare indices.

AGGREGATE INDICES FOR MEASURING THE FLOW AND STATE OF WELFARE

Aggregate indices for social conditions are crucial for assessing past performance and devising policies for the future, because improvement of social conditions is our objective. Both past and future should be judged by that criterion. Individual social indicators give us precise information about some of the elements of social conditions, but to have a reasonably full and precise picture of the whole, aggregate indices are needed. It is only when we have them that we can stop expressing development in terms of G.N.P. and start thinking of it as an improvement in the level of living, and this is, of course, a crucial and badly needed change in the quantitative treatment of development.

In spite of this consideration, there remain strong objections to devising aggregate welfare indices. It is true that having separate welfare indicators is better than having nothing at all; but it is also true that when we have a number of indicators, it is only natural to try to get an overall picture of the situation by finding an average of them all, which brings us back to the problem of aggregate indices.

The main reasons advanced against constructing them are the methodological difficulties involved.[21] These are indeed considerable, but in view of the importance of the aggregate indices an effort must be made to overcome them; and it is important to differentiate between valid and invalid methods of tackling this problem. An aggregate index is as good as the system of weights on which it is based. In devising a system of weights for a welfare index we cannot and must not try to be value-neutral.

But this is not always reflected in the discussions on the relative importance of welfare components which might lead to the determination of their weights. A common method of assessing the contribution of various welfare indicators to welfare or to development is to look towards the past, into the history their past growth in different countries. To that material all kinds of analytical techniques are applied[22] to discover the pattern of relative significance of the various indicators for what is called 'development'. However ingenious the analytical techniques can be the whole procedure seems to me misguided.

The past history of welfare (as expressed by welfare indicators) is influenced by the whole course of history, the rate of growth or stagnation of the economy and the distribution of income, class structure, the privileged or underprivileged state of various countries, the nature of the colonial system, etc. There is no reason at all why the resulting trend in welfare indicators should be considered in any sense 'normal' and an appropriate guide to what aggregate welfare is or should be. That kind of attitude might be justified only if we considered past development as the best possible, to be continued without any structural change; then the pattern of the past could serve as a norm for the present and the future. This is evidently not the case. What we can surely say is that people are now looking for a world different from that of the past, and therefore they should weight components of welfare in terms of their present aspirations (preferences), and not according to a pattern established in the past as an accidental outcome of contradictory forces.

The proper procedure for establishing a system of weights is to derive it from some system of preferences. As the indices which we are looking for are supposed to measure the welfare of a nation, the preferences which express the aspirations and govern the policies of that nation should be used. Preferences of this nature are contained in a nation's development plan. They are essentially political judgements determining the relative importance of improvements in various components of the level of living to be achieved within the plan. As they lie behind actual decisions and determine action to be undertaken it seems beyond dispute that when it comes to assessing the results of that action the relative importance of achievements should be judged according to the same system of preferences. This means that the level of living index should be computed with weights reflecting the same system of preferences by which planning was guided.

This is the way to solve the problem of weights for a level of living index, though obviously it is a solution only on the conceptual level. But it is necessary to be able to see correctly the theoretical side of the problem before proceeding to its practical solution.

The practical problems of establishing a system of weights for a level of living index remain formidable. First the 'preferences of the plan' are never stated explicitly. Perhaps some day the art of planning will advance to the extent that they will be written into the plan documents. Then the problem will simplified. At present they are implied in the plan, but must be 'revealed', and much work is still needed on the procedure for doing this.

Another problem is the international comparability of levels of living. If weights for the index are based on a national plan they would be valid for that particular nation but not for cross-country comparisons. To overcome this difficulty we have to construct a synthetic system of weights reflecting common features of a number of plans. The validity of such weights will also be limited in time and space but will transcend one nation. It may refer, for example, to 'developing countries in the eighth decade of the twentieth century'. This is again not an easy exercise but it is well worth trying.[23]

So long as we do not have a system of weights based on sound theoretical principles we have to use some conventional system. The simplest of these is a system of equal weights. It makes the level of living index an arithmetical mean of all the selected indicators.[24] There is nothing wrong in using it as long as we are fully aware of the nature of the operation.

WELFARE INDICATORS AND PLANNING

It is generally agreed that development should bring improvement in the conditions in which people live, yet the most obvious conclusion to be drawn from this statement has yet to be put into practice: namely, that the final targets of development plans (the targets which in optimization models are represented by variables of the objective function) should be expressed in terms of welfare indicators.[25] This also means discarding G.N.P. and similar variables from objective functions.

This principle is not yet to be found in planning textbooks, let alone in planning practice. One of the reasons why such a revision of planning models is not easy is the unfamiliarity of planning experts with such concepts as 'social indicators' in general and 'welfare indicators' in particular. But the difficulty goes deeper than that. If welfare indicators are to be given their proper place in the objective functions of the planning models, the planners would have to know the interrelations between economic and social variables, that is the parameters of welfare generation functions and of production functions of the new type (containing social variables). Not enough preliminary work has been done so far on these functions, which is why we cannot expect socially (or welfare) oriented planning to come into operation in the near future. But it is important that the conceptual problems of the social re-orientation of planning should be stated sharply and clearly, and this can only be done through the clarification of the problems connected with the construction, compilation and application of welfare indicators and indices.

NOTES

1. The origin of the critical approach to purely economic indicators of development should probably be traced to a pioneering United Nations report [*United Nations, 1954*], but by now this attitude is endorsed by practically every work discussing development objectives. As they are too numerous to be quoted here we mention only that this idea is raised by Myrdal [*1968*], by several United Nations reports on the preparation of the Second Development Decade, and by Rosenstein-Rodan [*1969*]. It must be admitted that so far this critical attitude has not brought about much change in the practice of development data collection or planning.

2. United Nations [*1963*] was probably the first major effort to provide world-wide data for what were then tentatively described as social indicators. Many publications followed within a short span of time contributing to the conceptual elaboration of 'social indicators' and/or providing more numerical material. Of these the most notable were Russet *et al.*, [*1964*], Bauer [*1966*], the crucial part of which was further extended by Gross [*1966*]; most comprehensive of them all: Sheldon and Moore [*1968*]. The literature on the problem has grown so much that a bibliography on this topic up to the year 1970 required 36 pages to list just the titles of publications [*Iowa State University, 1971*], and remains incomplete in spite of its size.

3. Perhaps the most remarkable work of this kind is provided by Adelman and Morris [*1967*]. The impressive ingenuity and technical skill did not unfortunately bring much in the way of tangible results. In my opinion this may be due to a great extent to an imperfect understanding of the varied nature of social indicators. In a sense the present article is an effort to bring clarity into this particular subject.

4. See United States [*1969*], where an interest is shown in the new approach; also U.K. Statistical Office [*1970*] and Moser [*1969*]. Quite considerable work on social indicators is also carried out by the French Commissariat du Plan, by the Social Affairs Division of O.E.C.D. in Paris and by the Council of Europe Secretariat in Strasbourg.

5. This kind of economic thinking is certainly not the only one possible. In the opinion of the present writer there is a strong argument in favour of alternative systems of measurement in economics. This would be simply a return to a well-established older tradition. Marshallian utility curves and Paretian preference functions were not expressed in monetary terms. It is only in modern times that the monetary approach has gained absolute preponderance to the detriment of economics as a social science.

6. It might be useful at this stage to clarify the relation of the 'aspects' of social conditions, as explained above, to the concept of 'modernization' which is commonly used when social conditions are analysed. It might be asked whether modernization should not be treated as another aspect of social conditions for which a special set of indicators could be devised. I would give a negative answer to that question. In the scheme presented here, modernization cuts across all three aspects. It consist of a specific kind of change which occurs in social conditions at a given stage of historical development and affects all three aspects. Consequently modernization changes can be observed in the demographic situation, in social relations and in welfare. To the extent that quantification is feasible they may be made measureable by means of indicators specific to each of the aspects.

7. For a more detailed discussion of this problem see UNRISD [*1970a*].

8. For the description of the interdependence between economic and social variables, see UNRISD [*1970b*].

9. Such as, for instance, indicators which are supposed to measure the level of living; see, for example, United Nations [*1961*],

10. All these classes of indicators can be found in, for example, Adelman and Morris [*1967*], but in many other publications the variety is comparable.

11. The distinction between flow and state (or stock) in respect of social indicators was discussed in UNRISD [*1966a, b; 1970a*].

12. The concept of level of living as it is commonly used is still very ambiguous. It is often meant to be represented by some economic national accounting variables. If, however, a serious effort at measurement is made it must be decided whether it is a 'flow' or a 'state' concept (it cannot be both). It has been considered more appropriate to assimilate it with the flow concept as it seems closer to the intuitive meaning of the level of living. A level of living index based on such ideas was elaborated by the present author in UNRISD [*1966b and 1970a*].

13. A suggestion for an index of the state of welfare (or the level of welfare as it was called then) was proposed in UNRISD [*1970a*].

14. See UNRISD [*1966a and 1970a*] for a further discussion of this problem.

15. A production function of this new kind was elaborated as an experiment in an unpublished UNRISD paper 'Suggestion for an Empirical Production Function Representing the Productivity Effect of Social Factors', computed on data from 32 countries. Problems of interrelation between economic and welfare variables have also been discussed in UNRISD [*1966a, 1970a, b*].

16. At least within a certain significant range of values. For example, an increase in calorie intake beyond a certain point cannot be regarded as increasing welfare. This does not, however, invalidate calorie intake as an indicator of nutrition.

17. See UNRISD [*1970a*] for a more detailed discussion of the distribution coefficient.

18. In practically all publications quoted in which social indicators can be found.

19. For example, the 'number of children in the family' indicator, quoted above as an example of a *non*-welfare indicator, might well be a welfare indicator in another culture where the number of children is considered a blessing and desirable.

20. In United Nations [*1969*] for example.

21. That view was put forward in United Nations [*1954*], and has been repeated ever since.

22. Such as factor analysis or multiple regression.

23. An attempt of that kind (not wholly successful) was made by Drewnowski and Subramanian [*1970*].

24. Such a system was used for the Level of Living Index as suggested in UNRISD [*1966b, 1970a*]. Another conventional system called 'Sliding Weights' was suggested there too, but it cannot be discussed here for lack of space.

25. See Drewnowski [*1970*].

REFERENCES

Adelman, Irma, and Morris, Cynthia T., 1967, *Society, Politics and Economic Development*, Baltimore: Johns Hopkins University Press.

Bauer, Raymond A. (ed.), 1966, *Social Indicators*, Cambridge, Mass.: Massachusetts Institute of Technology Press.

Drewnowski, J., 1970, 'A Planning Model for Social Development' in UNRISD [*1970b*].

Drewnowski, J., and Subramanian, M., 1970, 'Social Aims in Development Plans', in UNRISD [*1970b*].

Gross, Bertram M., 1966, *The State of the Nation: Social Systems Accounting*, London and New York: Tavistock.

Iowa State University, 1971, *Social Indicators: Bibliography I*, Department of Sociology.

Moser, P. A., 1969, *An Integrated System of Social and Demographic Statistics*, paper presented to Conference of European Statisticians, 273, May 1969.

Myrdal, G., 1968, *Asian Drama*, New York: Pantheon.

Rosenstein-Rodan, P. N., 1969, 'Criteria for Evaluation of National Development Effort', *Journal of Development Planning*, No. 1, New York: United Nations.

Russet, Bruce M., et al., 1964, *World Handbook of Political and Social Indicators*, New Haven and London: Yale University Press.

Sheldon, E. B., and Moore, W. E. (eds.), 1968, *Indicators of Social Change*, New York: Russell Sage Foundation.

U.K. Statistical Office, 1970, *Social Trends*, London.

United Nations, 1954, *Report on the International Definition and Measurement of Standards and Levels of Living*, New York: United Nations.

United Nations, 1961, *International Definition and Measurement of Levels of Living: An Interim Guide*, New York: United Nations.

United Nations, 1963, *Compendium of Social Statistics*. New York: United Nations.

United Nations, 1969, *Social Policy and the Distribution of Income in the Nation*, New York: United Nations.

United States, 1969, *Towards a Social Report*, Department of Health, Education and Welfare, Washington.

UNRISD, 1966a, *Social and Economic Factors in Development*, Report No. 3, Geneva: United Nations Research Institute for Social Development.

UNRISD, 1966b, *The Level of Living Index*, Report No. 4, Geneva: United Nations Research Institute for Social Development.

UNRISD, 1970a, *Studies in the Measurement of Levels of Living and Welfare*, Report No. 70.3, Geneva: United Nations Research Institute for Social Development.

UNRISD, 1970b, *Studies in the Methodology of Social Planning*, Report No. 70.5, Geneva: United Nations Research Institute for Social Development.

Development Indicators and Development Models

By Donald McGranahan*

SUMMARY

This paper is concerned with the semantics of indicators and the concepts of development. Procedures for the selection and validation of indicators are discussed. It is argued that the nature and scope of the indicators, as well as the nature of the quantitative analysis of relations between them, will depend on the conception and definition of development. The system model, which underlies the UNRISD measurement of development, is contrasted with other approaches.

INTRODUCTION: THE SEMANTICS OF INDICATORS

An indicator, Oxford and Webster tell us, is something that points out something else. When an economic and social variable is used as an indicator, it is not an indicator of itself, and it is also not an 'operational definition' of that to which it points. The temperature accurately given by use of a clinical thermometer is not an indicator of body temperature—it defines (is) body temperature; but it is an indicator of sickness. Similarly, death rates do not indicate relative numbers of deaths but may indicate public health levels. The school enrolment ratio is a *measure* of the amount of school enrolment but it may be used as an *indicator* of the educational level of a country, given various assumptions. In economic forecasting, orders in durable goods and plant and equipment contracts serve as indicators for detecting broad movements of the economy but they are not indicators of what they directly measure. In other words, economic and social indicators are not simply statistics, and statistics are not *ipso facto* indicators—unless some theory or assumption makes them so by relating the indicator variable to a phenomenon that is not what it directly and fully measures.

That, at least, is the way it ought to be, semantically. But in practice the borderline between the indicator and the operational definition is not too clear. For example, it is often not clear whether the *per capita* G.N.P. is intended in various writings as an operational *definition* of development (development is then simply and solely what is measured by *per capita* G.N.P.) or as an *indicator* of development (on the basis of an assumed—and empirically testable—relationship of the *per capita* G.N.P. to other defined aspects of general development). We can disagree with a definition of development in terms of the *per capita* G.N.P. by arguing that this is too narrow and not the way the word 'development' is understood and used by most people. If we question the *per capita* G.N.P. as the best single indicator of development (assuming that a single indicator is

* Director of the United Nations Research Institute for Social Development at Geneva, Switzerland.

This article is a revision of a working paper prepared by the author at UNRISD. While it takes advantage of work done at UNRISD, the views expressed are personal.

desirable, which is itself questionable) the problem is then empirical and we must demonstrate (as can in fact be done) that other indicators can be found that in practice perform better in describing, estimating and predicting the totality of aspects that constitute development, and are therefore better indicators of development as a whole, than the *per capita* G.N.P.

For an economic or social variable to be called a 'development indicator' commonly means that it represents some factor that is part of the process of development. This in turn implies a definition or theory as to what constitutes development. Since development tends to be an interdependent process, a good indicator in fact reflects, in varying degree, many more things than it directly measures. For example, agricultural productivity (per adult male agricultural worker) is conditioned by and reflects a country's level of technology, level of education, communications, etc., and in turn itself conditions a number of factors. Life expectation reflects not only the level of medical services but also, among other things, literacy, housing conditions, diet, income, occupational structure (all of which correlate more highly with it than do relative numbers of doctors or hospital beds). Conversely, if an item shows little or no relation to other aspects of development, it is questionable whether it should be called a development indicator. We shall return to this point.

What needs to be emphasized here is the fact that indicators involve two kinds of relationship to development:

(*a*) On the one hand, an indicator may constitute a direct and full measure—an operational definition—of a particular factor or aspect of development, and it is a 'development indicator' only in the sense that the factor it measures is a recognized goal or element of development.[1] Certain development goals like reduction of unemployment (in industrial societies), increase of *per capita* G.N.P., increase of school enrolment, reduction of infant mortality, can be stated quite adequately in quantitative terms. The main problem is whether they are in fact true goals or elements of development.

(*b*) On the other hand, the true goal or element of development may not itself be directly and fully measurable, so that the indicator serves in the first place to point to or represent, as best as possible, this non-measurable factor. Thus it may be considered that the true goal is not reduction of infant mortality but better health, and the infant mortality index is a substitute or proxy indicator for health. Reduction of infant mortality should not then figure as the health target of the plan but as an item of diagnosis and evaluation (among other items). The true objective here cannot be stated in quantitative terms. But proxy indicators may easily be turned into ends themselves and pursued (often with unfortunate consequences) instead of the true goals. The danger is particularly great in the case of indicators that represent means or instruments to the true goal and that by acquiring the sanction and status of goals, inhibit the use of, or search for, more effective means.

THE PROBLEM OF SOCIAL INDICATORS

While in the economic field many (but not all) factors of development are directly measurable or at least considered so, in the social development field most main goals like 'health', 'education', 'security', 'equity' and other objects of social policy are not directly measurable in their totalities or even clearly defined, and indicators commonly serve as proxy or partial measures of these entities. The theoretical or assumed connection between the indicator and the entity to which it points in these cases is usually based on a cause-effect or part-whole relationship. Health indicators, for example, represent presumed causes or instruments of good health (relative number of doctors or hospital beds), or consequences of ill-health (deaths, days spent in hospitals), or partial forms of ill-health (contagious diseases). The assumptions underlying such indicators may, of course, be wrong or largely wrong: the relative numbers of doctors and hospital beds in a country may not be the major factor conditioning the level of health; deaths (in particular of youth) may reflect primarily accidents, not sickness; the amount of contagious disease may not be a good representative of ill-health in general; and there is something odd about measuring ill-health by the relative number of days spent in hospital beds while good health is indicated by the relative number of hospital beds. These problems concerned with the relations of the indicators to their objects of indication are quite different from statistical problems of accuracy or reliability of data.

On the other hand, an indicator that has conspicuous deficiencies may nevertheless function quite well in practice. It is conceivable that school enrolment, which to all appearances is a poor indicator of education because it does not measure actual attendance at school or quality of schooling, may nevertheless perform its function relatively well *if* low attendance and poor quality consistently go with low enrolment while high attendance and good quality go with high enrolment.

THE VALIDATION OF DEVELOPMENT INDICATORS

Let us assume that the components, sectors or factors of development are roughly agreed upon, under a broad conception, and that several kinds of statistical data are available, or feasible to obtain, for each factor that is not directly measurable. The problem is then to determine which among these available series will provide the best indicators. Ideally, we should validate an indicator against a direct full measure of that which is being indicated. But since the reason for using an indicator of the type under discussion is the absence of such a direct measure, this is hardly possible. There are two ways of validation and selection of indicators under these circumstances: (1) use of expert consensus; (2) use of correlational analysis technique and related multivariate techniques.

These two approaches may be used as checks against each other. The second calls for explanation. Given that we do not have a single overall measure of an entity like health against which to validate and select indicators, that units of health in fact have no meaning at present, we may nevertheless have quantitative data on various aspects of health. What we know about health as a whole quantitatively will then be provided by the collection of these separate data. The indicator that best correlates with the rest of the collection, or, more precisely, has the highest average correlation with the others, may be considered to be the best health indicator of the group[2]. The procedure is illustrated by Table I, based on cross-national data for 1960.

Table I shows that life expectation has the highest average correlation. It is also the indicator generally chosen by experts as the best available.

TABLE I

Indicator	Average Correlation with other (six) health indicators	Average Correlation with 41 selected development indicators
Infant mortality rate	0·72	0·66
Expectation of life at birth	0·77	0·70
Crude death rate	0·56	0·45
Death rate from infectious and parasitic diseases	0·63	0·58
Inhabitants per physician	0·71	0·46
Inhabitants per hospital bed	0·43	0·43
Proportionate mortality ratio	0·65	0·65

Source: UNRISD Data Bank.

In fact, the list as a whole agrees with expert opinion quite closely: thus, infant mortality is usually rated second and hospital beds last.[3]

Any list of indicators used for such empirical testing should be a best available list (taking account of expert opinion and covering different aspects according to their judged importance). It may be objected that the seven variables listed in Table I have substantial overlaps, particularly those involving death counts. If a group of indicators concerned with medical services (nurses, clinics, drugs sold, etc.) were added to the list, (such data are not in fact available cross-nationally), then the average correlation of inhabitants per physician might conceivably rise and surpass that of life expectation. This is possible although physicians and hospital beds correlate better with life expectation than with each other. A major argument in favour of life expectation, however, is found in the final column of Table I, which shows that in a group of forty-two social and economic indicators covering a wide range of developmental factors, life expectation has considerably higher average correlation than does physicians. It seems to be a generally valid proposition that the technically superior indicators for a sector tend to have the higher cross-sectoral correlations. If, as discussed above, we assume that health is part of an interdependent system of development, and is influenced by factors like literacy, housing, food consumption, water supply and personal income, as much as or more than by direct health services, while also influencing other factors, then this is understandable and a high correlation of a health indicator with indicators for these interrelated aspects of development is justified as a criterion of validation and selection.[4]

An indicator is a matter of enquiry and knowledge, and as better knowledge is obtained, better selection of indicators becomes possible; also, an indicator may cease playing that role as new levels are reached or new relationships evolve, so that indicators must be constantly reappraised and tested in varying situations.

DEVELOPMENT INDICATORS AND STATISTICAL SYSTEMS

A statistic is not by itself an indicator and a statistical system is not a system of indicators. Any given statistical fact like a death rate or a life expectation figure can be indicative of a number of things and play as important a role in, say, social security analysis or employment analysis as in health analysis. Social research constantly uses social statistics for diverse purposes. Recent attempts to build up a system of social statistics, notably by the United Nations Statistical Office and the Conference of European Statisticians,[5] are attempts to introduce unifying principles into the field, as regards units or series, classifications, methods of collection and presentation of data.[6] These are formal and methodological tasks and should not be confused with the empirical and theoretical questions involved in building up systems of development indicators. Of course, the statistical systems will define the scope of available data for development indicators and should take account of indicator needs.

The best example of a unified statistical system is the national accounts system but it would be unfortunate to limit economic development indicators to this system. Discrepancies between monetary and 'real' indicators are frequent and in themselves indicative—indicative, for example, of the differential *efficiency*, in different places or at different times, of goods and services serving the same purposes at similar costs. The fact that one country spends as much money on health or education or electricity services as another country does not mean that it has the same level of health or education or electricity usage.

INDICATORS AND THE DEFINITION OF DEVELOPMENT

Since Indicators are an attempt to quantify some conception or definition of development, the nature and scope of the indicators, as well as the nature of the relations between them, will depend on this conception. The conception, however, may be rather vague and once the indicators are chosen, they are apt to take over the definitional function.

There are many definitions and theories of development and it is not possible to review them here. But certain major 'conceptual models' used or assumed in definitions may be noted. By conceptual model is meant some relatively concrete and coherent image which underlies the theoretical framework of the definition—an image by which one arranges and orders one's thinking about development, even if not very consciously or deliberately. A conceptual model is usually a metaphor (cf. the atom as a miniature solar system) and in the last analysis usually incorrect for that reason.

The concern here is with conceptual models applied to socio-economic development as a whole, not with models for economic growth or for particular social sectors.

Development Defined by Lists of Desiderata and Ideal Pictures of the Future

One of the simplest and most common conceptions of development is in terms of progress towards any or all of a list of national goals or values in the economic and social fields. Development indicators in this case are quantitative expressions, as best possible, of movement towards these various goals or values.

However, if development is defined simply in terms of some list of desiderata, then it is in fact nothing more than a short-hand name for this list—which is a kind of national shopping list. There is no reason to assume, in this case, a coherent totality corresponding to the word 'development' and there is little place for the idea of unity in such a definition. The list may contain arbitrary, contradictory, or impractical items. The items

G

will not necessarily have any relation to each other except perhaps through some ordering of priorities in terms of more important and less important values. Or they may be nominally brought together in some 'ideal picture' of the future society.

This conception of development as progress toward a collection of desiderata (usually defined sectorally) or an ideal picture of this future, raises a fundamental question whether development is purely a matter of progress towards ideals or is to be conceived as an objective process that may even exclude certain ideals that are impractical to achieve at the moment and may embrace various changes, including structural changes and changes in attitude, that are not values in themselves but are a necessary part of the process. Presumably a lack of progress towards unrealistic goals should be reckoned as failure not of development but of judgement, and a country has not developed the less because it has failed to do what it could not in any case have done.

The Organic Model

This is the oldest conceptual model and still favoured by many sociologists. Its most influential expression was in 19th century philosophy and sociology where national progress or development was conceived as the organic unfolding of the 'Volksgeist'.

The idea of distinctive stages or sequences is usually involved in organic models. This implies a different indicator approach from that of the continuous variable. Different stages of development call for different indicators. For example, it may be argued that employment rate is an appropriate indicator for an industrial society, but not for a pre-industrial agrarian society. (The extensive but generally unsuccessful efforts in recent years to measure unemployment—in the guise of 'under-employment'—in the rural parts of developing countries would tend to support this position.)

This model has the great advantage that it stresses functional inter-relationships and interdependencies and calls attention to the possibility of different styles or patterns of development. In its biological metaphor, however, it tends to assume the inevitability of the course of development of each country according to an innate genius or entelechy, so that there is not much one can do about it beyond watching it unfold. The assumption today is that development can be achieved by action, within the limits given by existing constraints. Also, experience shows that the organic model may promote a non-scientific mystique about development. The basic fact is that the organic metaphor is too far-fetched—societies do not have group minds and they do not unfold like a biological process.

The Technological-educational Model

Development is here likened to the learning process whereby the individual acquires new technological knowledge and skills. This conception, first evolved in France in the 19th century, focuses attention on what is perhaps the most critical element in development: technological change or innovation. It can be plausibly argued that if a process of change—say improvement of agricultural production and income because of climatic conditions—does not involve technological innovation, it should not be called development. Development would not be indicated by increased agricultural production due to a run of good weather, or even when due to long-term climatic change.[7]

There is a problem as to how to treat 'social innovations' and social progress under this model and how to deal, for example, with situations of unemployment associated with adoption of advanced capital-intensive technologies. The technological–educational model is deficient also because it does not deal satisfactorily with questions of structural changes and psychological reorientations which may be essential to development, and its emphasis is on knowing rather than doing. But it does suggest that a system of technological indicators might prove extremely valuable for developmental analysis. Unfortunately, relatively little has been done to set up a system of indicators to measure a country's technolgical level.[8]

The Input–Output Conceptual Model

This is the basic conceptual model favoured by economists since the second World War.[9] National growth is likened to factory production and the problem of development is to get the proper inputs to achieve maximum output rates and returns. This model has the great advantage that it is action-orientated. It is a useful paradigm for planning. And it has mensurability (primarily through the G.N.P.).

But the nation undergoing development is not a super-factory, just as it is not a super-organism or super-mind, and the input–output model fails when development is viewed in its socio-economic totality. An input of education into a society, for example, does not so much yield a particular output as it changes the whole society by changing the people who constitute it. That is, the response is more a change of the system than an output of the system. Similarly, the main response to an extension of communications in a socio-economic system, or a growth of urbanization, will be a change of the system itself. It is as if an increased input in a factory caused the factory itself to change and grow as the input is assimilated. The input-output model tends to lead to universalistic thinking about development, whereas it is apparent that different countries may respond quite differently to the same stimuli (inputs), depending on their circumstances.

Under this model the relations between social and economic variables are input–output relations and use of the model has been characterized by attempts to deal with problems of integration of economic and social development by trying to incorporate social variables into production functions. These efforts at the integration and incorporation of social variables have not been very successful, for one reason because they have been based upon an inappropriate use of regression analysis in the conditions of high interdependency that obtain among large numbers of social and economic development variables.[10]

The Capacity-Performance Model

Development is here defined as enhancement of the capacity of a society to function for the well-being of its members over the long run.[11] The advantage of this definition is that it lays weight on substantive change rather than superficial change, on authentic development rather than the trappings of development. It accommodates the idea of 'styles' of development.

This approach embraces not only technological and educational capacities but also structural and institutional capacities; it suggests the importance of structural and institutional indicators and of building up 'capacity indicators' in general. At the same time it is made quite clear that quantitative indicators have their limitations and should not be confused with development as a whole. The problem is to devise a scheme of developmental analysis that combines quantitative and non-quantitative elements.

Since we really do not know what 'enhancement of the capacity' is, in any definitive way, the function of the definition is to suggest a certain orientation and urge enquiry and investigation in a particular direction. It does not itself define development in such a way that by adopting it two people will then agree today whether a particular country has developed significantly over a given period of time. That is because, in the absence of capacity indicators and other means, it does not (or not yet) provide objective criteria of enhanced capacity (actual improvements of well-being are tautological criteria of capacity).

The model postulates a capacity whereby a society provides for the well-being of its members but much of 'well-being', when examined, will turn out to be part of the capacity, under the guise of 'human resources'. Enhanced capacity will flow from better well-being, as well as vice versa. A difficulty with the capacity-performance model, as a theoretical framework, is that it is a one-way model (like the input–output model) in a situation of interdependence or circular causation.

The System Model

Finally, a system model of development can be set up—using system in the dictionary sense of 'an assemblage of objects united by some form of regular interaction or interdependence'. A system can be of various kinds— organic, social, mechanical—and it is desirable in dealing with development to avoid undue influence of the engineering type systems, which are not growth systems.

Under this model, then, development is an evolving system of factors that influence and are influenced by each other, directly or indirectly. This means, conversely, that social or economic elements that are not (or not yet or no longer) interdependent with other factors, are excluded from the definition of development, although they may have a one-way relationship as causes or consequences. In other words, the scope of development indicators is immediately reduced by elimination of any elements that are (*a*) wholly unrelated to the system, or (*b*) contributory influences but not influenced themselves by development, or (*c*) effects or by-products of development but having no positive influence themselves on development.

Under this approach, some other expression, such as 'social progress', would have to be used for desirable changes not part of development, such as reductions in crime, protection of the environment, certain improvements in human relations, and progress towards other ideals of human society which do not appear to be part of development as an interdependent system. These values are no less important to society if they are not part of development so defined.[12] They should be involved in planning which would not then be coterminous with development planning.

For such items it is evident that developed countries as a rule do not necessarily show a greater degree of realization than do developing countries. With regard to some items, the less-developed countries may even be better off precisely because they are less developed and the correlation with development may be negative. These may include indicators of undesirable consequences of development—environmental problems are the most familiar example.

Structural changes, as well as changes involving progression towards goals or values, will be involved in the system model of development, to the extent that they influence and are influenced by change in other aspects. Certain structural transformations may occur only at a particular time or in particular circumstances (e.g. land reform), while other structural changes (e.g. occupational change out of agriculture) may be continuous, interacting with other factors of development.

One difficulty with this model is our imperfect knowledge of the influences of different factors upon each other. However, by means of statistical correlations (which eliminate items that are not significantly related), empirical observations and common sense, it is possible to get a fair idea of what such a system would comprise as a minimum in terms of internationally measurable variables.[13]

In a system model, absence of development can mean: (a) stagnant systems, 'vicious circles', where generally low levels are adjusted to and reinforce each other, inhibiting change in individual factors; (b) contradictions, discordances, in the system whereby growth of certain factors produces negative cross-effects instead of positive cross-effects—for example, increased unemployment resulting from extension of education (educated unemployed); lower agricultural production (and income) per person resulting from better health (because of population growth in conditions of land scarcity).

An increase of a given indicator does not necessarily mean there will be improvement in the rest of the system. It depends on the nature of the given change, its suitability to the rest of the system, the responsivity of the other factors, the nature of the linkages. Development is not a matter of explosive interactions of mutually reinforcing agents but of provision of favourable environments for growth of given factors by other factors. It is dependent on both qualitative and quantitative relations among factors. There can be the wrong kind of urbanization or education or too little or too much urbanization or education in a given situation. There is implied some kind of optimum set of developmental relationships for each given country in its circumstances—or at least a limited range of optimum combinations. The assessment of this optimum balance becomes a major task of development planning.[14]

The idea of 'balance', however, tends to be static and may convey the wrong image. Development can also be seen as a series of 'dynamic imbalances' as certain factors move ahead (because of technological innovations, new resources, redistribution of resources, etc.) and stimulate or provide opportunities for growth in other factors, depending on the linkages and responsivities of the system and the nature of existing factor deficiencies and surpluses.

The optimum development pattern will depend on the nature of the constraints (e.g. geographic size, population size) and natural advantages; different types of country will have different styles of development. (To take an extreme example, small tropical islands will not develop as centres of heavy industry.) One function of indicators is to help establish a *typology* of development.

Different quantitative methods of developmental analysis go with different conceptual models. It has been remarked above that at the macro level, relations between economic and social variables cannot be properly analysed through regression analysis. The different social and economic factors constituting national development cannot be divided into those that are independent variables and those that are dependent variables—in a system model all are dependent upon each other in varying degrees and the assumptions of regression are not valid.

For analysis of the relations between variables in a system model, instead of regression one may use a 'best-fitting line' which does not assume the independence of one variable and the dependence of another.[15] Such a line drawn through the distribution of two variables will show, not what change in variable Y will be created by a given increment of variable X, but what level of variable Y will tend to correspond with a given level of variable X, and vice versa ('correspondence points'). By putting a best-fitting line through a set of interdependent variables in multi-dimensional space, correspondence points for the set of variables can be established. Different variables will be seen to change at different rates in relation to each other. When transformations and adjustments are made to flatten lines between the correspondence points, a country's profile can be represented on the chart, showing where the country is higher and where it is lower than other countries at about the same general level of development. This can serve as a tool of *diagnosis*, which in a system approach plays a major role in developmental (cross-sectoral) analysis.

CONCLUDING NOTE

In view of the current popularity of development indicators, especially social indicators, let us note not only their advantages but also their limitations, in present circumstances.

Indicators are useful for developmental analysis, for general diagnosis of developmental conditions and needs, and for general evaluation of progress. But while they may measure progress, they should not be confused with targets for planning (this is especially true of the numerous proxy indicators). They may be used in evaluation but they should not be assumed ordinarily to reveal the impact of different factors upon each other—in spite of numerous studies attempting to show through regression the 'impact' of this factor upon that factor of development. They do not automatically or ordinarily reveal programme impact over time, because of the many influences at work in the interdependent process of development. Special studies are required for programme and project evaluation, perhaps using especially devised programme or project indicators. In other words, indicators are not a substitute for research but a tool of research.

While indicators can reveal progress in various separate value categories, it is not possible to convert indicators into a single value scale, to say that so much health is *worth* so much electricity consumption or so much education. Also, the concept of optimum styles or patterns of development introduces a value aspect over and above that of the single indicators. The problem of interdependency in a system further complicates the picture. The value of a 10-cent piece of wire in a multi-million dollar space rocket is not just 10 cents if the entire rocket blows up when the piece of wire is defective.

The discussion in this paper has been limited to national indicators. But for a better understanding of development, national aggregative indicators need to be supplemented by a system of measurement of real progress at the local level. Certain national indicators may prove invalid or meaningless when tested at the local level; national indicators generally fail to reflect distribution; and, particularly when social factors are involved, it is usually necessary to move down to the local level where the interactions take place in order to understand how different factors influence each other in real contexts, rather than as national abstractions.

NOTES

1. The indicator indicates the presence of development, one might say, but not the exact amount (unless the contribution of the factor has been weighted).

2. If the data are sufficient for the purpose, then a synthetic indicator may perhaps be constructed from the collection. This raises complex questions of both direct and indirect weighting (the latter form of weighting being dependent on methods of scale conversion).

3. This is not always the case with indicators, and discrepancy between correlations and expert opinion may call for special study. For example, educational experts tend to agree on teacher–pupil ratio as an indicator of quality of education, on the assumption that the more attention to the individual student, the better the education. But pupil–teacher ratio has relatively low correlation with other educational indicators or with development indicators in general. This may be because (a) quality of elementary education does not in fact improve with level of development and is therefore not a developmental factor; (b) the statistics on pupil-teacher ratio are poor or not comparable; or (c) poor quality education lowers enrolment and attendance, boosting the ratio, while high quality education has the opposite effect, so that the index has inherent contradictions.

4. The methodology behind the use of correlation in selection of indicators is set out in some detail in UNRISD [1970].

5. Under the project entitled 'A System of Demographic, Manpower and Social Statistics'.

6. Efforts at systematization by use of a stock and flow scheme, which introduces a temporal dimension into social statistics, or by use of data collection schemes like the Scandinavian number system or the grid-square system which serve to unify diverse economic and social data around the individual or locality (as contrasted with the prevailing tendency towards separate streams of statistics moving upwards), promise to be highly valuable for developmental analysis (if they should be feasible in more than one or two countries).

7. To be consistent, an area that is now much worse off in production than it used to be solely because of climatic change should not be considered any more underdeveloped, for that reason, than it was before. Nor should one country be considered agriculturally more developed than another country simply because it produces more, if its level of agricultural technology is no higher.

8. UNESCO is working on this problem.

9. To avoid confusion, it is perhaps necessary to stress that the concern here is with a conceptual model, a framework of thinking, extended to development as a whole, covering both social and economic aspects. The 'input-output model' as a set of techniques for quite precise purposes in economic analysis is not under discussion here.

10. For example, through regression analysis one reaches the conclusion that one of the most effective means to increase national production in industrialized countries is to prolong the lives of elderly persons since a small difference in life expectation is associated with very large differences in *per capita* G.N.P. in regression analysis (with *per capita* G.N.P. as the dependent variable).

11. This definition has been suggested by Marshall Wolfe in a working paper at UNRISD. It was not intended as a full definition of development, but as a minimum criterion.

12. If they should appear diminished because of the current value loading of the word 'development', then perhaps development should be used very broadly to include them while another word would be used for the system of interdependent factors.

13. In the UNRISD [*1970*] study, a core of eighteen highly correlated indicators was isolated.

14. The idea of 'an appropriate balance' is emphasized in a recent paper by Arthur Lewis where he writes:

Development occurs in all directions simultaneously. Growth runs into bottlenecks if there is not an appropriate balance between sectors, especially between industry, agriculture and infrastructure; and between production for the home market and for exports. All sectors must expand as income grows; so the question popular twenty years ago as to which sector should have priority has been displaced by the search for the appropriate balance. Less developed countries have not handled this aspect of their affairs adequately; their neglect of agriculture and of exports has produced severe balance-of-payments constraints [*Lewis, 1970, p. 1*].

15. The best-fitting line is defined as a line that minimizes the sum of the absolute deviations on both X and Y axes. It is always a median line and for that reason not derivable from a single equation. In 'Contents and Measurement of Socio-Economic Development' [*UNRISD, 1970*], a relatively crude moving-average method was used to derive the best-fitting line. Recent research at UNRISD has led to more exact methods (along with a computer programme) which are not much more difficult to apply than regression analysis in linear distributions.

Experiments with the best-fitting line have shown that as a rule it will estimate missing scores or predict future scores as accurately or more accurately than do regression lines, in spite of the fact that there are two regression lines (one minimizing the squares of the Y errors when X is the independent variable, and the other minimizing the squares of the X errors when Y is the independent variable). This is even true in the case of textbook examples of the proper use of regression. A report on the subject will shortly be issued at UNRISD.

REFERENCES

Lewis, W. Arthur, 1970, *The Development Process*, New York: United Nations.
UNRISD, 1970, *Contents and Measurement of Socio-economic Development*, Report No. 70. 10, Geneva: United Nations Research Institute for Social Development.

Indicators of Political Development

By Charles Lewis Taylor*

SUMMARY

Development implies goals and the positing of goals requires values. Economists have generally agreed that the increase of wealth (or perhaps welfare) is the proper object of economic development. Political scientists, probably happily, have no similar agreement in regard to the appropriate goal for political development. Moreover, it is doubtful that the various aspects of political change are located along a single continuum. This is an empirical question but investigation ought to begin at least with provision for an n-dimensional space. Finally, political scientists should concentrate on political change that has too often been neglected in favour of economic and purely social change.

INTRODUCTION

We have got no further than the title and have already begun to make debatable assertions. Few political scientists deny that social change can be measured on a continuum so that movement in one direction is denoted development or progress. Few also agree on the parameters of this continuum. International bodies such as the United Nations Statistical Office produce an enormous number of economic, social and cultural data series but publish virtually nothing that could be designated a political series. One can only assume the latter to be too 'hot' for an international organization; one man's responsible development is another man's repression. Political scientists, on the other hand, have felt less need to be reticent and have proceeded on the basis of their own values, even if they have not always been explicit on the identity of these values. 'Political development', then, has become a cacophony of definitions with numerous indicators designed to measure a number of facets of multiple phenomena.

The field now needs not so much definitional unity as the establishment of empirical relationships among the various dimensions of political change that have already been identified and more or less measured. We are not now and possibly never will be in position to find indicators of *the* political development process; we must work at indicators of *several processes*. Only after gathering these and analysing their functional relationships, if then, can we even attempt an overarching definition of that elusive term political development.

THE MULTI-DIMENSIONALITY OF POLITICAL DEVELOPMENT

Political change is not unidirectional towards progress. To think so is to be parochial in our understanding of history. The Western world had

---

* Professor of Political Science, Virginia Polytechnic Institute, and visiting Fulbright Lecturer at the University of Strathclyde.

its Dark Ages, that great political as well as economic depression, and other cultures have had similar long term political difficulties. We have had at least political recessions in our own time. But since it is always possible to talk of regression as the opposite of development, the problem of multiple directions is a great deal less serious than that of multiple dimensions.

No one can deny that profound differences exist between governments of primitive tribes and governments of modern states, but neither can one deny that significant differences exist among modern states. In Switzerland or Austria the primary concern of politics seems to be not to have any; partisan balance must be maintained at all cost. In the United States, on the other hand, the prerequisite of every administration is 'to do something'. Which system is the more developed? Where would the Soviet Union be placed on that particular continuum? The less-developed countries would appear to be in none of these implicit categories, but they are certainly not primitive tribes. They have already crossed that gap between primitive and twentieth century and they are in some sense modern states. They clearly have differentiated political structures of some degree and they are more or less independent units in the international polity and the international economy. Now will their political behaviour continue to move towards that of the United Kingdom, France, Japan, Czechoslovakia, East Germany, the Soviet Union and other politically developed states? Moreover, would this constitute development or be mere imitation? In a simple comparison of primitive government and government in modern, industrialized states, it is easy to believe that movement from one to the other must be along a single path or at least along a few parallel paths. It is when we try to place the present configuration of polities in the world along these paths that the troubles begin.

The mapping of political change into an n-dimensional space would appear more appropriate. Political development has been defined at one time or another as any one or more of the following facets of change: the growth of an impartial civil service and differentiation in the structures of government, the maintenance of stability and the provision for orderly change in leadership, fundamental changes in the style of thought, the increase of responsiveness in the personnel and institutions of government and the development of grass roots democracy, national integration that overrides primordial conflicts and brings purposive action to the state and its people, the provision of defence—military, economic, cultural— against the outside world, or simply constitutional development, the growth of rules by which authorative decisions can be made.[1] Whether all these facets of change and others besides can be got on to one continuum of development is an empirical question, but we may suspect their interrelationships are a bit more complicated.

THE VALUE-CONTENT OF POLITICAL DEVELOPMENT

Debate on whether or not to include negative components in estimates of gross national product for such things as pollution illustrate the value content of this concept. Yet, the economist probably faces far fewer of these problems of value than does the political scientist. After all, almost everyone agrees that the production of wealth, or at least the enhancement of the general welfare, is a good thing and that it is the proper goal of

economic development. What is the goal of political development? The
Europeans thought the Americans had worked that one out and the
Americans thought the British had got it. The less developed countries
may be doubtful about both. If we say political development is simply
the creation of social, cultural and psychological conditions necessary for
economic development, we omit a large part of the change that has been
discussed under the term. The complexity of politics cannot be reduced to
the causes and consequences of economic growth. Moreover, there is no
obvious political good to produce. Nothing is quite the analogy of wealth.
Political development is not the creation of more and more power or
authority or sovereignty (whatever that is). These may be redistributed,
refashioned, revolutionized but their aggregate increase is not development.
The maximization of freedom would be more popular as a goal among
readers of this journal, but most would prefer it made consistent with an
ordered society and we would all disagree on what that meant from
country to country and from time to time. This is not a proscription of
political activity; rather it is a caution for analysis.

It is possible to combine the notion of development with the n-
dimensional space suggested above. Development may be thought of as
the movement toward some point of balance among the co-ordinates, but
balance must be defined again in terms of value. The question of whose
values these will be must be answered in two contexts: that of the people
undergoing the process and that of the scholar observing it. The first
context is a pre-eminently political one. Who gets to decide the goals is an
indication of who holds power. The observation and analysis of conflicting goals and of the pursuit of them is the business of the political
scientist. In observing and analysing, however, he must inevitably impose
some of his own values if he is to talk of development. He may wish to
consider the number of people with identifiable notions on the proper
goals of the polity or the variety in the types of values put forth as indications of political development. If so, he will probably be operating within
the context of pluralist values. He might find some credible way to specify
a society's goals and assert that working towards those goals is development for that society, but that implies a rather liberal 'live and let live' set
of values. Besides, some polities such as the Burmese may choose the
goal of isolated traditionalism; would that be development too? What
the political scientist has normally done is to look at the great changes that
have accompanied industrialization in the West and has developed on
the basis of them concepts which are culture and time specific. This was
not surprising since he had to use somebody's values, but value is an
additional weight which anyone interested in the analysis of political development must carry and in future it should be more explicity recognized.

Henry Bernstein [1971] argues that the whole concept of modernization,
by which he means 'a total social process associated with (or subsuming)
economic development in terms of the preconditions, concomitants, and
consequences of the latter' (p. 141), flounders on the matter of value. The
paradigm of modernization, he says, was abstracted and universalized
from the Western historical experience so that the cluster of traits that
make up the ideal type 'traditional' are simply those characteristics such
as non-participation and lack of achievement motivation which do not
form a part of modern Western culture. Never mind the exceptions,
say the modernization theorists; these are written off as transitory or

pathological. Bernstein, on the other hand, feels these exceptions to be sufficiently numerous to require a serious reconsideration of the model and he proposes a systematic and comprehensive sociological theory of colonialism. I am a little less suspicious that theories of political development are simply tools of imperialism and believe that they may be useful for some purposes. There is surely some sense in which the attainment of grass roots democracy, of an ordered society, and of effective government represents progress. What one wants is all of these at once, but if trade-offs must be made, one wants the maximization of each consistent with the others. It seems not inappropriate to consider this maximization as a process of growth or development.

THEORY AND INDICATORS

If this change is to be analyzed in a comprehensive manner, then development must be thought of as a multi-dimensional concept and relationships among the dimensions must be sought empirically. This is not a call for a quick factor analysis of all the available aggregate data for the polities of the world. We already know something of how that would turn out.[2] The number and kinds of factors and especially the amount of variance for which each accounts is dependent upon the particular series included and those series already available may not be theoretically the most important. Moreover, such an analysis would consider only linear relationships, or if some of the series were transformed, some jumble of unidentified relationships. The interrelationships among dimensions of political development are likely to be far more complicated functions. Finally, there is a serious problem not only for 'barefoot' empirical methods such as factor analysis but for all statistical methods. The number of important dimensions is probably large relative to the number of independent observations. Two points alone will determine a line, of course, but we may be excused for having reservations about the relationship which it describes. One has greater confidence when there are a large number of points scattered about it. Very often in studies of development, it is characteristics of the polity as a whole that are of interest and there are a limited number of polities. Generalization to a few principles is difficult then because it is not easy to separate the effects of several factors operating simultaneously. The use of time series analysis and other historical methods helps somewhat, but even so usually there are still not large numbers of observations.

Statistical methods are designed to describe and to infer on the basis of the average behaviour of a large number of events each of which taken alone is unpredictable but which together fit into a system that has order and analyzable average properties. It is, indeed, appropriate to use these methods for some kinds of research, for example, that into the attitudes of political development. Lerner [*1967*] and Almond and Verba [*1963*] are classic, even if methodologically unsophisticated, examples. For work with system level data, however, statistics as such seem not very useful although some of the possibilities for line fitting and residual analysis that grow out of classical statistical procedures do hold significant promise [*Tukey and Wilk, 1970, and Taylor, 1972b*]. These allow a data analysis that can interact with thoughtful insight to produce meaningful models of political processes. To do this may be a more difficult task than political scientists have thus far been willing to recognize. At the system level, political development is probably of the nature of what Ronald D. Brunner and Garry D. Brewer call organized complexity, i.e. problems 'too complicated to yield to the old nineteenth-century techniques which were so dramatically successful on two-, three-, or four-variable problems of simplicity . . . [nor to the] statistical techniques so effective in describing the average behaviour in problems of disorganized complexity' [*Weaver, 1948*, cited in *Brunner and Brewer, 1971, p. 103*]. Brunner and Brewer developed a computer programmed simulation model for the process of political development in Turkey and the Philippines on the basis of partial data and incomplete theory. Not many of us would accept simulation as the only solution, but it is probable that the most plausible theories will be developed in an interaction between intensive searches of the data and inductive leaps of the imagination. Good explanations cannot be found without informed perspective (data) and data cannot be collected without some *a priori* notion of what to collect.

If the primacy of theory versus data is a chicken or egg question, as I believe it to be, it will be impossible to put together a comprehensive list of all the indicators that should be collected to measure all the relevant aspects of political development. The indicators come along as a direct result of theory building and this is a slow and painful process. A preliminary model is fitted to the data but residuals show that it is defective in some way. Changes are required either by restructuring the form of the model or by adding variables. As new variables are added, their measurement must be undertaken. Because of the slippage between variables and their indicators, there is even a sense in which the selection of measurements is itself involved in theory building.

At the same time we are not without ideas as to what this list of indicators should include. Bruce Russett, who has put together a list for political linkages,[3] wrote that the major problem of data collection 'is far less one of identifying possible indicators of variables that one would like to measure than a problem of deciding, among a virtual infinity of potential *indicators*, which ones can serve as measures of *variables* that are theoretically important' [*Russett, 1970*]. With several compendia of data series now available,[4] it might be appropriate in the immediate future to rely more heavily upon collecting additional indicators specific to the needs of particular models. In short, *at this time*, further development of indicators might best proceed from new theoretical requirements.

THE SALIENCE OF THE POLITICAL

Many indicators used in political development studies have been economic, social, cultural and psychological in nature. These have included such things as gross national product, ethnic fractionalization, literacy, achievement motivation scores, socio-economic status, religious affiliation, *et cetera*. In something as interdisciplinary as development studies, it would be singularly regressive to suggest that political scientists limit their economic interests to indicators with clear political overtones such as distribution of wealth or allocations among government expenditures. Nevertheless, it might not be presumptuous to encourage political scientists to be unashamedly political in their definitions if not in their explanations.

The first order of business in political development studies is to isolate and give substance to the separate dimensions in political terms. What do we mean by stability? It it simply provision for orderly change or must it contain some dynamic to encourage change? If the latter, what is the nature of the change and by whom should it come? Do we have to specify goals when we talk of government effectiveness? Are governments effective in some arenas and not in others? Is there enough relationship among them to be able to measure overall effectiveness? Participation is an aspect that has received a great deal of attention both in transitional and modern societies, but new things are happening among students in Western countries. Is this a case of over-modernization? Is the development of national autonomy within the international system and the institutionalization of procedures within the system subsumed under governmental effectiveness or is it a dimension of its own? How much differentiation of political, legal and administrative structures is useful and is there a threshold over which further differentiation becomes dysfunctional to effectiveness? How are stability, effectiveness and freedom reconciled? How responsive is the system to the common man? These questions hardly exhaust the larder but they point to a more *political* orientation in the study of political development.

CONCLUSION

Political change is more complicated than it has often been pictured in the literature on modernization. It is multi-dimensional and the relationship among the dimensions are probably not simple and linear. Moreover, the concept of development or progress when added to change raises the question of value. Enough agreement on the basic goals for which states should strive probably exists to allow continued use of the concept, but many kinds of political change might be exempted. Not all change is either progress or regression. Whether development or not, however, political change should be subjected to rigorous scrutiny in its own right and not simply as the adjunct of social, cultural and economic changes in societies.

NOTES

1. In the interest of brevity, I have assumed readers to be familiar with the theories of political development. For a short overview see the introduction to this issue. For longer bibliographies in political development, see Bernstein [*1971*] pp. 157–60, Holt and Turner [*1966*] pp. 383–406, and Rokkan [*1970*] pp. 432–464.

2. See Gregg and Banks [*1965*] and Russett [*1967*].

3. Russett [*1970*]. See Deutsch [*1960*] for a list more directly related to political development.

4. Collections of data include Banks [*1971*], Taylor and Hudson [*1972*], and Zapf and Flora [*1971*]. Data on interactions between states are being collected in the World Event Interaction Survey under the direction of Charles McClelland, the University of Southern California.

REFERENCES

Almond, Gabriel A., and Verba, Sidney, 1963, *The Civic Culture*, Princeton, New Jersey: Princeton University Press.

Banks, Arthur S., 1971, *Cross Polity Time Series Data*, Cambridge, Massachusetts: Massachusetts Institute of Technology Press.

Bernstein, Henry, 1971, 'Modernization Theory and the Sociological Study of Development', *The Journal of Development Studies*, Vol. 7, No. 2.

Brunner, Ronald D., and Brewer, Garry D., 1971, *Organized Complexity: Empirical Theories of Political Development*. New York: The Free Press.

Deutsch, Karl W., 1960, 'Toward an Inventory of Basic Trends and Patterns in Comparative and International Politics', *The American Political Science Review*, Vol. 54, March.

Gregg, Phillip M., and Banks, Arthur S., 1965, 'Dimensions of Political Systems: Factor Analysis of a Cross-Polity Survey', *The American Political Science Review*, Vol. 59, September.

Holt, Robert T., and Turner, John E., 1966, *The Political Basis of Economic Development: An Exploration in Comparative Political Analysis*, New York: Van Nostrand.

Lerner, Daniel, 1967 (1958), *The Passing of Traditional Society: Modernizing the Middle East*, New York: The Free Press.

Rokkan, Stein, 1970, *Citizens, Elections, Parties: Approaches to the Comparative Study of the Processes of Development*, Oslo: Universitetsforlaget.

Russett, Bruce M., 1970, 'Indicators for America's Linkages with the Changing World Environment', *The Annals of the American Academy of Political and Social Science*, Vol. 388, March.

Russett, Bruce M., 1967, *International Regions and the International System: A Study in Political Ecology*, Chicago, Rand McNally.

Taylor, Charles Lewis, and Hudson, Michael C., 1972, *World Handbook of Political and Social Indicators (Second Edition)*, New Haven: Yale University Press.

Taylor, Charles Lewis, 1972, 'The Uses of Aggregate Data Analysis', *Mathematical Applications in Political Science, VII*, ed. James F. Herndon, Charlottesville: University of Virginia Press.

Tukey John W., and Wilk, M. B., 1970, 'Data Analysis and Statistics: Techniques and Approaches', *The Quantitative Analysis of Social Problems*, ed. Edward R. Tufte, Reading, Massachusetts: Addison-Wesley.

Weaver, Warren, 1948, 'Science and Complexity', *American Scientist*, Vol. 36 (cited in Brunner and Brewer.)

Zapf, Wolfgang, and Flora, Peter, 1971, 'Some Problems of Time-Series Analysis in Research on Modernization', *Social Science Information*, Vol. 10, June.

The Measurement of Institutional Characteristics of Nations: Methodological Considerations

By Irma Adelman and Cynthia Taft Morris*

SUMMARY

A major barrier to the quantitative investigation of interactions between economic and non-economic influences in economic development is the lack of adequate indicators of institutional traits of nations. Our purpose in this paper is to consider the methodological procedures involved in the development of qualitative sociopolitical and economic indicators.

The first sections of the paper deal with various aspects related to the subject of measurement. This is necessary because misconceptions regarding the nature of 'qualitative measurement' are common, and misleading contrasts between qualitative and quantitative measurement are frequently made. The last four sections illustrate the procedures for the measurement of institutional indicators by applying them to the quantification of the concept of political participation in developing countries.

I. THE CONCEPT OF MEASUREMENT

As originally conceived by physical scientists, the concept of 'measurement' was restricted to the assignment of numerals to properties of objects or events, the behaviour of which could be described meaningfully by the operations of the real number system including the operation of addition.[1] The idea of measurement was later extended by physicists to selective non-additive physical properties such as density, which can be ordered serially on the basis of precise functional relationships with measurable cardinal properties. In the behavioural sciences, formal measurement procedures have been applied to an even wider range of nonadditive psychological and psychophysical attributes.[2] Recently, with increase in the sophistication and flexibility of statistical techniques for handling non-additive data, the concept of measurement has finally been widened to encompass the full range of non-additive and even non-orderable typological data.[3] Thus, measurement in practice in the behavioural and social sciences is now approaching the widest meaning of the theoretical concept of measurement, as encompassing 'most of those acts of identification, delimitation, comparison, present in everyday thought and practice. . . .' [*Nagel, 1960, p. 7*].

Formally viewed, measurement is the assignment of numbers to the properties of empirical objects or events in such a way that a one-to-one correspondence is maintained between the relations among the properties measured and the characteristics of the numbers assigned.[4] Forms of measurement may be differentiated by the type of measurement scale and by the type of link between the numerical scale and the concept measured.

* Senior Economist at the International Bank of Reconstruction and Development and Professor of Economics at the America University, Washington, D.C.

H

II. TYPES OF MEASUREMENT SCALES

Four kinds of measurement scales may be distinguished: nominal scales, simple ordinal scales, ordered metric scales, and cardinal scales.[5] Each of these is characterized by a particular set of restrictions on the numbers assigned to represent the relations among the properties of objects or events and therefore by a particular set of statistical operations which may legitimately be applied to the numbers assigned.

Nominal scales serve to classify a set of objects or their properties into classes within which objects are congruent. The rank order of the classes is not specified so that there are no restrictions on the numerical representation. Typologies having unranked categories and dummy variables are examples of nominal measurement.[6] In recent years, the use of nominal scales has become more common in econometric work because of developments in statistical techniques which permit use of highly differentiated nominal data in statistical analyses.[7,8]

Ordinal scales must meet both the equivalence requirement for nominal scales and the further requirement that the assignment of numbers preserve the serial order of the properties measured. Numerical representations are restricted to order-preserving transformations of any set of numbers consistent with the serial order of the properties. Permissible statistical manipulations include the calculation of medians and percentiles as well as contingency correlations.[9]

Ordinal scales are widespread in economics since the preponderance of economic composites are ordinal when interpreted as indices of some underlying property or concept. Examples are price indices interpreted to measure the cost of living, unemployment indices interpreted to represent the economic cost of unemployed labour either to the economy or to the individual, and G.N.P. interpreted to represent either national economic welfare or national productive capacity.[10]

In practice, economists generally treat widely accepted ordinal economic indices as if they were cardinal. The assumption, rarely stated explicitly, is that the results of statistical analyses are not very sensitive to alternative order-preserving transformations of the input data. This assumption should of course be justified case by case through studies of the actual sensitivity of statistical results to reasonable alternative specifications.

Ordered metric scales are the next most refined class of scales after simple ordinal scales. This class of scales must meet the requirement not only that the numbers assigned preserve the rank order of a set of points representing a property, but also that the rank order of distances between all pairs of points be preserved. Ordered metric scales are less familiar to economists than are simple ordinal scales. Psychometricians have used them in the measurement of attitudes where the basic data consist of pair-wise comparisons ranking objects or events. It has been shown that the rankings of distances among pairs of objects can impose sufficient constraints upon the location of the objects to derive a cardinal representation in a space of minimum dimensions.[11]

The final class of measurement scales are *ordered distance or cardinal scales*. These scales must meet the equivalence and order requirements of the simpler scale types and, in addition, the more restrictive requirement that different amounts of a property (or intervals between different amounts) be capable of meaningful combination by addition. The numerical representation of a cardinal scale is restricted to positive linear transformations of any given set of numerical values consistent with the properties measured. The attraction of cardinal scales is that they can, without arbitrariness, be subjected to a wide variety of statistical manipulations including the calculation of standard deviations, product-moment correlations and so forth.

In economics, most *elementary* measurements are cardinal; for example, quantities, prices, and measurements based on counting (such as numbers employed in a given occupation) are all represented by cardinal scales.[12] However, these primary measurements are seldom introduced into statistical analyses in their cardinal form. Production and price indices are introduced rather than quantities and prices in order to measure changes in multidimensional properties; ratios or porportions are used to represent the relative importance of underlying properties measured by the classes of objects or events counted; and so forth. As a consequence, the use of cardinal scales in econometric work is relatively rare.[13]

III. TYPES OF LINK WITH UNDERLYING CONCEPTS

When forms of measurement are classified by type of link between the numerical scale and the property or concept measured, three kinds of measurement may be distinguished: fundamental measurement, derived measurement, and measurement by fiat or definition.

Fundamental or direct measurement is based exclusively on principles relating different amounts of a single property to each other without involving other properties.[14] In establishing a scale for length, for example, the relationships between different 'lengths' can be shown to approximate the 'model' of a cardinal scale by the actual superimposition and combination of objects of various lengths.[15] Originally, physicists conceived fundamental measurement to be applicable only to cardinal ratio scales such as those for length, weight, and electrical resistance [*Stevens, 1960*]. However, psychometricians have established fundamental ordinal scales for subjective sensations such as loudness by tests of the relationships between varying amounts of the sensation measured [*Torgerson, 1958, pp. 35–7 and Ch. 13*]. In economics, the use of fundamental scales has to date been limited primarily to such elementary measurements as weight and length.[16]

Derived measurement is based upon precise functional relationships between the property measured and other, fundamentally measured properties. Classic examples in physics are the establishment of ordinal scales for density or force by exact numerical laws relating them to fundamental magnitudes.[17] Derived measurement is rare in economics because economic theories seldom provide exact functional relationships between fundamentally measured magnitudes and concepts or properties not capable of measurement on fundamental scales. By exception, utility under risk has been measured by derivative methods [*Coleman, 1964, pp. 65ff.*].

Measurement by fiat or definition is a form of indirect measurement by means of operational prescriptions based neither on fundamental procedures nor upon precise functional relationships with fundamental magnitudes.[18] It includes measurement by indices and typologies, and is widespread in the social and behavioural sciences for the measurement of multidimensional theoretical concepts for which neither fundamental nor derivative procedures are presently feasible. Measurement by fiat typically yields an ordinal scale for ranking the properties of objects or events with respect to the underlying concepts measured.[19]

IV. MEASUREMENT BY FIAT: ECONOMIC INDICES

In econometric work, measurement by fiat is the predominant form of measurement. The theoretical concepts important in generalizing about economic phenomena—for example, economic welfare, economic development, imperfect competition, capital, income distribution—are complex and multidimensional. Hence, they are not subject to representation by unidimensional, 'primary' cardinal data such as quantities, weights, or counts of events or objects. To represent such complex concepts, it is necessary to define 'empirical constructs' of a relatively low level of abstraction which specify operational rules or criteria for classifying observed behaviour with respect to the relevant concept.[20] Income, investment, and particular indices of unemployment, price, production, capital stock, and output per man-hour are examples of 'empirical constructs' or 'operational definitions' which provide multidimensional empirical equivalents of abstract economic concepts.

The rules laid down by empirical constructs for classifying observation may be based on theoretical models which help make the scope and limitations of the measures explicit, as in the case of indices of income or price. Or, they may be based on *ad hoc* judgement and experience, as when industrialization is measured by the proportion of the labour force in industry, or the equality of income distribution is measured by the share of a given percent of the population in total income. Even indices having theoretically based rules of aggregation usually suffer from ambiguous conceptual links between operational definitions framed in terms of observed behaviour and the relevant concepts of theoretical import, since theoretical models suitable for linking them together are frequently lacking. Connections between economic composites not having theory-based rules of aggregation and the underlying concepts they represent are typically still more uncertain.

To illustrate, G.N.P. is an empirical construct which provides operational prescriptions for ranking observed economic phenomena with respect to national economic welfare (or alternatively, national productive capacity). The rules of aggregation are based upon explicit theorizing which justifies the use of market prices (with some adjustments) in aggregating the value of outputs (or alternatively, inputs). As is well recognized, however, G.N.P. does not yield an unambiguous ranking with respect to even potential economic welfare and, in the presence of major changes in income distribution and externalities may be a poor measure of both potential and actual welfare. Similarly, in the presence of major structural changes in an economy, it yields a poor measure of both potential and actual productive capacity.

Measurement by fiat or definition yielding ordinal representations of complex abstract concepts is the stock-in-trade of the econometrician. Its widespread use in preparing data for statistical models which, strictly speaking, require cardinal data has been justified by the many meaningful empirical interconnections obtained and the stimulus to further theorizing which the 'illegal' statistical results have provided.[21] To quote Torgerson [*1958*]:

> . . . *measurement* by *fiat* . . . has led to a great many results of both practical and theoretical importance. . . .
>
> The discovery of stable relationships among variables so measured can be as important as among variables measured in other ways. Indeed, it really makes little difference whether the present scale of length, for example, had been obtained originally through arbitrary definition, through a relation with other, established variables, or through a fundamental process. The concept is a good one. It has entered into an immense number of simple relations with other variables. And this is, after all, the major criterion of the value of a concept. If the result is the same, the way in which a concept is originally introduced is of little importance (*1958, pp. 23–4*).

V. MEASUREMENT BY FIAT: SOCIOPOLITICAL AND INSTITUTIONAL INDICES

Although measurement by fiat has proved fruitful in econometric work, economists and econometricians frequently oppose application of this type of measurement to a wider range of 'qualitative' institutional phenomena which they fully recognize to be important for understanding primary economic events. There are several reasons for their position.

First, economists suspect measurements which are aggregates of ordinal or 'qualitative' primary data on the grounds that they are neither as sensitive nor as reliable as measures which are composites of cardinal or 'quantitative' primary data. This view cannot, however, be established in general, since there is no *a priori* reason to suppose that composites of 'quantitative' primary data provide more sensitive measures of the theoretical concepts they represent than do reasonably well conceptualized composites of qualitative components. As regards reliability, most economists consider that composites of numerical or 'quantitative' data vary less with repeated measurements than do composites of qualitative data. Given relatively unambiguous concepts and accurate methods of recording such as are sometimes found in advanced countries, numerical data may in practice be more reliable than qualitative rankings, although they are not necessarily so. In underdeveloped countries, however, techniques for recording numerical data such as quantities produced, population, or number of births and so forth are frequently so inaccurate that they may vary considerably more than expert judgements on qualitative rankings based on reasonably explicit criteria.[22]

Second, economists suspect aggregates of qualitative inputs because the rules for aggregation are seldom based upon theories as explicit as those used for such measures as G.N.P., production, factor productivity and cost of living. The disadvantage of *ad hoc* rules of aggregation is that the scope and limitations of the indices are less explicit and hence less well understood than in the case of indices composed on the basis of theoretical models. As indicated by Torgerson,

> The major difficulty with measurement by fiat is the tremendous number of ways in which such defined scales can be constructed. . . .
> . . . Although . . . investigations may establish that many lead to virtually

the same result and hence may be considered to be equivalent operational definitions of the same concept, many will also lead to quite different results, in which case they are operational definitions of different concepts [*1958, pp. 24–5*].[23]

Since social science theory suitable for preparing measures of institutional phenomena is at a rudimentary stage of development, this criticism is important and will be discussed further below. It should be kept in mind, however, that a considerable number of so-called 'quantitative' indices which are widely used in econometric work are also no more than *ad hoc* measures of theoretical concepts without explicit theories for the aggregation or combination of their components. Such measures as the percentage of the population in cities of a given size and over as a measure of urbanization and various indices of economic concentration are accepted in econometric work by convention and because they show meaningful connections with other variables rather than by reason of any explicit theoretical base.

Third, economists tend to avoid indices based upon qualitative data because of difficulties in obtaining primary qualitative data. Governments as a rule collect numerical or simple taxonomic data; such data are therefore widely available, although of varying reliability. In contrast, there is no regular and widespread collection of primary qualitative data suitable to representing abstract concepts. The collection of qualitative data also involves techniques with which most economists and statisticians are not overly familiar, and for which many of them have little taste. The result is that some economists maintain *a priori* that qualitative data are necessarily less reliable than quantitative data—without the case-by-case testing necessary to validate such a view.

VI. THE CONSTRUCTION OF MEASURES OF SOCIO-POLITICAL AND INSTITUTIONAL DEVELOPMENT

The establishment of operational criteria for the scaling of actual observations with respect to key multidimensional concepts is the essential feature of the 'measurement' of institutional phenomena. Since the measurement procedure involves the explication or operational definition of the concepts themselves, it can legitimately be called 'measurement by definition'.

The structure of the social sciences is such that indirect measurement not based on precise functional relationships of necessity plays an extremely important role. Complex multidimensional concepts of a relatively high level of abstraction are important to the social sciences because of their ubiquitous role as crude explanatory variables in understanding significant social phenomena. Such concepts have acquired the status of 'theoretical' constructs in spite of the fact that most of them do not have generally accepted empirical equivalents relating them to observable primary facts or data.

Alongside this wealth of intuitively important theoretical constructs, there is in the social sciences a larger number of 'empirical constructs' which are defined in terms of observable facts. Frequently, however, the connections between the abstract hypothetical constructs used in theorizing and these particular empirical definitions are, at best, tenuous. To quote Torgerson:

. . . The concepts of theoretical interest tend to lack empirical meaning, whereas the corresponding concepts with precise empirical meaning often lack theoretical import. One of the great problems in the development of a science is the discovery or invention of constructs that have, or are likely to have, both [*Torgerson, 1958, p. 8*].

Not only are the links between the key concepts of the social sciences and their associated empirical constructs uncertain but the key concepts are themselves often not rigorously linked to each other by explicit theoretical systems. In economics, for example, concepts such as economic growth and economic welfare have neither fully accepted empirical equivalents nor explicit generally agreed theoretical interconnections. Where theoretical systems linking key concepts do exist, as with the neoclassical theory of resource allocation, unique empirical equivalents are frequently lacking. This uncertainty of the links both among key concepts and between key concepts and their empirical equivalents contrasts with the structure of knowledge in the physical sciences. In the physical sciences a multiplicity of formal logical relationships link key theoretical concepts and provide rules of correspondence or empirical procedures for relating the concepts to observable data. The establishment of such rules of correspondence is the familiar process of measurement itself.

The social sciences are thus at a stage of development at which there is an overwhelming need for more exact and generally acceptable empirical equivalents of the abstract, and often complex concepts in terms of which current theories of behaviour and change are formulated. The need is particularly great since empirical investigation of hypotheses involving the relevant theoretical relationships cannot proceed without operational definitions connecting the institutional concepts to observable facts.

The Translation of Concepts into Empirical Indices

The process whereby the concepts of importance to social science investigations are translated into empirical indices may be viewed as consisting of the initial visualization of the concept, the specification of the components or dimensions of the concept, the selection of indicators to represent these dimensions and the formation of an index from the battery of indicators. By far the greatest difficulties in developing indicators of social, political and economic structure are those of conceptualization and operational definition. In addition, the scarcity and irregularity of primary data greatly constrain the number of feasible alternatives for the measurement of each influence.[24]

The initial visualization of a concept may be derived from explicit theoretical reasoning, from the observation of regularities among empirical events, from an intuitive feel for some set of interrelated phenomena or from some combination of the three. Many of the key concepts of contemporary economics are derived from explicit theory. In contrast, many of the concepts currently used to analyse modernization are derived from everyday language and understanding and originate in common observation of historical and contemporary phenomena. Examples are the concepts of industrialization, urbanization, social mobility, and political democracy.

Research need not, however, start with more than vague notions regarding the general thrust of an investigation. When the research is exploratory, the investigator may focus on data describing a wide range of behaviour—the varied social and psychological characteristics of American soldiers under stress during World War II, or the varied observable economic and non-economic characteristics of a set of low-income countries. A study of the raw data may itself suggest theoretical categories of interest.

The specification of the dimensions of the concept may also be either deduced from explicit theory, logical reasoning, or from observed regularities among empirical phenomena. The specification of the dimensions of economic welfare, for example, comes from explicit theories of economic welfare. On the other hand the specification of the dimensions of economic development or industrialization come less from explicit theory than from observations regarding the typical characteristics of successful growth.

The concept of social mobility provides an example of the need for specification of dimensions for concepts whose general meaning is complex and derives from common parlance. The upward movement of individuals or family units through a hierarchy of positions stratified by wealth, power, or esteem, is one dimension of social mobility stressed in American history. The movement of entire classes either gradually, as with the 'professionalization' of an occupation, or abruptly, as by revolution, is another dimension of social mobility. A third major dimension is the introduction of new systems of stratification involving changes in the criteria for evaluating social roles as well as the redistribution of roles, rewards and personnel.

The selection of indicators to represent the various dimensions of a complex concept normally requires selection from a considerable battery of possibilities. Where measurement is indirect, as in the measurement of most social science phenomena, the selection of indicators involves theoretical reasoning about causes and effects. Knowledge of empirical regularities or correlations may also provide guidance in the choice.

Efforts to measure the extent of social mobility, for example, have most frequently concentrated on the measurement of the *effects* of social mobility. Comparison of the distribution of fathers' and sons' occupations involve indirect measurement by observation of the characteristic effects of social mobility. Less usual are efforts such as those by the present authors [*1967 Ch. 2*] to measure mobility indirectly through its presumed *causes*: the spread of education, the size of the middle class, and the presence or absence of specific ethnic or religious barriers to mobility.

The distinction between cause and effect approaches to social measurement parallels the structural–functional dichotomy. The measurement of the effectiveness of the financial institutions of low income countries provides an example of possibilities for measuring a multidimensional concept by the *structural* characteristics of an institution. Estimates of the number and types of financial intermediaries or of the volume of savings and demand deposits measure indirectly the capacity of financial institutions to perform certain functions by means of selected structural characteristics of the system. The effectiveness of financial institutions could alternatively be judged by the performance of key *functions* such as the channelling of loans into productive investment. Data on the volume of loans to businesses per unit of time could be used for such a purpose.

Sometimes the two approaches to the selection of indicators are merged.

In the measurement of G.N.P., for example, the measurements by value of inputs and of outputs are combined into a single aggregate.

Ultimately, the choice between types of indicators for indirect measurement must rest on the reliability of the interconnection between the theoretical concept and its indicators—its causes, its structural characteristics, its effects, and/or its functional properties.

The final step in the process is *the formation of indices* from component elements representing the selected dimensions of the concept. In this step also theoretical reasoning together with empirical or pragmatic considerations interact.

Lazarsfeld and Barton [*1951, p. 173*] cite three kinds of approaches to the reduction in the multidimensional attribute space used to represent complex phenomena. The first kind of reduction is *functional reduction* on the basis of an actual relationship between two or more of the attributes in an attribute compound. Examples of functional reduction are provided by Guttman scales and by the groupings of variables into dimensions in a factor analysis.

The second kind of reduction is an *arbitrary numerical reduction* through the selection of numerical weights for the component attributes. Weights may be derived in a variety of ways including the use of explicit theory (e.g. production and cost-of-living indices) and methods based on a mathematical model fitted to empirical data (latent structure analysis).

The third kind of reduction is *pragmatic reduction* whereby 'certain groups of combinations are contracted to one class in view of the research purpose' [*Lazarsfeld and Barton, 1951, p. 174*]. This is the type of reduction most applicable to the present state of measurement of institutional phenomena.

The Method of Successive Definition

The procedure we recommend for the development of empirical equivalents for complex and often fuzzy theoretical concepts is that of successive definition. In the preparation of the qualitative multidimensional indicators we have used in our work, we began with *a priori* definitions suggested by the literature. Next, we studied the descriptive data in order to see how well actual country situations fit our formulation of the concept. The inadequacies of the initial fit were then used to reformulate the concept to fit better the characteristics of the real world. We then consulted expert opinion and again reformulated the definitions. We continued this process of confronting successive reformulations with information on actual country situations until we were able to classify all the 74 countries in our sample with reasonable confidence.

The process of conceptualization and definition which we followed in constructing our composite indicators is a procedure well tried in the history of scientific inquiry—in the physical as well as the social sciences. Abraham Kaplan has the following to say about the early stage of scientific inquiry:

In short, the process of specifying meaning is a part of the process of inquiry itself. In every context of inquiry we begin with terms that are undefined—not indefinables, but terms for which that context does not provide a specification. As we proceed, empirical findings are taken up into our conceptual structure by way of new specifications of meaning, and former indications and references in turn become matters of emprical fact. . . .

What I have tried to sketch here is how such a process of 'successive definition' can be understood so as to take account of the openness of meaning of scientific terms. *For the closure that strict definition consists in is not a pre-condition of scientific inquiry but its culmination.* To start with we do not know just what we mean by our terms, much as we do not know just what to think about our subject-matter. We can, indeed, begin with precise meanings, as we choose; but so long as we are in ignorance, we cannot choose wisely. It is this ignorance that makes the closure premature [*Kaplan, 1964, pp. 77–8*].

It may also be worth noting that the procedure of successive definition is that which was followed historically in economics in the development of measures of national income. The theoretically derived empirical construct was confronted with actual data on income and output; the inconsistencies between construct and primary data then stimulated reformulations of the construct, which were again tested for consistency with primary facts. This is not, of course, to say that our indicators are either as reliable or as precise as measures of G.N.P. in advanced countries. It is only to say that at the exploratory stage in development of new measures of institutional phenomena the method of successive definition must be applied in order to obtain operational definitions consistent with observable phenomena and therefore suitable for classifying them.

VII. AN EXAMPLE—THE CONSTRUCTION OF AN INDICATOR OF POLITICAL PARTICIPATION

The successive steps by which we formulated and defined an indicator of popular political participation illustrate well the blend of conceptualization and testing against the characteristics of the real world required for the construction of multidimensional indicators. We shall therefore describe in detail the procedures followed in the derivation of this measure.

The basic requirement of a definition of political participation usable in studies of economic development was that it be capable of providing a continuum along which contemporary underdeveloped countries could be ranked. Our major difficulties arose from the fact that the literature did not offer a conceptualization of political participation both sufficiently relevant to the study of underdeveloped countries and sufficiently sensitive for differentiating among them.

An important part of the literature on political participation relates to the growth of parliamentary institutions in the Western democracies. It thus concerns, in words of a recent article on political participation, 'those voluntary activities by which members of a society share in the selection of rulers and, directly or indirectly, in the formation of public policy' [*McClosky, 1968, p. 252*]. However, increases in participation in the political process which do not impinge upon either the selection of rulers or the formation of public policy typify the growth of the rudimentary participant institutions characteristic of many countries at very low levels of socio-economic development; it follows that a conceptualization of political participation which excludes such activities is not appropriate for a study of underdeveloped countries.

On the other hand, writings on political participation in contemporary communist countries and in non-communist countries with single-party political systems give exclusive emphasis to forms of political participation which do not provide for a share in the selection of rulers and formation of public policy. These concepts do not allow for inclusion in a single classification scheme both countries with multi-party and those with single-party systems.

The absence of a clearly formulated model of political participation applicable to underdeveloped countries required that we, first, attempt an *a priori* conceptualization of political participation suitable to our needs. Next, we studied the descriptive data on participation in underdeveloped countries in order to see how well actual country situations fit our formulation of the concept. The inadequacies of the fit between data and concept were then used to reformulate the concept to conform better with the characteristics of the real world. We continued this process of confronting successive conceptualizations with actual country situations until we were able to classify the seventy-four underdeveloped countries in our sample with reasonable confidence and without fitting them into a Procrustean bed.

Once we arrived at a conceptualization of political participation sufficiently clear to permit the unambiguous classification of the overwhelming majority of countries in our sample, the actual task of classification was relatively straightforward. First, a large number of country studies were examined to obtain tentative classifications. Then, experts working in the individual countries were consulted in order to confirm and, as necessary, revise the classifications. In all, close to 100 experts on particular countries were consulted in the process of preparing and finalizing the 74 individual country classifications.

Initial Definitional Scheme

In our previous investigations of the development process, we had used several rather narrow indicators of political democracy. These represented the strength and competitiveness of the national political system, the extent of freedom of political opposition and press, and the predominant basis of the political party system. The major deficiency of this set of variables appeared to be their almost exclusive emphasis upon participation through national political parties. Consequently, our first formulation of an index of political participation broadened these measured to include both the attributes of the national party system and, in addition, the characteristics of alternative mechanisms for influencing national political decisions: for example, special interest associations such as labour unions and farmers' associations and local political institutions. This initial formulation of our participation indicator specified three broad sets of criteria for distinguishing among countries with respect to political participation:

(1) The breadth of representation and extent of choice offered by the national and political party system;

(2) The variety, political effectiveness and degree of autonomy of voluntary interest groups having as one of their functions political representation of members with some common socio-economic or cultural-ethnic identification; and

(3) The extent of local political participation through formal political institutions and informal associations carrying out political functions.

Our success in constructing a composite index from these elements depended upon the fulfilment of several conditions. First, to be valid, the proposed approach required that, in most instances, countries scoring high (or low) with respect to the representativeness of their national political parties also score high (or low) on special interest groups and local political institutions. Second, it required that it be possible to rank the several multi-party categories and the several single-party categories with respect to overall popular political participation; our provisional assumption was that multi-party systems could be ranked consistently above single-party systems. The third requirement was, of course, that, for countries with single-party systems and for those with multi-party systems, respectively, meaningful distinctions between different degrees of participation be possible.

Once our initial definition was completed, a wide variety of secondary sources were examined and a series of interviews with country and regional experts conducted in order to test whether actual country situations could be classified reasonably in terms of this definitional scheme. It soon became evident from both written sources and interviews that two of the three requirements for successful use of the preliminary scheme were not fully met. In the first place, a fair number of countries with quite broadly based systems of representation did not also have reasonably effective special interest associations and non-tribal local political institutions. In the second place, our provisional assumption that all multi-party systems could be ranked above single-party systems was clearly not satisfactory. Additional difficulties in classifying individual countries successfully were caused by the failure of the scheme to include explicitly the extent to which participant mechanisms actually influenced political decisions.

Reformulation Maintaining Multi-party/Single-party Dichotomization

Our next step was to reformulate our definitional scheme for political participation in order to achieve more meaningful distinctions between degrees of participation both in countries with two or more national political parties and in those having only one national party. At this stage, we were not successful in resolving the basic difficulty of ranking participation in multi-party systems compared with that in single-party ones.

In redefining degrees of political participation for countries with multi-party political systems, we decided to differentiate between countries in which there were important voluntary interest associations and local political institutions as well as national political parties, and countries in which participant mechanisms other than parties were negligible or very weak. We then divided the former countries into two groups: (1) those in which participant mechanisms taken as a whole represented the major groups in the population reasonably well and also influenced national political decisions to some significant extent, and (2) those in which either representation was incomplete or there was no significant influence on national political decisions or both. We thus obtained, in all, three major categories of political participation for countries with multi-party systems.

Revisions in the definition of degrees of political participation in single-party systems proved more difficult. According to a number of African experts we interviewed, variations among countries in the overall effectiveness of participant mechanisms could not be related primarily to the presence and strength of special interest associations and/or local political institutions. In the opinion of some, the real factor differentiating among single-party systems was the attitude of the leadership; that is, the countries with the more effective mechanisms for involving the population politically were generally those in which the leadership had worked from the top to create a network of participant groups at national and local levels. We decided to accept this view provisionally and revised our criteria for classifying single-party systems to distinguish between three groups of countries: (1) those in which the leadership had taken positive and successful measures to develop national and local mechanisms for broad popular participation, (2) those in which the leadership had taken measures but with quite limited success in actually involving members of the population, and (3) those in which participant mechanisms had either not been encouraged or had been suppressed. We specified further that, to be effective, popular participation in a single-party system did not require any particular kind of participant mechanism: that is, effectiveness might be achieved in one country by promoting local units of a political party and in another by developing special-interest adjuncts to the dominant party.

With respect to the unresolved problem of comparing participation in single-party and multi-party systems, the almost unanimous judgement of the experts consulted was that those single-party systems with quite well developed institutional mechanisms for popular participation ranked higher with respect to overall political participation than those multi-party systems having a very narrow representative base. We were not able, however, to find a solution to this ranking dilemma at that time and continued to collect data on the basis of a six-way classification of countries, with three groupings for multi-party systems and three for single-party systems. In consulting experts at this stage, we simply pointed out that there was a problem in ranking the lowest multi-party category and the highest single-party category.

The Conceptual Problem and Its Resolution

Our inability to rank participation in multi-party and single-party systems relative to each other clearly derived from our difficulty in conceptualizing the phenomenon of political participation adequately. Evidently, the dichotomization between countries with a single party and those with several parties did not coincide closely with any grouping of countries according to fundamental aspects of political participation.

The component of political participation most consistently associated with the single-party/multi-party dichotomization appeared to be the extent of individual choice among channels for the representation of political interests. The presence of more than one political party seemed *a priori* to offer more choice than the presence of only one party. However, even this generalization turned out to be questionable. Several experts pointed out that multi-party systems in which each party had a clear-cut cultural and/or ethnic identification did not in fact offer individuals with given cultural-ethnic identities any choice between parties.

Differences among countries in the number of channels available for political representation did not coincide with differences among them in other components of political participation. In some countries the various political parties all catered to the same narrow socio-economic group, so that most of the population had no genuince choice of a channel to represent their interests. Furthermore, the extent of choice between different types of channels for representation, such as political parties and labour unions, could in practice be considerably greater in a single-party system than in a multi-party system.

Two other important components of popular political participation were even less closely related to the multi-party/single-party dichotomization: the extent and effectiveness of representation of the major cultural-ethnic and socio-economic groups in the population; and the degree of actual participation by the population in the political process.

In pinpointing the source of our ranking dilemma, we became convinced that the solution to our conceptual problem lay in a definition of political participation in terms of its basic components rather than in terms of such specifics as the number of parties. In particular, positive improvements in popular political participation appeared to us to involve at least three kinds of political transformations: extensions in the coverage of representative institutions to include all the major groups in the population; the provision of greater choice between mechanisms for the representation of individual interests; and an increase in the actual involvement of the population in participant associations and institutions.

The classification schema finally adopted for political participation therefore groups underdeveloped countries in terms of the following broad criteria.

I. The extent to which, through participant associations and institutions, the major socio-economic and cultural-ethnic groups have their interests represented in, and are able to influence, the making of national political decisions affecting them.

II. The extent to which those individuals belonging to nationally represented cultural-ethnic and/or socio-economic groups can choose between political channels in seeking national representation of their interests.

III. The extent of actual participation by individuals in the national political process through participation in political parties, special interest groups and/or other institutions or associations carrying out political functions, or through voluntary voting between genuine political alternatives.

For each of the seventy-four underdeveloped countries, a composite score for the extent of popular political participation was derived from the rankings of that country with respect to the three criteria listed above. The precise make-up of the composite score was determined by *a priori* judgements regarding the relative importance of the different aspects of political participation represented. Table 1 of Appendix A abstracts the several categories of the composite indicator in terms of the three elements composing it. Immediately following Table 1 is the detailed explanation of the symbols contained in it. Finally, a brief literary description of the categories of the overall participation index completes the presentation of the classification scheme for the participation indicator.

A fundamental premise underlying the construction of our measure was that (as with G.N.P.) the capacity of a system to enhance individual welfare depends upon its success in transmitting and aggregating the choices of individuals. Extensions in the coverage of representative institutions to include all major groups in the population (the first element in the composite) clearly augment the capacity of a political system to provide for participation in the national political arena. Increases in actual individual participation (the third element in the composite) also enhance the possibilities for involving a still wider circle of individuals in national political institutions and associations. Finally, it seems reasonable to suppose that a great diversity of personal preferences is more likely to be transmitted to national decision-makers in a representative manner when individuals face a variety of different associations and institutions (the second element) through which their choices can be expressed.

The view that the capacity of a political system to provide for political participation increases with greater diversity of participant mechanisms is consistent with theories of consumers' choice in the economic domain. In analyses of consumer behaviour, the economic welfare of individuals taken as a whole is presumed to increase when the variety of goods and services available expands. There is thus a symmetry between our view of expanded political participation as an increase in the *capacity* of a country to engage its population in political activities influencing national political decision-making and the view of economic development as increases in the *capacity* of a country to provide economic welfare as measured by changes in *per capita* G.N.P. It is generally recognized that increases in *per capita* G.N.P. are not necessarily accompanied by *actual* increases in the economic welfare of the majority of the population. Similarly, we recognize that neither extensions of a representative system to cover additional cultural-ethnic groups nor expansions in the choice of participant mechanisms necessarily lead immediately to increases in *actual* political participation; both developments may nevertheless be expected to expand the capacity of a political system to eventually induce wider individual participation in the political process.

VIII. THE VALIDATION OF THE INDEX OF POLITICAL PARTICIPATION

The validity of measuring abstract concepts by empirical indices cannot be determined independently of the uses to which the measurement is put. On the relationship between validation of measurement procedures and the uses made of the measurements obtained, Abraham Kaplan has the following to say:

> The validity of a measurement consists in what it is able to accomplish, or more accurately, in what *we* are able to do with it. Plainly, this 'what' depends on the context of the measurement's use. Validity is not determined just by the instrument and scale of measurement, nor even also by the 'intrinsic nature' of the magnitude being measured. We must take into account as well the functions in inquiry which the measurement is intended to perform, or with respect to which—whether by intention or not—its validity is being assessed. The basic question is always whether the measures have been so arrived at that they can serve effectively as means to the given end [*Kaplan, 1964, p. 198*].

The usual characterization of a valid measurement is one which 'measures what it purports to measure' [*ibid*]. There are two ways of establishing validity in this sense of the word. One is to specify the meaning by the measurement procedure itself; e.g. if the meaning of 'national product' is specified by the rules for estimating G.N.P., then there is no question that G.N.P. measures national product. This does not, of course, validate the use of G.N.P. to represent theoretical concepts of economic welfare or productive capacity. The second way to validate a measurement, more suitable for most economic composites, is by its empirical connections with other indicants of the concept being measured. 'Here the validity of a measurement is a matter of the success with which the measures obtained in particular cases allow us to predict the measures that would be arrived at by other procedures and in other contexts' [*Kaplan, 1964, p. 199*]. The use of G.N.P. as a measure of national productive capacity, for example, can be validated by the extent to which estimates of G.N.P. enable economists to predict other aspects of capacity to perform economically, such as the capacity constraints revealed by input–output studies, or the constraints on the consumption of goods revealed by surveys of family budgets.

Validity also requires that measurement be relatively free of error in its several senses. That is, the measurement procedure should be sufficiently (but not unduly) *sensitive* to differences in the amount or degree of the property measured; the procedure should be sufficiently *reliable* in the sense that repeated measurements under constant conditions yield relatively unvarying results; and the procedure should be *accurate*, or free from systematic error due to omitted influences whose effect is presumed to be incorporated in the measurement procedure. Ultimately, therefore, validity depends both upon the characteristics of the measurement procedure and upon the uses to which the measurement is put.

The validity of the classification of underdeveloped countries by extent of popular participation may be gauged by the extent to which its use in statistical analyses yields sensible interconnections with other social science concepts, and by the extent to which results obtained with the aid of this indicator are consistent with knowledge based on historical and comparative studies. We shall therefore briefly summarize the results of several discriminant analyses in which this indicator was employed.

The classification of underdeveloped countries according to the extent of popular political participation was used to perform discriminant analyses for the full sample of seventy-four countries and for each of three subsamples representing successive levels of socio-economic development for two sub-periods (1957–63 and 1963–68) [*Adelman and Morris, forthcoming*]. The purpose of the discriminant analyses was to find for each sample that linear combination of country attributes which best differentiated between the groupings according to political participation. The variables allowed to enter the discriminant functions were chosen in a stepwise fashion from about twenty indicators of social, political and economic characteristics of underdeveloped countries during 1957–62. The twenty indicators represent various aspects of change which may, on theoretical grounds be expected to affect the degree of political participation.

The results indicate that the favourable influences and the constraints on the development of popular political participation change as countries move from lower to higher levels of socio-economic development.

At the lowest level of development, in which the extent of the economic and social transformations potentially favourable to expanded political participation is extremely limited, and which is composed mostly of 'new' countries with little political experience, we found that the important political forces are the initial development (primarily in urban centres) of representative political institutions, of specialized political organizations, and of reasonably good government administrations combined with a modicum of political freedom. Also of some importance at the low level are attitudinal changes favouring individual participation in urban political groupings; at this level, however, these are typically limited in their impact to an extremely narrow urban élite.

For countries at the intermediate level of development, the characteristics which discriminate best with respect to political participation express the presence of a positive connection between the wider spread of political participation and the expansion of the middle class. The study indicates that the expansion of participation to the urban middle-class groups is typically accompanied by a rise in the political role of the military, and by an increase in political instability and social tension. We find, however, that once higher levels of political participation are achieved a decrease in social tension and an increase in political stability result.

Increases in participation at the 'highest' level of development represented by our data are characterized in our results by the evolution of the more sophisticated and more robust political party systems in which political parties tend to articulate and aggregate the special associational interests characteristic of modern industrial societies. The growth of unions and spread of participation to peasants become important elements in determining the prospects for channelling increased political mobilization within the system. In addition, the extent of social mobility, which depicts the degree to which the economy and society are participant, becomes important in discriminating among countries with respect to political participation.

The results just summarized reinforce findings by political scientists based on comparative case studies. In a recent comprehensive (but descriptive) study of political development in developing countries, Huntington [1968, p. 202] stresses that modernization is associated with marked redistribution of power, and often requires the mobilization of new social forces into politics. To be able to accommodate economic and social modernization a political system must therefore be able to assimilate the socio-economic forces generated by modernization. Huntington suggests that in middle level underdeveloped countries the expansion of participation involves the broadening of participation from a small élite to middle-class groups and that 'the middle class makes its debut on one political scene not in the frock of merchants but in the epaulettes of the colonel' [Huntington, 1968, p. 201]. For countries which correspond to our 'high' level of development, Huntington stresses [p. 429] the role of political party structure in accommodating the expansion of participation. Electoral competition between parties tends to expand political participation and at the same time to strengthen party organization. 'Party competition of this sort enhances the likelihood that new social forces which develop political aspirations and political consciousness will be mobilized into the system rather than against the system.' He also stresses that 'the party and the party system are the institutional means of bridging the rural-urban gap'. Huntington's analysis thus confirms both the general finding that different forces are responsible for broadening participation at different levels of socio-economic and political development, and the specific set of variables singled out by the discriminant analysis at successive levels of modernization. The comparison of our statistical results with his analysis thus offers

I

partial validation of our index of political participation. Although our measure is necessarily crude, it appears to be sufficiently reliable for use in exploratory quantitative studies aimed at tracing its interconnections with other phases of the development process.

Summary and Conclusion

The discussion of measurement in this paper indicates the general similarity between conventional economic measurements of multi-dimensional concepts and the measurement of institutional, economic and non-economic, phenomena. There are no essential differences between the two classes of measurement in the general characteristics of the scales used to quantify them, the general procedures used for the derivation of the measurements and the validation requirements inherent in their statistical use. Both types of measurements are ordinal; both are measured by indirect techniques and rely on measurement by definition; and the validity of using them for a given purpose must be demonstrated for both through case-by-case sensitivity studies. The primary differences among the two classes of measurement lie in the fact that, for institutional measurement, much of the theoretical work required for adequate conceptualization needs yet to be done and that neither ready-made categories nor ready-made data currently exist.

APPENDIX A
Classification of Underdeveloped Countries with respect to the Extent of Popular Political Participation

The following classification groups countries by the extent and effectiveness of *national* popular political participation as judged by the following broad criteria:

I. The extent to which the major socio-economic and cultural-ethnic groups have their interests represented in, and are able to influence, the making of national political decisions affecting them through participant associations and institutions.

II. The extent to which individuals belonging to cultural-ethnic and/or socio-economic groups which have some form of national political representation can choose between different political channels in seeking national representation of their interests.

III. The extent of actual participation by individuals in the national political process through participation in political parties, special interest groups and/or other institutions, or associations carrying out political functions, or through voluntary voting between genuine political alternatives.

For each of seventy-four underdeveloped countries, a composite score for the extent of popular political participation is derived from the rankings of that country with respect to the three criteria listed above. Table 1 below specifies the characteristics of the several categories of the composite indicator in terms of the three elements composing it. The precise make-up of the composite is determined by *a priori* judgements regarding the relative importance of the different aspects of political participation represented. Immediately following Table 1 is the detailed explanation of the symbols contained in it. Finally, a brief literary description of the categories of the overall participation index completes the presentation of the classification scheme for the participation indicator.

I. Effectiveness of National Political Representation of the Major Cultural-ethnic and Socio-economic Groups in the Population

1. Countries charactérized by reasonably effective national political representation as indicated by the presence of political institutions and associations (such as political parties, voluntary interest groups or traditional associations carrying out political func-

TABLE I

DEFINITION OF INDICATOR OF POPULAR POLITICAL PARTICIPATION
IN TERMS OF ITS THREE COMPONENT ELEMENTS

Categories of Popular Political Participation (composite)	National Political Representation	Choice of Channel for Representation	Actual Participation
A	1	1	1
B	2	1	1
C	3	1	1
D	1	2	1
E	2	2	1
E—	2	3	1
F	3	2	1
F	4	1	1
F—	3	3	1
G	1 or 2	2	2
G—	1 or 2	3	2
H+	3 or 4	1	2
H	3 or 4	2	2
H—	3 or 4	3	2
I	4	3	2
J	5	1 or 2	2
J	5	3	1
J—	5	3	2

Note: See the pages following for an explanation of the symbols in this table.

tions, and local political institutions)* through which the major socio-economic and cultural-ethnic groups are represented and through which they influence to some significant extent national political decisions directly affecting their interests. Countries are excluded if socio-economic and/or cultural-ethnic groups probably comprising over 10 per cent of the population are excluded from the system of representation.*

2. Countries in which national political representation of the major cultural-ethnic and socio-economic groups in the population is defective in one but not both of the following respects:

(a) Political associations and institutions fail to represent some major socio-economic and/or cultural-ethnic group(s) of the population which, however, probably comprise between one-tenth and one-third of the population,† or

(b) most political associations and institutions which are potentially key channels for representation of major groups in the population fail in practice to influence significantly national political decisions directly affecting their members. This category also includes one-party systems which are used almost exclusively as channels for one-way communication from above.

3. Countries in which national political representation is defective in both of the respects listed in category 2. Excluded from this category, as from category 2, are countries in which the socio-economic or cultural-ethnic groups without national political representation probably comprise more than one-third of the population.

---

* For the purpose of this classification, traditional non-Western-type groupings or associations are considered as part of the system of national representation providing they operate at national level as direct (not necessarily formal) channels for influencing national political decisions.

† Exclusions from the national political process based upon literacy requirements for voting are considered a defect in representation for the purpose of this classification if they result in the exclusion of major identifiable socio-economic and/or cultural-ethnic groups to a degree described by the various categories of this scheme. Exclusions of foreigners count as a defect if the foreign residents are permanent immigrants to the country.

4. Countries in which major cultural-ethnic and/or socio-economic groups in the population probably comprising more than one-third, but not more than two-thirds, of the population are without formal national political representation. Also included in this category are countries in which a system of parliamentary representation was set up during the period but had not led by the end of the period to the development of political parties of formal political pressure groups.

5. Countries in which major cultural-ethnic and/or socio-economic groups in the population probably comprising over two-thirds of the population are without formal national political representation.

II. EXTENT OF CHOICE OF CHANNELS FOR NATIONAL POLITICAL REPRESENTATION (for GROUPS IN POPULATION HAVING SOME FORM OF REPRESENTATION)

1. Countries in which, for members of socio-economic and cultural-ethnic groups which have national political representation, there is significant choice of channels for political representation of their interests; specifically, significant choice exists both between different channels of a given type (such as national parties with organizational networks covering an important part of the country) and between different types of channels (such as political parties with organizational networks covering an important part of the country and labour unions). Included in this category are countries meeting its criteria in which one of two or more independent national political parties dominate the political scene.

2. Countries in which, for members of socio-economic and cultural-ethnic groups which have national political representation, there is little or no choice between different channels of a given type for political representation of their interests (such as political parties with organizational networks covering an important part of the country); there is, nevertheless, significant choice between different types of channels for political representation (such as political parties and labour unions and/or traditional tribal or other channels of representation which actively and directly influence national politics).

The countries meeting these criteria are of three different types:

(a) Countries with multi-party political systems in which there is little or no choice between political channels of any given type because each channel is accessible exclusively to individuals of a specific cultural-ethnic or socio-economic identification.

(b)* Countries with single-party (or multi-party) political systems in which there is little or no choice between political channels of any given type because all national channels are dominated by the ruling political party; excluded are countries in which, for all practical purposes, special interest groups are units of the dominant political party and thus do not provide alternative channels for representation.

(c) Countries with multi-party systems in which the party system as a whole is relatively unimportant compared with traditional channels for influencing national political decisions.

3. Countries in which, for individuals in the major socio-economic and cultural-ethnic groups in the population, there is little or no choice of channel for political representation of their interests.

Included in this category are

(a) Countries with either no representative political system or a negligible one. Also included in category 3a with a plus score are countries with choices between two or more political parties which were, however, poorly established or newly established and operated almost exclusively in urban centers involving less than 20 per cent of the population; other channels of representation (including traditional) negligible. Also included in category 3 (a) with a plus score are countries without formal political parties or alternative representative channels such as labour unions, but with nevertheless significant choice between individual candidates to a national parliament existing for at least half the period; other channels of representation negligible.

(b) Countries with a single party political system in which there are very few or no channels for political expression other than the various units of a single dominant na-

---

* Note on Category 2b: the kinds of choices available in a one-party system include choices between candidates in parliamentary elections; and the wider choices possible in elaborated systems of branch, district, regional, and national elections; as well as choices of subchannels for various interest groups (labor unions, unions of cooperatives, women's unions, youth leagues, agricultural federations).

tional political party. Also included in 3 (*b*) with a plus score are countries in which special interest groups are so thoroughly integrated into the national party that they are, for all practical purposes, units of the dominant party rather than alternative channels.

III. Extent of Actual Participation by the Adult Population in the National Political Process*

1. Countries in which it is probable that at least one-quarter of the adult population participates in some minimal way in political groups, associations, or institutions representing their interests at national level (by voluntary voting between genuine alternatives,† or membership, or other even marginal forms of participation).‡

2. Countries in which it is probable that less than one-quarter of the adult population participates in some minimal way in political groups, associations, or institutions representing their interests at national level (by voluntary voting between genuine alternatives, or membership, or other even marginal forms of participation).

Classification Scheme for Composite Index of National Political Participation

The following category definitions are brief literary equivalents of Table 1. More detailed specifications can be derived by the combined use of Table 1 and the detailed definitions of the three elements included in the present composite index summarized above in Table 1.

A. Countries in which national political representation of the major socio-economic and cultural-ethnic groups in the population is reasonably effective and in which there is significant choice for given individuals belonging to these groups between a variety of channels for national political representation.

Excluded from this category are countries in which it is probable that less than one-quarter of the adult population participate in some minimal way in the national political process.

B. Countries in which, first, national political representation is defective *either* because

(a) some major group of the population probably comprising not more than one-third of the population is without national political representation, *or*

(b) representative organs fail to influence significantly national political decisions.

Second, in countries in this category there is significant choice (for individuals belonging to groups having political representation) between a variety of channels for national political representation.

Excluded from this category are countries in which it is probable that less than one-quarter of the adult population participate in some minimal way in the national political process.

C. Countries in which national political representation is defective in *both* the respects listed for category B.

With respect to choice of channels for political representation and actual political participation, the criteria for the present category are the same as those for category B.

D. Countries in which national political representation is reasonably effective but in which there is little or no choice for individuals belonging to groups having political representation between political channels of any given type (although there is choice between different types of channels).

This category includes both single party systems and multi-party systems which have reasonably effective national political representation; the multi-party systems are those in which each party is accessible exclusively to individuals of a given socio-economic or cultural-ethnic identification.

---

* Political participation in tribal or other traditional organizations and groupings is only counted as actual national political participation for the purpose of this definition if these organizations and groupings actively and directly influence national political decisions.

† 'Genuine alternatives' in voting means that there are candidates from at least two national political parties under independent control operating on a country-wide basis.

‡ 'Marginal forms of participation' would include attendance at political rallies or informal public meetings or membership in unions or cultural-ethnic associations working to influence national political decisions.

Excluded from this category are countries in which it is probable that less than one-quarter of the adult population participate in some minimal way in the national political process.

E. Countries in which national political representation is defective *either* because some major group(s) in the population probably comprising not more than one-third of the population are without national political representation or because representative organs fail to influence significantly national political decisions.

With respect to choice of channels for political representation and actual political participation, the criteria for the present category are the same as those for category D.

F. Countries qualify for the present category by meeting *one* of the following two sets of criteria:

(1) National political representation is defective both because some major group(s) in the population probably comprising not more than one-third of the population are without national political representation and because representative organs fail to influence significantly national political decisions.

At the same time, there is little or no choice for individuals belonging to groups having political representation between political channels of any given type (although they do have choice between different types of channels)

or

(2) National political representation is substantially defective in that major socio-economic or cultural-ethnic groups in the population probably comprising more than one-third, but not more than two-thirds of the population, are without formal national political representation; however, for individuals in those groups with representation, there is significant choice between a variety of channels for national political representation.

Excluded from the present category are all countries in which it is probable that less than one-quarter of the adult population participate in some minimal way in the national political process.

G. Countries in which it is probable that less than one-quarter of the adult population participates in some minimal way in the national political process and in which national political representation is defective because of either of the two following reasons:

(*a*) major groups in the population probably comprising more than one-third, but not more than two-thirds, of the population are without formal national political representation *or*

(*b*) major groups in the population probably comprising less than one-third of the population are without formal national political representation and in addition representative organs fail to influence significantly national political decisions.

The final characteristic of countries in the present category is that for given individuals in those groups with representation, there is significant choice between a variety of channels for national political representation.

H. Countries meeting the same criteria as those given for category G with respect to actual political participation and national political representation.

With respect to the extent of choice of channels for political representation, the countries in the present category are characterized by little or no choice for given individuals belonging to groups having political representation between political channels of any given type (although they do have choice between different types of channel).

I. Countries meeting the same criteria as those given for categories G and H with respect to actual political participation and national political representation.

With respect to the extent of choice of channels for political representation, the countries in the present category are characterized by little or no choice either between political channels of any given type or between different types of political channel; specifically, they have single-party political systems in which there are very few or no channels for political expression other than the various units of the national political party.

J. Countries in which major groups in the population probably comprising over two-thirds of the population are without formal national political representation and in which it is also probable that less than one-quarter of the adult population participates in some minimal way in groups, associations or institutions representing their interests at national level.

Of the countries meeting these criteria, those countries having systems of national representation for groups probably comprising less than one-third of the population in which there is at least some limited choice of channels of representation are classified J; those countries with little or no choice of political channels are classified J—.

NOTES

1. See, for example, Campbell [*1921, Ch. 6*].

2. See Cohen and Nagel [*1934, Ch. 15*], for a useful summary of classic approaches to measurement.

3. For a discussion of various procedures for the measurement of psychological and psychophysical attributes, see Torgerson [*1958, Ch. 3*].

4. The basic reference for the following discussion is Pfanzagl [*1968, Ch. 1*]. See also Torgerson [*1958, Ch. 2*], and Stevens [*1960, pp. 141–9*].

5. This classification follows Pfanzagl [*1968*]. Stevens gives the more classic division of scale types into nominal, ordinal, interval, and ratio scales; the last two are treated here in the class of cardinal scales. Coombs [*1952*] introduced the concept of an ordered metric scale; he makes a finer breakdown between scale types using both the distinction between partially ordered and fully ordered sets of points and between partially ordered and fully ordered distances.

6. Banks and Textor [*1964*] provide a good deal of political typological data. Lazarsfeld and Barton [*1951*] cite examples of typological data in social psychology. In economics, nominal measurement is limited largely to the fairly widespread use of dummy variables.

7. The analysis of hierarchical interactions, for example, is a form of analysis of variance which utilizes nominal as well as ordinal independent variables.

8. All measurement theorists are not agreed that nominal scales constitute a form of 'measurement'. The question, while semantical, is much disputed because to call nominal scales 'measurement' confers on them a status which some would deny. In practice, the validity of using nominal scales is determined in the same manner as the validity of using any measurement scale, i.e. by the extent to which they serve effectively as means to a given end. In econometric work, for example, it is generally accepted that the use of dummy variables can yield meaningful information about the relationships among variables.

9. See Stevens [*1960*] for a discussion of the statistical operations applicable to measurements made with different types of scale.

10. Economic indices are cardinal only if viewed merely as the result of the mathematical operations involved in the formulae used for their definition. However, when they are viewed cardinally, it is difficult to ascribe meaning to them or to study the relationship between such indices and other variables.

11. See, for example, Kruskal [*1964, pp. 1–27*].

12. For a discussion of the implicit comparison and combination operations involved in measures formed by counting which justify treating them as cardinal measures, see Coleman [*1964, pp. 71–5*]. Ratios based on counts are not cardinal, but rather ordinal, when interpreted to represent the relative importance of the underlying property measured by the class of objects or events counted.

13. The generality of this statement can be seen by examining any typical issue of the *Review of Economics and Statistics* or *Econometrica*.

14. Fundamental measurement as understood by measurement theorists means that the original construction of a scale depends only on relationships between different amounts of the property measured. Practical procedures for measuring particular objects may, however, be based on an empirical law relating the property measured to another property, even though the scale of measurement for that property has been established fundamentally.

When economists speak of 'direct' measurement, they do not mean fundamental

134 MEASURING DEVELOPMENT

measurement. They usually mean that the primary data used in constructing some index has been obtained by direct survey, census, or questionnaire.

15. As Stevens [*1960*] points out, strictly speaking, fundamental scales could be set up without the possibility of physical combination.

16. An exception is the measurement of utility under risk by fundamental procedures. See Coleman [*1964*].

17. Cohen and Nagel [*1934, pp. 299–300*] describe the construction of a scale for density.

18. Pfanzagl [*1968, p. 320*] writes: 'We speak of measurement by fiat, if the assignment of numbers is defined by some operational prescription which is neither based on homo-morphic mapping of an empirical relational system into a numerical relational system (fundamental measurement) nor on the functional relationship to fundamental scales (derived measurement).'

Torgerson [*1958*] writes: '. . . *measurement by fiat* . . . ordinarily . . . depends on *presumed* relationships between observations and the concept of interest. Included in this category are the indices and indicants so often used in the social and behavioural sciences This sort of measurement is likely to occur whenever we have a prescientific or common-sense concept that on *a priori* grounds seems to be important but which we do not know how to measure directly . . .' [*p. 22*].

19. As indicated above, indices are cardinal only when viewed as sets of formulae; however, when so viewed, their meaning is undefined.

20. The terminology for discussing the links between concepts important in theorizing, 'empirical constructs' which specify rules of correspondence, and 'primary facts' is far from uniform. Richard Stone [*1951, p. 9*] uses the terms 'empirical construct' and 'primary facts'. Torgerson [*1958*] speaks of 'rules of correspondence' or 'operational definitions' which link together 'observable data' and 'theoretical constructs'. Coombs [*1964, pp. 4 ff.*] refers to 'recorded observations' and restricts the word 'data' to that which is analysed, that is, to the output from a scaling 'model'. Torgerson [*1958, Ch. 1*] was particularly helpful for the discussion in this section.

21. The phrase 'illegal statisticizing' is used by Stevens [*1960, p. 145*]:

'. . . In the strictest propriety, the ordinary statistics involving means and standard deviations ought not to be used with these scales, for these statistics imply a knowledge of something more than the relative rank-order of the data. On the other hand, for this 'illegal' statisticizing there can be invoked a kind of pragmatic sanction; in numerous instances it leads to fruitful results. . . .'

22. The divergences between commonly used quantitatives estimates for underdeveloped countries and the estimates eventually produced by field research are often very large. For example, U.N. field surveys have revealed crude fertility rates double those published and widely used prior to the surveys. We doubt that the qualitative rankings provided in the present study are subject to anything like such a margin of error.

23. Torgerson intends this statement to include economic indices which are *ad hoc* rather than based in explicit theory. It should be stressed again that, at best, theorizing provides rules for aggregation for economic indices; it rarely provides unambiguous links between operational definitions and the underlying concepts of interest.

24. Even where relatively explicit and acceptable theories exist as in the case of measurement of social mobility, we were obliged by reason of data deficiencies to select indices other than those which would be most desirable theoretically.

REFERENCES

Adelman, Irma, and Morris, Cynthia Taft, 1967, *Society, Politics and Economic Development: A Quantitative Approach*, Baltimore: Johns Hopkins University Press.

Adelman, Irma, and Morris, Cynthia Taft, forthcoming, *A Conceptualisation and Analysis of Political Participation in Underdeveloped Countries.*

Banks, Arthur, and Textor, Robert, 1964, *A Cross-Polity Survey*, Cambridge, Mass.: Massachusetts Institute of Technology Press.

Campbell, Norman, 1921, *What is Science?* London: Dover Publications.

Cohen, Morris R., and Nagel, Ernest, 1934, *An Introduction to Logic and Scientific Method*, New York: Harcourt Brace, London: Routledge.

Coleman, James S., 1964, *Introduction to Mathematical Sociology*, New York: Free Press of Glencoe.

Coombs, Clyde H., 1952, 'A Theory of Psychological Scaling', *Engineering Research Bulletin*, No. 34, Ann Arbor: University of Michigan Press.

Coombs, Clyde H., 1967, *A Theory of Data*, New York: Wiley.

Huntington, Samuel P., 1968, *Political Order in Changing Societies*, New Haven: Yale University Press.

Kaplan, Abraham, 1964, *The Conduct of Enquiry: Methodology for Behavioral Science*, San Francisco: Chandler.

Kruskal, J. B., 1964, 'Multidimensional Scaling by Optimizing Goodness of Fit to a Nonmetric Hypothesis', *Psychometrika*, Vol 29, March.

Lazarsfeld, Paul F., and Barton, Allen H., 1951, 'Qualitative Measurement in the Social Sciences: Classification, Typologies, and Indices' in David Lerner and Harold D. Lasswell (eds), *The Policy Sciences*, Stanford: Stanford University Press.

McClosky, H., 1968, 'Political Participation', *International Encyclopaedia of the Social Sciences*, Vol. 12.

Nagel, Ernest, 1960, 'Measurement' in Arthur Danto and Sidney Morgenbesser (eds.), *Philosophy of Science*, New York: Meridian.

Pfanzagl, J., 1968, *Theory of Measurement*, New York: Wiley.

Stevens, S., 1960, 'On the Theory of Scales of Measurement' in Arthur Danto and Sidney Morgenbesser (eds.), *Philosophy of Science*, New York: Meridian.

Stone, Richard, 1951, *The Role of Measurement in Economics*, London: Cambridge University Press.

Torgerson, Warren S., 1958, *Theory and Methods of Scaling*, New York: Wiley.

On the Relationship between Human Resources and Development: Theory, Methods and Data

By Johan Galtung*

SUMMARY

The article challenges simplistic one-way models of the relation between education (human resources) and economic development. Diachronic analysis clearly indicates different patterns or trajectories linking the two variables through time in individual nations, with significant thresholds or transition points. The relation between educational levels and economic development is seen as part of the international division of labour, depending on the degree of national autonomy, and on the relations between countries rather than the differences between them. Education may influence development through changes in the system of social stratification as well as through the expansion of knowledge. The diachronic approach is used to test these relations in a number of developing countries.

1. INTRODUCTION

One way of approaching the current discussion of the relationship between human resources (HR) and development (D) is to phrase it in terms of two models, Model I and Model II. Model I is the 'naïve' model, and Model II the 'sophisticated' model—but they are used here only as expository devices. Obviously, Model I, referred to as 'naïve', is implicitly rejected, and Model II, the 'sophisticated' one, is seen as superior to Model I—which is not the same as accepting it. It should also be emphasized that when Model I is rejected there is no assumption that any concrete research tradition is rejected since Model I is obviously too naïve in its formulation to reflect something with which any competent researchers in the field would be willing to identify.

These 'assumptions' are obviously interrelated, and some comments will clarify this.

Our formulation of the models is as shown in Table 1.

2. EDUCATION AS A CONVERSION MECHANISM

As to the *first* assumption we are contrasting a view according to which human resources are converted into development in a way that can approximately be studied by using methods of linear regression, with a view that takes no stand as to whether human resources are converted into

* The present article was originally written for a UNESCO Project on the relation between human resources and development, and I am grateful to Zygmunt Gostkowski and Serge Fanchette for encouragement to engage in this study as well as for the permission to have it printed. All conclusions drawn are the responsibility of the author, however. The article can be identified as PRIO—publication No. 27–4 from the International Peace Research Institute, Oslo.

Table 1

	Model I ('naïve')	Model II ('sophisticated')
1. Assumptions about HR-D relations	linear, and mainly one-way conversion from HR to D	also curvilinear, different types, and two-way conversion, also from D to HR
2. Assumptions about method of study	mainly *synchronic*	mainly *diachronic*
3. Assumptions about LDCs and MDCs	mainly a question of *difference* between them	also a question of *relation* between them
4. Assumptions about HR	any type of knowledge can be converted into development	only special types of knowledge are convertible
5. Assumptions about conversion process	essentially through instrumental knowledge, learning to operate	also through other methods, e.g. education as a new "stratifier" in society

development or vice versa, and does not assume a linear relationship. Of course, a linear relationship can be assumed as a basis for *prediction*, it does not necessarily involve any assumption about the linear *process*. But the value of a prediction that does not at the same time give substantial insight into the process can be questioned. One is led astray by assuming human resources to be independent variables, and also the assumption of a linear relationship will make one miss the insight that can be derived from the study of *transition points*, i.e. points where there is a change from predominance in growth of HR to predominance in growth of D (or vice versa). Thus, basic insight about Japan[1] is lost if the method of study disguises this phenomenon.

All this is of course very closely connected to the *second* assumption the choice of basic method of study. A *synchronic* method of study will not *force* the investigator to question assumptions about one-way conversion, nor assumptions about linearity although the latter will have more consciously to be imposed on the data. With a *diachronic* approach points in the scattergram are no longer scattered but are connected by trajectories, because they belong to the same national unit at different points in time. If the trajectory shows very clearly that development indicators were increasing much before human resources indicators, then it is difficult to maintain the assumption that human resources are the 'independent' variables. And correspondingly: if a scattergram showing the trajectories of various nations through time shows a variety of shapes, some of them possibly even linear, it is equally difficult to maintain the assumption of linearity as a general model and meaningful expression of anything except, possibly, as a basis for making predictions. But it also seems hard to maintain that this would be a good basis for prediction since it would not enable us to take into account what happens to a nation when it comes to a transition point.

Fundamental in connection with these first assumptions is the notion of *conversion*. According to this notion society is seen as a market where HR and D are both inputs and outputs. The basic question is whether one can be converted into the other, in other words whether society has mechanisms for these processes. But there is a difference between the two conversions that may look trivial but actually is full of implications.

When capital resources deriving from development are converted into education by building, physically and socially, educational institutions and producing educated human beings, there resources are somehow expended; whereas human resources that are brought to bear on development are not expended. On the contrary, they grow in the process. Once the process has started it should be a highly 'profitable' one, like a customer who gets more and more money back the more he buys of a commodity. This self-reinforcing nature of the HR→D process would, then, be a strong argument in favor of starting with human resources.

On the other hand, there is also reinforcement in the D→HR process if the proceeds from development are invested into the type of human resources that can be reconverted into more development. To what extent this is the case depends, of course, on the educational system model that the decision-makers in that nation have had in mind. Thus, an underdeveloped nation that suddenly gets rich, e.g. through the discovery and extraction of natural resources, may make the mistake of investing in the type of education that above all is compatible with a very low level of development. Case studies show that Venezuela[2] is a country that illustrates this type of process.

Just as the first two assumptions are tied together, so are the next three. One way of studying them would be by starting with the basic dilemma of whether the whole problem of development, and more particularly of the gap between MDCs and LDCs, should be seen in terms of *differences* or in terms of *relations* (the *third* assumption above). In the first case the assumption is that the world consists somehow of detached nations, essentially free to form their own strategy. Hence, if some of them rate low on some dimensions, then they can make up for that regardless of what happens to the rest of the system. Under the second perspective this is not the case. The world is seen as strongly coupled, and more particularly in such a way that some nations rate high on human relations and development indicators *precisely because* other nations rank low. The two presuppose each other, and it is only by studying them in conjunction that one can really grasp the phenomenon.[3]

Our own view is located somewhere in-between, in the sense that 'it all depends on where and when'. But since the second view is the more interesting one, particularly against the background of the flatlesss of studies that implicitly presuppose the first view, it should be explored further.

Basic in this connection is the idea of 'international division of labour'. The nature of this division of labour is well known: LDCs produce primary commodities and recive in return secondary and tertiary commodities, as illustrated in Figure 1.

The raw materials in the LDCs have a domestic basis expressed by the verbs 'to have' and 'to extract', where the upper classes (land owners, owners of mines, etc.) take care of the 'having' and the working classes (unskilled labour, often non-white) take care of the 'extraction'. In the MDCs the raw materials are then processed in a complex system of organizations based on division of labour, and some of it is re-exported, mainly to be consumed by the upper classes in the LDCs. This picture is, of course, oversimplified, but not unrealistically so, and the basic question to ask is what this '*division* of labour' (needless to say, a euphism) implies in terms of *differences* in human resources.

Figure 1. *Relation (not only differences) between LDCs and MDCs*

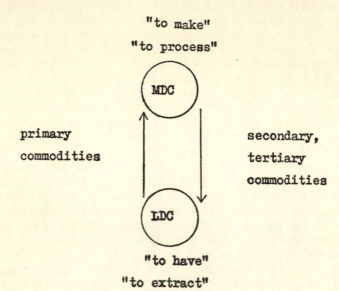

One type of reasoning is indicated in Table 2 below:

TABLE 2

HUMAN RESOURCES AS A FUNCTION OF 'INTERNATIONAL DIVISION OF LABOUR'

	LDCs	MDCs
Primary education	Low: unskilled labour sufficient	High: preparation of skilled labour
Secondary education	Low: mainly as preparation for tertiary education	High: preparation of white collar
Tertiary education	specialists on 'having': *lawyers*	specialists on 'making': *scientists, engineers*

The point is simply that when LDCs tend to have low rates of education at all three levels, it is to a large extent because they do not need more. With the international division of labour all that is needed for an average LDC is sufficient access to unskilled labour, perhaps equipped with enough primary education to understand security precautions, a level of secondary education sufficient to prepare for tertiary education, and a tertiary education with a high incidence of lawyers—specialists on defining property rights and resolving conflicts in that connection.[4]

MDCs need much more, in principle without any limit. The more the economy is geared towards processing, the more scientists and engineers are needed, and the more skilled blue collar and white collar will be needed in order to process and administer. The MDCs are the places where specialists on 'making', scientists and engineers, are put to work. Merely to train them and educate them for the LDCs (whether the training takes place in LDCs or MDCs) is meaningless unless something is done to the international division of labour so that their insights can be put to use. If not there will be a surplus of skills in demand of jobs, and when the jobs are not forthcoming because of the internationally induced production structure, 'brain drain' to countries with a surplus of jobs in demand of skills will be the highly predictable results.

Left behind will be the usual high reservoir of lawyers and others with a corresponding type of intellectual orientation, such as theologians. The point is, as stated before, that not all types of knowledge can be converted into development or are in any sense development producing. Some types of knowledge should rather be seen as specialization in underdevelopment than as specialization in development. And the maintenance of this may be in the interest both of the MDCs and of the upper classes in the LDCs and this is essentially the *fourth* assumption of Model II.

3. EDUCATION AS A MECHANISM OF STRATIFICATION

All that has been said so far disregards one important point expressed in the *fifth* assumption: the idea that education serves many other functions than that of imparting knowledge, and consequently *may* be instrumental in a development process through other intervening variables than higher knowledge levels. Some examples are the ideas of education as an instrument for the inculcation of national values, national consensus and higher levels of homogeneity in the population; education as an instrument for the inculcation of hygienic standards so as to improve the health level (as distinct from the knowledge level) of the human resources; and education as a way of liberating parents *from* daily care of children and, at least potentially, *for* productive work.

But there is still another function of education that seems to be more important. Education can serve as a *stratifier*, since educational institutions are stratified and individuals can be classified according to the highest institution they were able to graduate from. This has deep implications, one pointing towards stability, another pointing towards change.

The point of departure in what is today called a development process is usually a 'traditional' society which is highly vertical, and where position in society is ascribed at birth. 'Like father, like son' is the leading principle. This may be carried as far as to a perfect caste system where it even prescribes the precise occupation of the son, or only as far as to a closed class system where the ascription is to a wide class of occupations, roughly located in the same stratum.

But this social structure does not only allocate individuals at birth, but also prescribes the social relations between them. Essentially these are Herr/Knecht relationships, embedded in a structure that is feudal: a predominance of vertical interaction relations, *from* the top *to* the bottom, very little horizontal interaction at the bottom, and very little multilateral interaction. And the basic point about education as a stratifier is that it can induce exactly the same structure, a point that can be elaborated in some detail in connection with the Japanese social structure in the Tokugawa and Meiji eras.[5]

The correspondence is not perfect, but very high at many points. Thus, education can be said not to have altered the basic aspect of Japanese society: a feudal structure. Moreover, relations between the strata are not too far from isomorphic.

TABLE 3

Class by Birth and Class by Education in Japan	
Tokugawa	*Meiji, etc.*
shi (samurai)	Tōkyo, Kyōto universities
nō (agriculture)	other tertiary education
kō (crafts)	secondary education
shō (trade)	compulsory education

But there is, of course, one basic difference that points in the direction of change: allocation to a layer is not by birth. In Japan it is by 'social birth', by the entrance examination procedures that young Japanese undergo in their late teens and early twenties. By this process they are allocated, essentially for life. Needless to say, this permits redistribution of talent, and particularly the channelling of talent in the directions deemed desirable by 'society' (i.e. by the leadership of society). Japan can, in fact, be said to be a country that demonstrates the compatibility of an essentially feudal interaction structure with the liberal society principle of equality of educational opportunity. It is not biological birth, but social birth as defined by the educational process that matters, but that is the only liberal element. Allocation is postponed until the individuals can be more correctly classified according to ability—or rather, this is the ideology. This point will now be elaborated.

Rechannelling of talent is only one aspect of the change that may be induced by the introduction of comprehensive educational systems. It may even not be so important, and should perhaps rather be seen as an ideological rationalization of the second factor: that development-relevant knowledge gives and is given access to leading positions in society. Expressed differently: it may not be so important that people on top of society are so brilliant, or that brilliant people have relevant knowledge, but it does seem important that people with development-relevant knowledge also are in a position where that knowledge can be implemented. To paraphrase Marx: The leading knowledge (for development) must also be the knowledge of the leading class.

This does certainly not mean that all in the leading class have to be specialists in engineering, etc., but that at least top engineers are members of the top class, and able to communicate upwards, sidewards and downwards.

From this something very concrete follows about the education system. In fact, one prediction one could make would be that the stratification induced by education should not deviate too much from the pre-existing stratification in society. There are two aspects to this: the numerical proportion of those who have primary, secondary and tertiary education respectively should not differ too greatly from the proportions in the lower, middle and upper classes; the relations between the education groups should not differ too much from the relations between the traditional class groups, *and* (at least for a transition period) there should *not* be equality of opportunity. The children of the lower classes will get primary education, the children of the middle classes will get secondary education and the children of the upper classes will get tertiary education— by and large. How this is achieved in practice, i.e. how the class structure shapes the recruitment to the education structure is a well demonstrated subject in many societies.

To put it in still more concrete terms: even if a society could afford to do so, it would *not* launch an educational reform whereby secondary and tertiary education would be given to all. Rather, the hypothesis would be that secondary and tertiary education would expand till they exhaust their social bases. But primary education can be given to all, so it would seem possible, in principle, to launch an educational reform whereby everybody was given primary education, and that was it. This type of structure however, would run against the principle mentioned: the educational system would induce a social structure too egalitarian, too much at odds with the pre-existing social structure. Hence, higher levels are indispensable.[6]

However, even though this type of explanatory principle probably can be used to some extent, it is definitely better as an explanation of how traditional social structures are shaken than of how thay are preserved. In a society stratified by family background an educational system introduces a new element, a parallel stratification system. The three principles of correspondence mentioned above (numerical correspondence, relational correspondence and recruitment correspondence) can never be maintained with mathematical accuracy. There will be disequilibra in the system: there will be people who have higher or lower education than their social background and the three principles should lead one to believe. More particularly, it is well known that the upper classes often take their position for granted and fail to see that tertiary education is the new key to solidification of that position. Traditionally it is the middle classes who have seen education as a ladder to top positions, or some isolated minorities like the Jews. The demand for higher education may therefore simply be an expression of the demand for new ladders of social mobility, and may be one of the mechanisms whereby development is converted into more investment in human resources because the middle classes have at their command sufficient surplus to afford idling years away at educational establishments. What this leads to is certainly not the breakdown of stratification, but the gradual transfer from *family background* to *education achieved* as the pillar carrying the stratification system of the society.

4. HUMAN RESOURCES AND DEVELOPMENT: A GENERAL VIEW

Essentially, what we have now tried to express is that the contribution of education to the social structure may be even more basic than its contribution to the economic structure. One should not from that derive the conclusion that a society with a high level of educational stratification will also be a society high on economic growth. This would rather be seen as a historical incidence. In principle one could well imagine that compulsory education might have been introduced in societies with an extremely stable, traditional (or even primitive) economic basis. In such a society there could also be primary, secondary and tertiary education with very high enrolment rates, but what they would teach would be instrumental to the maintenance of that social order and that economic basis, not to the emergence of, for instance, a liberal social order with a capitalistic economic system.

This is not only a hypothetical speculation, but a reflection that leads to an important, and well-known distinction between less developed

K

countries with an educational system geared to the needs of a traditional social structure, and less developed countries with little or no formal educational structure at all. Among the former, however, the distinction should also be drawn between less developed countries that have been at the bottom of an international division of labour system and for that reason have brought forward a tertiary education with a high emphasis on the type of specialists needed in that system, e.g. lawyers, on the one hand, and on the other hand less developed countries that have been more autonomous in their traditionalism, and have had a tertiary education system (more or less formalized) cultivating persons who have become specialists in that country's culture. India is probably a blend of these two types, being both a raw material producing country within the British Empire and a country with vast pockets of cultural autonomy. Ancient Greece may be a more pure example of the latter.

If we now return to the first of these two distinctions a question that can very meaningfully be put is whether a 'modern', development-orientated educational system can more easily be introduced by changing and redirecting an already existing educational structure, or by building educational institutions from scratch. Or, stated in different terms: what is better, to have a relatively numerous elite trained for a lower position in the international production structure with lawyers, theologians, cultural specialists, etc.), or to have a very small elite trained for more autonomous development? This is the type of problem that research ideally should be able to tell one something about, but it seems that neither theory nor methodology nor data are sufficiently developed for this purpose. The development potential of a human resources investment may perhaps be proportionate to the product of one *qualitative* indicator (for example development relevance) and one *quantitative* indicator (e.g. enrolment ratio or frequency in the population), but this should remain a figure of speech rather than a premature effort to capture very complex phenomena in some type of simple mathematical formula. The important point is that quantity alone (in the form of enrolment ratio, etc) says virtually nothing: one must know whether the content is development-relevant.

Finally, some words about 'development' in this connection. If 'development' is interpreted in the usual sense, so as to mean economic growth as measured by rate of change in the G.N.P. *per capita* then all analyses, synchronic as well as diachronic, seem to point to the significance of investment in human resources. It is not obvious that this investment will precede economic growth, but if the model of educational development is not too traditional, economic growth can be invested in educational development and then be reinvested into economic growth, as mentioned above. This is partly done by bringing relevant knowledge to bear on problems of processing rather than extraction, and partly by reshuffling the allocation structure in society so as to bring new types of orientation to the top of the social order. The extent to which this can be done depends very much on the position of the nation in question in the international structure, and much of the experience we have so far seems to indicate that in order for a dramatic new departure in the field of education to take place nations have first, somehow, to detach themselves from a position as the providers of raw materials in vertical international regions or blocs. If this is not done a major effect of educational investment will probably have to be brain-drain. The development in Eastern Europe seems to testify to this, as does the development in some other countries like Cuba and the People's Republic of China— but the exact data basis for saying this is very meagre.

It should also be emphasized that we are not thereby implying that the detachment does not have to be within a socialistic formula, and accompanied by an internal socialist revolution. Japan is an example of the opposite where another economic system, admittedly not capitalist, but certainly not socialist either, has been built on an educational basis in a way that could hardly have been possible if Japan had not so jealously guarded her national autonomy and, by strength, by luck or by default of others, had been able to avoid an assignment to the bottom tier of an international stratification system (one simple reason being that Japan had virtually no raw materials to deliver).

If one should venture some general type of conclusion from these theoretical speculations then it might perhaps be that it seems more likely that autonomy can lead to educational investment and further on to economic growth than the opposite pattern, that educational investment will lead to economic growth and further on to autonomy. And the reason for saying so can be expressed in one sentence: brain-drain is not really a question of emigration from one country to another, but of *migration within a transnational system* with a clearly defined centre surrounded by a vast periphery, and with brains being drained to the centre which is the only place where they become relevant.

If, on the other hand, development is interpreted not in terms of *politics of growth*, but in terms of *politics of equality*, then the role of education changes. If a society should decide to try to create a structure where level of living as well as power over level of living are more equally distributed, then it is hard to see that a stratified education structure is possible. In stratified educational systems, production as well as the consumption of knowledge are very unevenly distributed. Almost only those who have completed tertiary education, and only a fraction of them, can hope to participate in the more advanced forms. If this participation should be distributed more evenly, then educational investment would also have to be distributed more evenly. Society would not proceed to higher levels of education unless all members could participate; a class of specialists would not be tolerated. The reason why we mention this is to put both theory and methods of the present exercise in a more proper perspective. Our theory is essentially about how educational specialization is related to economic growth. But the future may very well call for a theory about how educational equalization (as distinct from equality of educational opportunity) may lead to more general social equality. And that, in turn, will call for a quite different type of training than the academic specialities known today; perhaps more like what is currently being developed in the People's Republic of China.

5. METHODS OF ANALYSIS

One consequence of the theoretical views that have been expressed above is that it is relatively limited how far one can go in the study of the relationship between human resources and development relying on statistical data alone. On earlier occasions we have contrasted the synchronic methodology prevailing in the field with suggestions for a diachronic approach [*Galtung and Hoivik, 1967*] elaborated a methodology of diachronic analysis for this type of data [*Galtung, 1970*] and presented some results [*Galtung, 1969*]. Since those results apply to what today are developed countries, we shall in the third section of this paper give some data from what today are developing countries. But we do not necessarily accept the view that the general problem of the relationship between human resources and development cannot be studied advantageously by using really long-term data (as we had for the study mentioned above), for some different types of countries. All MDCs have once been LDCs, and since one is particularly concerned with how LDCs do become MDCs this approach seems in a sense better than a reliance on short-term data for the LDCs of today.

Let us tie this approach more closely together with the models discussed above. Thus, first of all it should be noticed that the predilection for diachronic approaches does not imply any all-out rejection of the synchronic approach. On the contrary, the synchronic approach has one advantage that no diachronic diagram can ever yield: it gives us a map of the concrete situation in the world *at a given point in time*. Thus, it can tell us something about how the international division of labour and educational structure are related to each other today. This refers to the third dimension for the two models on page 1, and although it does not prove anything it is suggestive because it does not only emphasize the well-known differences in educational level and in economic basis, but how tightly *correlated* these two differences are. It is this type of method that would lead one to a perspective of *relation* rather than simply *difference*, but although it is a necessary data basis it is certainly not a sufficient one. That type of data can only be obtained through more intensive studies of what actually happens, taking as a fundamental perspective that the unit of analysis in the world is no longer the country (with the underlying assumption that countries are autonomous), but a *set* of countries, a *dyad*, a *bloc*, with a vertical division of labour. It is only by studying the flows of goods (called trade) and the flows of man-power (migration, technical assistance, fellowships, brain-drain) that this can be explored.

Basic to this type of thinking is the concept of *autonomy*, the freedom to form one's own development strategy. This concept is hard to catch in statistical terms, but is, perhaps, to some extent operationalized through voting in the U.N. (the extent to which voting is independent of bloc formation), dispersion of trade partners and, possibly, also dispersion of export commodities (as opposed to mono-culture). Countries can rank high on these three indicators without necessarily haveing a high load of manufactured goods in their exports. That may come later, as the result of increased level of autonomy. In that process there may be concomitant change in education structure, both in terms of higher enrolment ratios and in terms of a teritary education with a much higher emphasis on development relevant specialization. But however this may be it will take us outside what statistics can reaily offer, and also beyond the limits of reasonably coherent theory. We would only like to emphasize that one possible method here might be the diachronic study of the relationship between MDCs and LDCs that are within the same bloc, e.g. of *dyads* consisting of the U.S.A. on the one hand and Latin American countries on the other, England on the one hand and members of the Commonwealth on the other, France on the one hand and members of the Communauté on the other, and possibly Japan on the one hand and certain South-east Asian nations on the other. By this method relations, not only differences, would be captured.

As to the methodology for dimensions nos. 4 and 5 (Table 1), it seems clear that we are here closer to theoretical perspectives that can be tested in terms of their consequences than to propositions that can be tested directly. Thus, it is well demonstrated that there is a relationship between development level and the proportion of lawyers, *and* that the relationship is a negative one. From this it does not follow that 'lawyers' in general have a negative effect on development. Rather, it emphasizes that there is something in *some* aspects of law (for instance static, Roman law?) that may correspond to a certain position in the international structure, as it has been expressed above. It is easy to imagine other types of law, where law is seen as an instrument of *social change* rather than as an instrument of the maintenance of *status quo*,[6] that might have brought opposite results. However, it looks as if the type of law that the world has most of, at least in the developing countries, serves 'having' rather than 'making'. But the elaboration of that type of thesis can only be in more qualitative studies, and on a case to case basis.

The same applies to the perspectives on precisely *how* education can be converted into development. These theories have to be accepted on the basis of their general plausibility and explanatory value rather than on the basis of hard data—or rejected because they seem implausible, or because other theories suggest themselves that are equally good or better in terms of explanatory value. But in principle it should be possible to carry out detailed studies of the correspondence between family background-induced and education-enduced stratification, particularly in order to see the strains that might follow from significant discrepancies in the numerical proportions when a society moves from the former to the latter.

6. DATA

In the analysis which follows, the diachronic approach is used to analyse the relations between economic growth and enrolment ratios in a number of developing countries. Since the B.D.A. (bivariate diachronic analysis) approach is based on an analysis of *shapes* of trajectories, it goes without saying that one needs at least three points, preferably four, in order to be able to classify the trajectory of a nation. This means that only those nations are included where data for at least three to 5 years points are available: 1965, 1960 and 1955. In some cases data for 1950 could also be included.[7]

On the *human resources* side enrolment ratios at the primary level were generally available; data on enrolment ratios at the secondary and the tertiary levels were available for a smaller number of countries.

On the *development* side G.N.P. *per capita* was available for many nations. However, energy consumption *per capita* was also available for many, and this raises the general problem of whether the two are mutually interchangeable. This problem could not be solved in general by plotting trajectories for G.N.P. *per capita* × energy *per capita*, since the problem is to what extent nations will be classified the same way as to trajectory regardless of whether one uses G.N.P. *per capita* or energy consumption *per capita* as the economic indicator. To look into this five countries were selected for which both economic indicators were available (Uruguay, Trinidad, Mexico, Honduras and Guyana) and both development indicators were compared diachronically with primary level enrolment. Although two of the trajectories might have been classified differently by the two indicators, the discrepancy was never fundamental, e.g. from concave to convex trajectories. Hence, although in general we made use of G.N.P. *per capita* we have on some occasions had to use energy consumption *per capita* as the development indicator (as the only one available), since there is at least a certain level of interchangeability.

The results in terms of diachronic curve shapes are given below.

FIGURE 2 AND TABLE 4. DIACHRONIC RELATIONSHIP BETWEEN PRIMARY EDUCATION AND DEVELOPMENT, 1950–65, 38 LDCs

	1	2	3	4	5	6
SOUTH AMERICA	Mexico Ecuador Costa Rica Colombia Brazil Cuba	Panama Chile	Honduras Puerto Rico Nicaragua Guatemala Dominican Republic El Salvador Argentina	Jamaica Venezuela Peru Guyana	Uraguay Haiti Bolivia	Trinidad Paraguay
	6	2	7	4	3	2
AFRICA	Ethiopia Sierra Leone Zambia Tunisia U.A.R.	Ghana	Sudan Uganda Nigeria Malagasy	Libya Tanzania Kenya		Malawi
	5	1	4	3	0	1

Altogether this gives the distribution for 24 South American countries and 14 African countries; a total of 38 developing countries (data on Asian countries were not available for this exercise). Some of the classifications may be disputed, but generally the intersubjectivity of this type of classification is quite good.

We have three comments to offer.

First, when we look at the general distribution on the curve shapes, one sees very clearly how unwarranted any linear assumption is. Even if a synchronic matrix should yield a linear clustering, it is doubtful whether that has any subtantive interpretation of interest at all. Out of 38 countries at most 14 (and actually ony 11, if one does not include the second curve type) can be said to have undergone a process in recent years that would correspond to this type of model. More particularly, a larger group of countries (18) exhibit curvilinear patterns of considerable theoretical interest, particularly since there are turning points involved (types 3 and 4).

Second, it is also seen how unwarranted the assumption about one-way conversion is. Although 11 countries have been classified as showing initial development on the human resources variable, and then on the economic growth variable, 7 countries show the opposite pattern. Of course, it may be objected to this that the curve shape depends on the phase of development in which the country finds itself, and that in the long run any twist and turn is a part of a more extended trajectory that may show a quite different pattern. This is true, but two such typical oil countries as Venezuela and Libya are nevertheless among the latter type of trajectories, and this should indicate that the classification is not in any sense random, but has a substantive basis.

In this connection one should not fail to notice that there was a need for two more patterns than have been envisaged in the general theory of the B.D.A. method: the last two patterns (types 5 and 6) that are parallel to either axis. There are countries that show no sign of change during this period in enrolment ratio, whether that enrolment ratio is very high or very low, and there are countries that show no sign of economic growth. Typically, of the six countries of these types in the present sample of countries five are found in Latin America: Paraguay, Uruguay, Haiti, Bolivia and Trinidad (the latter not 'Latin', though)—as good illustrations of what Latin Americans refer to as 'estancamiento'.

In this connection a third point can be made. If we compare the frequency distributions in the table accompanying Figure 2 they are actually remarkably similar except for the important point mentioned: there are no African countries in this sample that show the Latin American no-growth pattern. Whether the latter is because resources have not yet been exhausted or because the saturation point within an existing division of labour structure has not yet been reached, because of recent reshuffling of the structure (the 1960 independence wave, as opposed to the 1810–40 independence wave in Latin America) we shall not be able to say from this type of data. But the similarity is important: the curve shapes are encountered under very different conditions, showing that although *nations* show considerable variety, *regions* may be somewhat similar in their internal dissimilarity.

Is it possible to say more about nations classified in the same group; do they have other characteristics in common? We have tried to correlate the classification with the absolute level of the indicators of human resources and development, but with no significant result. It does not look as if a classification can be seen as a function of development level alone. It rather seems to depend on more peculiar circumstances, and for that reason the only approach that can give more insight would be more intensive case studies. Consequently this should only be seen as a preliminary exercise in the distribution of basic types, showing that the highest frequencies are accorded to curve shapes of type 1, 3 and 4 above. Cast studies should therefore be selected so as to illustrate different aspects of the relationship between human resources and development in nations with highly different trajectories, selecting one from each of the three most frequent types.[8]

Let us then turn from primary education to a consideration of secondary and tertiary education. As already indicated, we are now more constrained by the scarcity of data but can still assemble some material for the testing of a definite suspicion arising from the theory developed. More precisely, we have three hypotheses in mind:

(1). The curve shapes for the secondary and tertiary levels would be very different from the curve shapes of the primary level, for the same country;

(2). The curve shapes for the secondary and tertiary levels, for the same country, would be rather similar, and

(3). There would be a difference between South American and African countries in the sense that we would expect a more balanced relation between secondary and tertiary level of education and economic growth for African countries, i.e. more trajectories of types 1 and 2.

The reasons for these hypotheses or suspicions should be spelt out. The first and second are actually closely related. We assume that in most countries secondary and tertiary education are geared to each other, since the former is to a large extent a recruitment basis for the latter. But they are not geared to primary education which in all countries in the world, although to varying degrees where implementation is concerned, is subject to the goal of general, compulsory education. The latter goal can be implemented relative to economic growth according to patterns 1, 2, 3, 4 or 5—that all depends on how it interacts with economic growth, or how economic growth takes place regardless of what happens to primary education. As we have seen, all types are possible.

But secondary and tertiary education are not subject to programmes of a general and compulsory nature—except in some very few highly advanced countries, and even then only for secondary education. Demands for graduates from those institutions in order to promote economic growth would be important, and so would the demands, not necessarily explicitly stated, for an education structure that can maintain a stratified social structure. Secondary and tertiary education would have to go hand in hand, to a large extent, regardless of which of these two types of pressures explored in the theory section is stronger; this is the rationale behind the second hypothesis.

When it comes to the third hypothesis our thinking is along different lines. Very briefly formulated we would assume that for African countries secondary and tertiary education would be implemented more according to definite economic planning, with a view to economic growth; whereas for Latin American countries the second kind of pressure may be more important. If this is the case we would expect secondary and tertiary education to go more hand in hand with economic development in African countries, leading to curve shapes of types 1 and 2; and to be related to economic growth in a less balanced way in Latin American countries, leading to curve shapes 3 and 4. The reason for saying this is highly speculative, but let us nevertheless venture the hypothesis: we would feel that in many Latin American countries the potential for economic growth that can be derived from tertiary education (which in turn presupposes secondary education) is to some extent *exhausted within the existing international division of labour*, whereas this is not the case in Africa—at least not as yet. And one basis for this hypothesis, in turn, is the finding we have reported in an earlier study of the 'turbulent' pattern for certain types of academic specialization in, for instance, Argentina.[9]

Let us then turn to the test of these hypotheses. In order to make maximum use of the data, one nation was selected from each of the 11 groups in the preceding table, 6 for Latin America and 5 for Africa. The trajectories were drawn, and the results were as follows:

TABLE 5

DIACHRONIC RELATIONSHIP BETWEEN SECONDARY/TERTIARY EDUCATION AND DEVELOPMENT, 1950–65, 11 LDCs

Curve-shape Primary level	1	2	3	4	5	6
Country	Ecuador	Panama	Argentina	Peru	Bolivia	Paraguay
Curve-shape Secondary level	4	3	1	4	5	4
Curve-shape Tertiary level	4	3	3	4	5*	3
Country	Tunisia	Ghana	Sudan	Tanzania		Malawi
Curve-shape Secondary level	1	2	2	5*		4
Curve-shape Tertiary level	2	2	1	4		5

* With turbulent moves towards the end.

In a sense the results were above our expectations, and although they certainly need to be explored further with better data and for more countries, there is at least some indication that there is something to the type of reasoning.

First, there is certainly very little relationship between the primary level curve-shapes and the secondary and tertiary level curve-shapes, and this holds both for the six Latin American countries and for the five African countries. Secondly, apart from the case of Paraguay there is no *gross* discrepancy in the curve-shapes for the secondary and tertiary levels for any country. And thirdly, whereas only one case of a balanced curve-shape can be found for the Latin American countries, six out of ten curve-shapes are balanced for the African countries.

In a sense this only confirms what is intuitively already highly plausible: that secondary and tertiary level education enter into the general development pattern of a nation in a way which is very different from primary level education. The types are geared to different needs, they enter into the history of the nation in different phases, and they are interrelated in different ways from one nation to another but, possibly, with the patterns pointed to above.

Finally we explored the general notion that these different patterns are a question of *relation* rather than *differences* between MDCs and LDCs.

We know that there are considerable differences in the three educational enrolment levels between the two groups; that there are differences in the composition of tertiary level enrolments between the two groups; *and* that whereas MDCs can engage in nearly unimpeded growth in the number of development-relevant specialists, LDCs somehow seem to run their head against the wall (with a resulting brain-drain to the LDCs).

To look further into this we studied the *synchronic* relationship between the three educational levels on the one hand, and the percentage of the working population actively engaged in the non-primary sectors (in other words in the secondary and tertiary sectors). The latter is together with the trade composition index (the extent to which a nation conforms to the image given in Figure 1), one of the best measures of the position of the nation as a whole in the international division of labour. When some nations have less than 10 per cent of their active working population in the primary sector, *what this means is mainly that the primary sector work is being done for them in some other nations*. And the three diagrams leave no doubt as to which these nations are: the educational indicators on the one hand and the economic indicators on the other are very heavily correlated, with the poorest among the LDCs in the lower left hand corner and the richest among the MDCs in the upper right hand corner—as one would expect.

What is of interest in the present context, however, is that while the nations in the world as a whole are not separated neatly into two groups by this process, the nations in the same vertical bloc are quite neatly separated. U.S.A. is on that diagonal far above the Latin American countries, England is far above the Commonwealth members, and so on— but this does not mean that the top Latin American countries could not merge into the group of Southern European countries, and even pass them. What this indicates is only what we have already pointed to in earlier theoretical discussion: it is relatively meaningless to lump together all countries in the world in a scatter diagram, except for very preliminary, exploratory purposes. Countries should be grouped together that are related together in their general patterns of interaction and then be studied in the light of that pattern, at least at the dyadic level. But that would lead outside the scope of the present study.

NOTES

1. For an example, see 'Human Resources and Socio-Economic Development: the Case of Japan', by Johan Galtung, prepared for the UNESCO project.

2. See the case study by Kristin Tornes, 'Human Resources and Socio-Economic Development: the Case of Venezuela', also prepared for the UNESCO project.

3. For a general theoretical exploration of this issue, see J. Galtung, [*1971, pp. 81– 117, esp. pp. 86 ff.*].

4. See Galting, [*1969*].

5. For an exploration of this theme, see Galtung [*1970a*].

6. Thus, we feel there is a relation between the very early introduction of compulsory and general education at the primary level in Japan, with its great significance for Japanese development in general (see special essay on Japan) *and* the extremely elitist position accorded to the top Japanese universities. The Meiji leaders were very foresighted in introducing the Educational Act of 1872, but the Japanese social structure would also have been basically threatened if the system did not provide for some way of maintaining a distance within an educational system. The top two or three universities, and the general ranking system for universities, has served this need very well (see, for instance, O.E.C.D. [*1970*]).

7. The data referred to have been collected by the Princeton University group under the direction of Professor F. Harbison, and made available for the present analysis.

8. Thus, the case studies mentioned in notes 1 and 2 above are taken from types 3 and 4 respectively. In addition there is a case study, 'Human Resources and Socio-Economic Growth: the Case of Mexico', by Tord Høivik, representing type 1.

9. Thus, see Gallung [1969, pp. 39–48], for an elaboration of how tertiary specialization simply stops in Latin America—presumably because it is non-functional. Also, see Table 2 in the same document for a typology of intellectuals.

REFERENCES

Galtung, Johan, 1969, 'Diachronic Analysis of Relationships between Human Resources Components and the Rate of Economic Growth in Selected Countries', Paris: U.N.E.S.C.O., mimeo.

Galtung, Johan, 1970a, 'Social Structure, Education Structure and Life-Long Education: The Case of Japan', Paris: O.E.C.D., E.D. (70)2.

Galtung, Johan, 1970b, 'Diachronic Correlation, Process Analysis and Causal Analysis', *Quality and Quantity*.

Galtung, Johan, 1971, 'A Structural Theory of Imperialism', *Journal of Peace Research*.

Galtung, Johan, and Høivik, Tord, 1967, 'On the Definition and Theory of Development, with a View to the Application of Rank Order Indicators in the Elaboration of a Composite Index of Human Resources', Paris: UNESCO, mimeo.

O.E.C.D., 1970, *Examiners' Report on Japanese Education*, Paris: Organization for Economic Co-operation and Development.

Industrialization and National Development in the British Isles

By Michael Hechter*

SUMMARY

This article examines the relationship between industrialization and regional inequality in England, Wales, Scotland and Ireland, from 1851 to 1961. Data on several indicators of economic and social development have been collected by county units from published government statistics. Whereas industrialization is often thought to contribute to national development through the gradual effacement of regional inequality, no such pattern is evident in this case study. On the contrary, the structural position of the Celtic fringe did not improve as a consequence of long-term industrialization in Britain. The Celtic lands within the British Isles have instead undergone a type of dependent development similar to that described among societies of the Third World. The spatial diffusion of industrialization has been sharply constrained in the Celtic territories, resulting in economic and social dualism. Celtic counties have consistently had lower per capita *incomes than comparably industrialized counties within England. It is suggested that the historically persistent disadvantages of these regions may in part be due to the existence of racial stereotypes of Celtic culture which have been institutionalized within England.*

INTRODUCTION

Sociological theories have long stressed the signal importance of industrialization as the first cause, or *primum mobile*, in a linked chain of events leading to the eventual creation of the national state. To be sure there have been some disagreements about the precise causal connections between industrialization and national development. Some have tended to see the establishment of the large nation state as a reflection of the power of the first national ruling class, the bourgeoisie, in its ceaseless quest for political stability.[1] Others have stressed the integrative consequences of growing structural differentiation, while a third perspective emphasizes the diffusion of bureaucratic rationality as a unifying moral order in industrial societies. There is some excellent evidence to support the general contention of the linkage between industrialization and increasing state power: by and large only those states which have industrialized are characterized by effective central governments. England is, of course, the first such example.

Common to these approaches is the tendency to consider economic and social development as automatically snowballing processes which, once under way in a given territory, inevitably 'tear down all Chinese walls', in

* Assistant Professor of Sociology, University of Washington, Seattle. This study was partially supported by a grant from the National Science Foundation. The author would like to thank Immanuel Wallerstein for comments on an earlier draft.

Marx's phrase, and revolutionize the nature of political authority as well as the society's mode of production. Just as positive evidence of the correlation between development and national integration can be found in the consideration of Western European history, strong negative evidence is everywhere abundant in the societies of the Third World. It is generally acknowledged that the intense regional and ethnic conflicts so characteristic of these new states inhibit their prospects for social and economic development. At the same time it has been felt that, in the absence of industrialization, there is little hope of replacing the 'primordial sentiments' of ethnic, religious, or linguistic loyalty by attachments of national scope which are more conducive to the realization of political stability [Geertz, 1963].

The consequences of industrialization for national development presumably may be conceptualized on two levels. At the microscopic level, industrialization implies great disruption in individual life-styles. Rural–urban migration, the anomie of city life, and the required adjustment to new modes of production and types of working conditions all serve to loosen the individual's traditional political attachments. As a result the legitimacy of the central government is thought to be strengthened at the expense of local authorities. At the macroscopic level industrialization stimulates a wide range of transactions which are presumed to significantly narrow differences between regions within state territory. These lead not only to a more homogeneous national culture, but also, it has been argued, to a more equal distribution of regional income over the long run [Williamson, 1965].

It is quite evident that regional variations in income and rates of economic growth can become critical obstacles to the realization of political stability. To the extent that a regional population sees itself as relatively disadvantaged, political opposition to the central regime may become crystallized around the issue. Effective national integration can probably come about only when regional inequality decreases to some, as yet unspecified, tolerable level, and the benefits of economic growth are more equably shared throughout the society.

However, advanced industrial societies are themselves facing some of the same political cleavages thought to be characteristic of the new nations. The intensity of ethnic and regional cleavages in these societies suggests that problems of regional inequality may continue to have considerable political salience despite the existence of industrialization [Hechter, 1971a]. Movements for regional separation are typically based on the twin claims of economic and cultural discrimination against peripheral areas perceived as emanating from the central government. It has become evident that the relationship between industrialization and regional inequality is far more complex than had generally been supposed. While industrialization results in a substantial increase in inter-regional transactions, and hence widens the effective scope of national markets, this cannot always be assumed to result in greater welfare among peripheral regions. What has sometimes been overlooked is that even should industrial development proceed to an appreciable extent, geographical and cultural factors function to confine growth spatially to specific regions for long periods of time [Zipf, 1941; Hicks, 1959; Alonso, 1964]. Even in the most developed societies, regional growth differentials have tended to persist.

Such is the case in the British Isles. Despite centuries of inter-regional economic transactions a recent compilation of regional statistics of the United Kingdom ranks Wales and Scotland generally lowest among ten British regions (Northern Ireland is excepted from the data) on a host of indicators of economic and social development, relating to employment, housing, education, health, environment, and personal income [*Hammond, 1968*].

This article will attempt to estimate the extent to which industrialization has affected the structural position of the Celtic fringe relative to England from 1851 to 1961. This will be done by considering several different economic and social indicators of development which have been collected by county units from published government statistics. In general, the conclusion is that the disadvantaged position of the Celtic fringe relative to England has been unchanged during this period, despite rapid industrialization in parts of Wales and Scotland beginning around 1851. Industrialization did not, therefore, serve substantially to eliminate Celtic economic inequality. The *per capita* income of Celtic counties has been consistently lower than that of English counties. This regional income inequality persists even after the level of industrialization is eliminated as a source of variation between regions. Rather, the situation of the Celtic fringe in the British Isles is analogous in several respects to that of the less developed countries in the world system. Development occurred in a largely dependent mode [*Dos Santos, 1970*], and created dualistic structures within the Celtic periphery. As a consequence the spatial diffusion of industrialization in the Celtic lands was considerably restricted. Further, production in Wales, Scotland, and Ireland may be considered virtually monocultural, whereas England alone developed a diversified industrial economy. Finally, it is argued that the continuation of these systematic disadvantages may result from the institutionalization of policies which have the effect of discriminating against the Celtic periphery in a manner similar to that which has been described as institutionalized racism. The perception of cultural difference in the Celtic lands by significant English institutions may discourage prospects for development in these regions.

THE PROBLEM OF REGIONAL STRUCTURAL INEQUALITY

There are essentially two independent bases for the development of regional structural inequality. First there are economic causes, which are geographical in nature. Regions typically vary with respect to resource base, soil composition, climate, accessibility to navigable waters and other factors which potentially have a bearing on the production and distribution of goods. These factors give advantages to some regions as compared with others. 'Poles of growth' tend to occur in regions with geographical advantages relative to specific means of production [*Perroux, 1955*]. Once begun, growth may continue in a region even after the loss of one-time geographical advantage due to the benefits of other external economies, such as the availability of skilled labour, or the presence of a variety of goods and services which need not be imported, or to decisions of the central government concerning tariff and investment policies. Thus regional differences may not only persist, they may also increase with time [*Lasuén, 1962; Baer, 1964*].

Although regional geographic attributes do not undergo objective change in the course of social development, the degree to which a society makes use of its natural resources is a function of the mode of production. It is clear that in pre-industrial times, when agricultural production dominates the economy, that region which is richest in topsoil, mildest in climate, and smoothest in relief and of appropriate rainfall will be best suited for cultivation, and hence will be the most coveted. On the other hand, in an industrial society these attributes are relatively much less valued, as industries tend to be located near sources of minerals or energy, with good natural accessibility to markets. This shift in the valuation of land has important consequences for the regional distribution of wealth. A region largely unsuited for efficient arable cultivation in one century may find itself a favoured area in the next, with the advent of industrial production. The distribution of comparative geographical advantages may therefore be affected by gross changes in social organization and production. This shift in comparative advantage, in fact, occurred in both Wales and Scotland during the nineteenth century upon the discovery of extremely rich sources of high quality coal.

The second major source of regional structural variation is socio-cultural. In traditional societies there may be major differences in patterns of agricultural production, kinship systems, inheritance customs, and—generally speaking—modes of social organization which affect the level and type of production. Thus in similar geographical environments investigators have found radically different modes of social organization. Explanations of these variations usually rest on theories of group migration. One plausible account of the disparity of agricultural villages in East Anglia from those of the geographically similar Midlands relies on a hypothesis that Frisian migration led to a separate type of social organization in one corner of the British Isles [*Homans, 1957–58 and 1969*]. Therefore, in any investigation of regional inequality both geographical and cultural variables must be weighed as potential differentiating factors.

One initial structural inequality has evolved the transmission of growth from dynamic to stagnant regions becomes problematic. The process by which this is thought to occur has been the subject of some controversy. The crux of the debate concerns the role of *politics* in the regional redistribution of resources. Some writers [*Tachi, 1964; Williamson, 1965*] feel that regional equality will result through the action of economic forces alone. They hold that the diffusion of economic growth is impeded by the constraints of traditionalism in the stagnant regions, and will naturally follow the extention of efficient markets there. With the expansion of the national economy, and consequent heightening of the rate of inter-regional transactions, disparities in the rates of regional development should decrease.[2]

The alternative argument is pessimistic with regard to the consequences of increasing economic penetration of the periphery. These areas are seen to be already suffused with extensive market connections to the dynamic region. In this view the structural inequality of the stagnant regions will tend to be exacerbated by the play of market forces in the absence of intervention by the central government [*Myrdal, 1957, pp. 23–38; Hirschman, 1958, p. 187*]. Hence, since increased economic efficiency between regions can only serve to impoverish the stagnant regions, some form of political action is required to bring about regional parity.

When the periphery is not only economically disadvantaged but culturally distinct as well, the likelihood of the evolution of regional equality is even more remote. This is characteristic of a situation which has been described as 'internal colonialism' [*González-Casanova, 1965*]. In these circumstances the dynamic region exercises monopolistic control over production in the peripheral areas. It practices discrimination against the ethnically distinct peoples who have been forced on to less accessible, inferior lands. Such ethnic discrimination need not be directed against individuals. For example, no one would argue that there is much discrimination against Welshmen *as individuals* in the United Kingdom today. Nevertheless, the fact that Wales *as a region* is disadvantaged in terms of income, employment, housing, and education has decisive consequences for the individuals living there. To the extent that the region is deprived, the average Welshman competes with the average Englishman at a disadvantage in any free market situation. When such long-term differences in aggregate rates of development are the result of ethnic stereotypes, we may speak of the phenomenon of institutional racism [*Carmichael and Hamilton, 1967, pp. 4–5*]. It is the contention of this article that such processes may be involved in the persistent pattern of economic disadvantages which can be demonstrated in the Celtic lands during the past century.

REGIONAL STRUCTURAL INEQUALITY IN THE BRITISH ISLES: THE NINETEENTH AND TWENTIETH CENTURIES

In pre-industrial Britain some regional structural inequality already existed though there is little quantitative evidence of its extent. Wide geographic variations in the British Isles have led to the classic distinction between Lowland and Highland zones, set apart by a natural boundary, the Highland Line.[3] Generally speaking, the Highlands are characterized by a series of comparative disadvantages for agricultural production. The terrain is difficult to plough and drain, the soil chalky, the climate stern, the rainfall too heavy for good cultivation. A quick glance at a map indicates that the Celtic-speaking regions are disproportionately clustered in the Highland zone. It may be reasonable to regard these Celts as a conquered indigenous people pushed into these territories by subsequent, more powerful invaders.

The social organization of the Welsh and Scottish Highlands and Ireland was substantially different from that of the rest of Britain. Whereas impartible inheritance, primogeniture, was the rule throughout most of the Lowland areas, partible inheritance, *gavelkind*, was an integral part of the Celtic social structure. Partible inheritance had two general consequences for agricultural production. There was a marked tendency for large plots of land to be subdivided into small portions in the course of a very few generations. H. L. Gray [*1915, p. 191*] mentions the example of a 205-acre Irish farm which after the course of only two generations became subdivided into 29 holdings and 422 different lots. The average arable quantity was four acres, while the single largest arable plot owned by any one man was only eight acres. Secondly, instead of the English pattern of two or three large, commonly worked open fields, the Celtic system led to individual small plots held in widely varying locations, considerably hindering the prospects for efficient cultivation as well as agricultural improvement. This situation often led to early enclosure, with the consequent polarization of the stratification system and proletarianization of the peasantry [*Thirsk,*

L

1967]. All these factors had undoubtedly resulted in differences in regional standards of living before the nineteenth century.

However, even in pre-industrial times, it is impossible to argue that the relative poverty of the Celtic regions was largely due to their isolation from material or ideational transactions with England. Britain was one of the earliest states to achieve a national economy. In large part the foundation of this national economy had been laid very early. England virtually led Europe in eliminating internal barriers to trade such as the random tolls which strangled continental commodity movements during the Middle Ages. By the fourteenth century the state had imposed a uniform toll system on both roads and rivers, and as a general consequence transport costs were much less than elsewhere in Europe, save perhaps Sweden. During the period 1275–1350 a national customs system was evolved under the guidance of the state, without ever being abandoned afterwards [*Heckscher, 1962, Vol. I, pp. 52*].

Customs barriers between England and Wales were removed following the annexation of Wales in 1543. The customs barriers between England and Scotland disappeared totally after the Union of 1707, and complete freedom in trade, communication and shipping was established thereafter. Commercial contacts between England and Ireland had existed since the fourteenth century through the legal status of Ireland *vis-à-vis* England went through several changes until 1801, when free trade was established throughout the British Isles.

Adam Smith, who was otherwise a scathing critic of English mercantilism and the general inefficiency of the economy, was very well placed as Customs Commissioner for Scotland to observe the exceptional extent of British internal trade:

> The inland trade is almost perfectly free, the greater part of goods may be carried from one end of the kingdom to the other, without requiring any permit or let-pass, without being subject to question, visit, or examination from the revenue officers. There are a few exceptions, but they are such as can give no interruptions to any important branch of inland commerce of the country. Goods carried coastwise, indeed, require certificates or coast cockets. If you except coals, however, the rest are almost duty-free. This freedom of interior commerce, the effect of the uniformity of the system of taxation, is perhaps one of the principal causes of the prosperity of Great Britain; every great country being necessarily the best and most extensive market for the greater part of the production of its own industry [*Smith, 1950, Part II, Art. IV, pp. 432*].

England was far ahead of her Continental rivals in the realization of central control over local privileges in many other spheres of the economy as well. From the fourteenth century onwards a host of ordinances attempted to establish national, and hence, regionally uniform standards of weights and measures. A unified system of coinage was achieved under Henry II in the second half of the twelfth century. The effectiveness of the English central authority by the Elizabethan period can be estimated by the extent to which municipal privilege, an intractable vestige of feudal decentralization on the Continent, was effectively eroded in favour of national policies regulating both urban and rural areas.[4]

The creation of the Justices of the Peace represented further royal attempts to intrude upon regional privileges and ensure national compliance to the law. Though there is doubt as to the effectiveness of the J.P.s in carrying out their prescribed functions, their existence is ample testimony to the desire of the central government to extend its power and authority throughout English territory.

Furthermore, the increasing size of English cities, particularly London, was instrumental in creating a national market for foodstuffs as early as 1600; and production in Wales began to be influenced by this growing demand [*Fisher, 1954, pp. 139–40*]. Wool was also produced in North Wales for sale in the London market [*Mendenhall, 1958*]. By the eighteenth century, much of the agricultural production of Ireland and Scotland was similarly bound for England.

In the nineteenth century, inter-regional transactions between the Celtic regions and England were substantially increased [*Hechter, 1971b*]. The construction of canals and railroads facilitated the expansion of inland trade by significantly lowering transport costs. Inter-regional economic integration proceeded apace with the growing industrialization of the British Isles. However, this increase in transactions between the Celtic lands and England was not merely confined to commerce. Shifts in the rates of inter-regional migration also support the thesis of an increase in the level of more socially diffuse interaction. The decision to migrate from a backward region to an advanced but culturally alien one is assumed to be difficult even given changes in objective environmental factors. Despite the inertial pressure of traditional constraints, movements of population between the regions varied throughout the nineteenth century. Massive Irish emigration to Britain after the Great Famine impoverished the British working class and caused it to be divided sharply along ethnic lines. The point is not so much that there was a steady secular rise in the rate of inter-regional migration, but rather that there were fluctuations which demonstate the increasing permeability of regional barriers. Similarly, the rates of letters mailed, on a *per capita* basis, increased at about the same degree in Celtic regions as the over-all English rate.

These few examples, which could no doubt be multiplied many times over, serve to illustrate (1) that the Celtic regions were to a considerable extent already tied to the English economy before the Industrial Revolution, and (2) that the advent of the industrial production led to a dramatic heightening of the intensity and quality of the interconnections between British regions. Hence, the proliferation of regional structural inequality following industrialization can in no way be accounted for by reference to the isolation of the Celtic fringe from rapidly developing England. Whatever is responsible for the development of further structural inequality, it is evident that the Celtic regions must, by the mid-nineteenth century, be considered an integral part of the unified economic system of the British Isles of which England was such a conspicuous participant.

THE SPATIAL DIFFUSION OF INDUSTRIALIZATION, 1851–1961

Although Britain was the first society to experience industrialization, and remains to this day among the most highly industrialized and urbanized of all societies, certain parts of the British Isles amost totally escaped industrialization, while others have been only partially transformed by industrial production. In some ways the United Kingdom is unique in that the great majority of necessary agricultural goods required to sustain her relatively dense population has for the past century come from overseas. If Britain, and more specifically England, were the workshop of the world in the nineteenth century, other lands, mostly in the Empire, served as sources not only of primary products for manufacture, but as providers of bread, meat, and dairy products for teeming British cities.

The story of rapid economic take-off of the north-western counties around the textile industry—and the subsequent redistribution of wealth, and, to a lesser extent, political influence from London and the south-east to the provinces—has been told previously, and at great elaboration.[5] Comparatively little attention has been paid to the actual spatial diffusion of industry through the nineteenth and twentieth centuries. In part this neglect is due to the perception that Britain was an industrial society if there ever was one, and that to analyse those peripheral areas where industrialization had not taken root was to exhibit a preference to study the failing past rather than the auspicious future. Autopsies have a much grimmer aspect than obstetrical deliveries. And for many comparative sociological interests the question of the extent to which the British Isles are industrialized seems very low on any imaginable scale of empirical priorities.

But for the purposes of the study of national development the question is a vital one. Friedlander has recently presented a method of distinguishing between industrial and largely rural counties in England and Wales over the period 1851 to 1951.[6] Adopting the logic of his method, we have classified British and Irish counties as *industrial* if their percentage of employed adult males in non-agricultural occupations was equal to or exceeded 85 per cent for the years 1851–81; 87·5 per cent for the years 1891–1921; and 90 per cent from 1931–61. Figure 1 presents the spatial distributions of industrial counties in Britain and Ireland in 1861 and 1961. If we conceive of this map as representing merely an undifferentiated geographical surface arbitrarily divided into counties, then the spatial distribution of the heavily industrialized areas in 1861 appears reasonable. The few industrial counties seem almost randomly distributed on this surface, with the single exception of Ireland, where no heavily industrialized location can be seen. By and large these industrial counties are either rich in coal resources (Glamorgan, Durham), loci of the textile industry (Lancaster, Lanark, Renfrew), or large commerical centres (London; and Midlothian, which includes Edinburgh).

The situation in 1961 is strikingly different. A great proportion of the geographical area of England has become heavily industrialized, whereas gains in the Celtic lands are conspicuously modest. It appears as if the diffusion of industrial concentration was affected, in some way, by the old national boundaries of Wales, Scotland, and Ireland.

We can rather quickly scan the changes in regional structural inequality by considering the changes in county means for ten indicators of economic and social development in England, Wales, Scotland, Ireland, and Northern Ireland, taken at decennial periods from 1851 to 1961. *Non-agricultural occupations* (Table 1) is perhaps the best general indicator of development over time since it does not differentiate between secondary employment, which was the major component of the industrial sector until World War I in Britain, and tertiary employment, which has since increased dramatically. The mean level of non-agricultural occupations is over 50 per cent and virtually identical for England, Wales, and Scotland in 1851, whereas the

THE SPATIAL DIFFUSION OF INDUSTRIALIZATION, 1861-1961

FIGURE I

Southern Irish mean hovers at about 25 per cent, far beneath the rest of the British Isles. Thereafter England develops at a faster rate than all the other regions save Northern Ireland. By 1961 the Welsh mean is only 79 per cent, the Northern Irish 76 per cent, and the Scottish but 57 per cent of England's. Southern Ireland remains untouched by British industrialization, forcefully implying that the diffusion of industrialization throughout state territory is far from an automatic process.

TABLE 1

MEAN COUNTY PROPORTION OF EMPLOYED MALES ENGAGED IN
NON-AGRICULTURAL OCCUPATIONS

	England	Wales	Scotland	N. Ireland	Ireland[a]
1851	58	57	55	33	22
1861	59	55	49	33	24
1871	66	62	51	33	26
1881	68	61	57	38	30
1891	75	64	53	36	28
1901	76	67	65	39	31
1911	76	67	65	39	31
1921	74	64	64	43	26
1931	78	62	55	42	25
1951	85	67	57	60	32
1961[b]	(85)	(67)	(57)	65	39

Source: *Censuses of England and Wales, Scotland, Ireland and Northern Ireland.*

a In this and all following tables 'Ireland' refers only to the 26 Southern Irish counties.

b The 1961 *Census of England and Wales and Scotland* did not publish occupation data by administrative county.

Turning to the secondary sector and the development of *manufacturing occupations*, a somewhat similar pattern emerges.[7] The early figures in the series show England, Wales, and Scotland at near parity, while both Irish regions are considerably lower. Thereafter, until about 1931, the first three regions have similar means. In the next 30 years the decline in manufacturing occupations is much greater in Wales and Scotland than England. *Commercial and professional occupations*, in essence comprising the service sector of the economy, are similarly differentiated by region, though in an opposite pattern in the time series. The English advantage is greatest in the earlier periods, and becomes somewhat diminished by 1961.

Regional structural inequality is most evident when we consider the mean *urban population*, defined as that proportion of a county's population dwelling in cities of 20,000 or over, in British regions. Even by 1961 the average Celtic counties fall between only 20 and 33 per cent of the English statistic. If these peripheral regions were less urbanized, they were also somewhat more prone to *unemployment*, with greater inequality especially noticeable after 1921, *illiteracy* (Scotland is a notable and interesting exception),[8] and *infant mortality* than England. *Decennial population growth* was highest for England throughout most of the period. Southern Ireland lost population at each observation; Northern Ireland in all but the last three decades; while Scottish demographic growth was relatively low, suggesting the continual emigration characterizing these areas in the nineteenth and twentieth centuries.

Finally, if we seek to understand something about the relative standard of living two indicators also give evidence of regional inequality. The crude *marriage rate*, a variable empirically related to industrialization in these data as well as a kind of barometer of economic optimism, is consistently highest in England, though only slightly so by 1961. A measure of *per capita* income constructed from county tax returns (see Appendix) shows hardly any decrease in Welsh and Scottish inequality relative to England over the continuum, while both Irelands made substantial gains, from near starvation and subsistence to something more, perhaps genteel poverty.

On the basis of these data, coupled with the more extensive indicators collected by Hammond, it is indisputable that substantial regional structural inequality exists today in the British Isles, despite almost two centuries of industrialization. It is slightly more difficult to estimate whether, *on the whole*, structural inequality has been aggravated or diminished because each measure behaves somewhat differently. I have argued elsewhere that whereas there was in general a tendency towards regional convergence along dimensions similar to those Karl Deutsch has identified as 'social mobilization' variables—perhaps literacy is an outstanding example—the indicators of regional economic development show, at best, slight convergence [*Hechter, 1971b*]. Further, the growth of the Celtic lands' dependence on extra-regional markets had certain unfortunate consequences in the twentieth century.

CONSEQUENCES OF INDUSTRIALIZATION—THE ENCLAVE AND THE HINTERLAND

While the average county data indicating regional structural inequality gives little evidence of a Celtic convergence with England along the several dimensions of development selected, nonetheless the impression which can be gained is that, at the very worst, the Celtic regions were developing at more or less the same *rate* as England. And since the rate of English development, particularly in the period 1851 to 1911, was unequalled in all the world, it might be argued that the Celtic regions gained much by their association with the premier industrial power of the nineteenth century. In terms of these objective structural variables much can be said for this position. However, if we look at the statistical *dispersions* from the mean rates of development of the Celtic nations and England, it becomes very evident that industrialization had somewhat different social consequences in the periphery than the metropolis. While industrialization became diffused through English territory, in Wales, Scotland, and Northern Ireland development was confined to a highly limited and relatively unchanging number of counties. Hence those shaded areas in Wales, Scotland, and Northern Ireland shown in 1961 might be visualized as small enclaves of industrialization in regions pervaded by hinterlands. Industrialization in the Celtic regions basically created these small urbanized enclaves which were oriented to English and international markets and featured cosmopolitan life-styles. With the passing of time the social gap between enclave and hinterland grew steadily wider. To the extent that the Irish economy maintained its traditional role as a source of agricultural produce for England—such that its regional monocultural specialization was agricultural rather than industrial or extractive—no industrial enclave emerged there. This relative social and economic homogeneity had decisive consequences for the development of a politically cohesive nationalist movement.

One way of looking at the development of enclave-hinterland differences on a regionally comparative basis is through the use of a coefficient of variation with regions, V_w.[9] It is perhaps most instructive to begin with *non-agricultural occupations*, as an over-all indicator of industrial development (Table 2). In 1851 the levels of V_w for England, Wales and—to a lesser extent—Scotland are all comparable. English regional heterogeneity

TABLE 2

COEFFICIENTS OF VARIATION (V_w) FOR
NON-AGRICULTURAL OCCUPATIONS

	England	Wales	Scotland	N. Ireland	Ireland
1851	0·26	0·26	0·36	0·39	0·61
1861	0·27	0·28	0·46	0·36	0·52
1871	0·23	0·22	0·49	0·38	0·53
1881	0·23	0·27	0·43	0·40	0·49
1891	0·22	0·35	0·43	0·46	0·50
1901	0·21	0·29	0·61	0·53	0·58
1911	0·20	0·27	0·34	0·51	0·52
1921	0·26	0·33	0·35	0·51	0·61
1931	0·18	0·39	0·53	0·40	0·65
1951	0·12	0·38	0·53	0·30	0·50
1961	—	—	—	0·30	0·46

Source: As in Table 1.

continues at a constant degree until about 1931, when V_w drops beneath 0·20. Welsh heterogeneity fluctuates somewhat above the English level until the same year, when it doubles the English V_w. Scotland's industrial diffusion is more spatially skewed, and in 1931 reaches triple the English level of heterogeneity. By 1951 Welsh and Scottish regional heterogeneity increases substantially relative to England. If we examine the absolute, rather than relative statistics, English heterogeneity decreases from 0·26 to 0·12 in the 100 years from 1851 to 1951, while the Welsh and Scottish levels increase significantly—the former, from 0·26 to 0·38; the latter from 0·36 to 0·53. The absolute rate for Northern Ireland looks somewhat curvilinear, while the relatively high levels of V_w attained by Ireland are a function of the over-all extremely low mean of non-agricultural occupations.

Similar absolute increases in regional heterogeneity in the Celtic regions may be found along dimensions of *manufacturing occupations*, *commercial and professional occupations*, and the *infant mortality rate*. In each of these examples the trend in England was towards homogeneity, while the reverse was true for all Celtic regions. Increasing trends towards regional homo-geneity can be found in considering levels of *employment*, *urbanization*, *illiteracy*, *demographic growth*, and *per capita income*. Jeffrey Williamson's hypothesis of the curvilinear path of regional economic inequality over time is incidentally supported in these data.[10] However, this pattern by no means holds *within* all the various regions of the British Isles. England actually has a higher V_w in 1961 than in 1851—in other words there is more variation in county incomes with increasing time—though the relationship over time approaches Williamson's expected curvilinear pattern. Wales and Scotland, on the other hand, simultaneously experience a steady decline in county income variation.

Table 3 shows the extent of enclave-hinterland differences in all five regions of the British Isles for non-agricultural occupations. It was con-structed by subtracting the mean proportion of non-agricultural occupa-tions in non-industrial counties from the industrial (according to the previous definition) county mean. Whereas the extent of enclave–hinterland difference between England, Wales, and Scotland is small in 1851, by 1961 it has stretched out considerably. Similarly, whereas the English statistic falls over the period from 35 to 16, it rises in Wales and Scotland with

TABLE 3

	England	Wales	Scotland	N. Ireland	Ireland
	ENCLAVE-HINTERLAND DIFFERENCES: IN NON-AGRICULTURAL OCCUPATIONS[a]				
1851	35	(28)	36	(52)	(63)
1861	35	33	43	(52)	(61)
1871	29	30	45	(52)	(59)
1881	28	33	44	(48)	57
1891	25	37	43	(49)	(57)
1901	24	35	55	(51)	(59)
1911	24	33	39	(48)	60
1921	27	37	38	(47)	64
1931	21	39	47	(48)	(65)
1951	16	34	50	(30)	62
1961[b]	[16]	[34]	[50]	33	59

[a] In years when there were no industrial counties in a region, the non-industrial mean is subtracted from the minimum level of non-agricultural occupations necessary to define the county as industrial. The result appears in parentheses.

[b] [ ] indicates estimates from 1951 data.

time. The gaps in the Irish statistics occur because there is *no* industrial county, or enclave, in certain years. Table 3 thus demonstrates that the higher V_ws for Wales and Scotland do not merely represent random county variation, but are systematically related to levels of industrialization. In other words a relatively high V_w indicates the necessity of investigating sub-regional phenomena.

Thus, in general structural terms, we can see that the course of development had somewhat different consequences for England than for the Celtic periphery. The aggravated internal differences arising from British industrialization in Wales and Scotland are reminiscent of the discussions of dualistic or pluralistic economies in the literature of contemporary Third World societies, a function of their colonial mode of development.[11] Metropolitan investment in these areas led in the main to monocultural export economies. The primary products are obtained in hinterland areas, then passed on to coastal ports for shipment to metropolitan markets or manufacturers. The enclaves in colonial areas are urbanized, Western-oriented cosmopolitan centres which become highly differentiated from their respective hinterlands, such that they may be considered appendages to the metropolitan economy and—to a lesser extent—culture. The existence of enclave–hinterland conflict in Third World societies is an important structural obstacle to the development of a fully national solidarity.

Certain structural parallels may be made between the experience of the typical Third World colony or neo-colony and that of Celtic periphery in the British Isles. Since the colony develops as an appendage to the metropolitan economy, and in this sense is used instrumentally by the metropolis, it most frequently serves as a source for primary or extractive products for metropolitan industrial manufacture and distribution. In contrast to the highly specialized nature of Celtic economic structure, the English industrial economy was diversified—built on textiles, general manufacturing, steel, coal, and commercial and financial services—and hence, the economy as a whole was much less vulnerable to the vicissitudes of the free market.

England also had the advantage of producing mass commodities for the large domestic market, an option not so readily available to Wales which would have had to compete with Durham and Northumberland in the internal market for coal, and Scotland which all too quickly saturated the domestic market for ships and locomotives, its most important exports.

In the interest of economic efficiency, and in response to metropolitan demand, there is frequent resort to economies of large scale, effectively reducing the *variety* of colonial exports, while substantially increasing their *quantity*, and hence value. The plantation, utilizing vast resourses of land and labour, is a modal type of productive system for a monocultural economy; and evidences of it may be found in colonies and ex-colonies throughout the world. In this regard it is significant that the first English plantations were not in the American colonies, but in Ireland. Since colonial development occurs as a result of territorially exogenous forces, initiated by conquest, it tends to be dissimilar to that type of development which emerges endogenously in a society, free from external political manipulation or control.

The basic distinction is this: there tends to arise a 'national' division of labour, such that the majority of manufacturing, processing, and distributing functions in that economic unit formed by the union of the colony and the metropolis are performed in the latter nation, whereas the former is in the subordinate position of supplying materials and cheap labour. The issue is not just that the metropolis 'owns the means of production' for the colony, though in a general sense this has occurred. Nor is is that the international prices for primary products might be declining relative to those of manufactures.

The structural consequences of colonial development are different from those implied in a system with a national economy:

> The country and the people were laid bare and defenseless to the play of the market forces as redirected only by the interests of the foreign metropolitan power. This by itself thwarted individual initiatives, at the same time as it prevented the formation of a public policy motivated by the common interests of the people [*Myrdal, 1957, pp. 60*].

There are some significant analogies to structural development in the Celtic periphery in this very general discussion. First, with regard to *monoculture*, both Wales and Ireland clearly served in this capacity for the English metropolis. Ireland's traditional role as a provider of grain was threatened with the repeal of the Corn Laws (1846)—thereafter the island was converted into a livestock and dairy producer. Even today, 80 per cent of Eire's exports are consumed in Britain, and its economy remains but a regional appendage of the United Kingdom. Welsh development in the years after 1851 was dominated by export of coal from Glamorgan and Monmouthshire. Wales became the world's greatest exporter of coal until World War I. Scotland's development was not monocultural in this sense, though coal was a major source of revenue. The existence of textiles and heavy industry (ship and locomotive construction) in the Clydeside involved much skilled labour, engineering talent, sophisticated organization, none of which are typical of colonial economies. But when domestic and international markets dried up for Scottish ships, depression affected the entire regional economy, just as it did the over-specialized economies of Wales and Ireland.

The hinterland areas of Wales, Scotland, and Ireland were sources of reserve labour for boom periods, and offered the possibility of cash-crop farming during slumps. The hinterlands became more and more distant, in a social sense, from the industrial enclaves of Wales and Scotland. The industrial cities were far more cosmopolitan, English-oriented in culture, and secular than the rural hinterlands. This split would have decisive political implications for Wales and Scotland with the evolution of a three-party system following World War I. Welsh and Scottish antipathy to the central government tended to be split up between two opposition groups, the Liberal and Labour parties.

Further, the proliferation of railways as a result of industrialization did not serve to narrow this social distance. Railway development in the Celtic regions followed a very specific pattern. In most cases the rail routes linked the productive centres of the periphery to England. Thus in Wales north–south rail links were late to be constructed, and relatively sparse when compared with routes in the coal-mining areas of Glamorgan and Monmouthshire. Railway extension was much less responsive to population density in Wales, Scotland, and Ireland than in England. Finally, it must be emphasized in this context that the major financial institutions in the United Kingdom have always been English, and that London has served as the primary repository of credit and investment capital. Thus when most individual investment decisions concerning the Celtic lands are made they are largely decided in London by Englishmen who may be expected to have little knowledge, sympathy, or interest in these peripheral regions.

To this point in this article we have discovered several important differences in Celtic and English patterns of development: (1) Whereas industrialization has become diffused throughout a large proportion of English counties, it was spatially confined to much smaller and relatively compact areas in the Celtic periphery. (2) While the English economy became highly diversified, the peripheral economies were nearer a mono-cultural norm, highly vulnerable to extra-regional price changes. (3) When industrialization touched English counties, it served to dampen traditional sub-regional political and cultural differences, such as those between the northern counties and London and the south-east; whereas in the Celtic periphery (save Ireland where the monocultural export was agricultural) differences between industrial enclaves and hinterland areas became exaggerated, thereby contributing to the erosion of national solidarity, and (4) industrialization did not function to narrow systematic patterns of regional structural inequality between England and the Celtic lands.

THE INTERPRETATION OF STRUCTURAL INEQUALITY

In the previous sections it has been demonstrated that the spatial diffusion of industrialization was highly skewed in the British Isles, and that large sectors of the Celtic periphery remained non-industrial. The possibility remains that the systematic structural inequalities persisting between the Celtic areas and England are merely a reflection of the rural–urban differences found to some extent in all societies, and that, in and of themselves, little can be inferred about patterns of regional dominance from these statistics. In part this may be the case because of a downward bias in rural economies on indicators such as *per capita* income, where much individual income essentially goes unreported since it is consumed in kind. Clearly differences in occupational categories and level of urbanization also follow from this essential difference in the mode of production.

The implication, then, is that there can be no *a priori* grounds for believing that industrial development alone is in each region's best interests, and that those areas remaining rural in character are necessarily exploited or otherwise discriminated against by market forces or the actions of the central government. Capital-intensive agricultural production may be a perfectly suitable alternative to industrialization in so far as prospects for capital accumulation are concerned. Indeed, as it becomes evident that industrialization has resulted in greater costs to the environment, in terms of environmental pollution, than had previously been appreciated, the non-industrial path to development—such as that followed in Denmark, New Zealand, and, to an extent, Eire, as well—may well prove the wiser social investment in the long run.[12]

Hence it is difficult to interpret the data on structural inequalities unless the mode of production can satisfactorily be eliminated as a source of variation in these regions. That is to say, we must compare the wealth of English industrial counties to those—admittedly fewer—of the Celtic periphery, while simultaneously repeating the process for the non-industrial areas. What is ultimately required is a method for holding the variations in county levels of industrialization constant.

Since industrialization is a multi-dimensional concept, it is clearly advantageous to employ multiple indicators in its definition. In the attempt to specify significant indicators of industrialization, 27 social and demographic variables were subjected to a principle axis factor analysis for the years 1851, 1861, 1871, 1881, 1891, 1901, 1911, 1921, 1931, and 1951. The factor loadings were rotated to Kaiser's varimax criterion facilitating empirical interpretation [*Harman, 1960*]. From these ten factor analyses a factor of industrialization was determined, with mean loadings of 0·857 for the percentage of the male labour force engaged in manufacturing occupations, and —0·850 for the percentage of the county's male labour force in agricultural occupations (Table 4). Four other variables were consistently related to this factor over time: proportion of the population aged 65 and over; decennial demographic growth; crude marriage rate per 1,000 inhabitants, and proportion of the county population living in cities over 200,000. A seventh variable, the percentage of employed males in commercial and professional occupations, was included as an indicator of industrialization on the basis of its increasing significance over time. The remaining twenty variables are either not related or are inconsistently loaded on the industrialization factor over the continuum.

Multiple regression analysis was then employed to control for differing levels of industrialization. The indicator of *per capita* income was regressed on these seven variables, empirically related to the industrialization factor, for all counties in England, Wales, and Scotland at all eight points in time where data was available (1851–1901, 1951 and 1961). Data for all 32 counties in Ireland, South and North, was available only for 1861, 1871, 1881, and 1961, hence Ireland was not included in this series of regressions.[13] The multiple regression serves, in effect, as a means of holding these seven variables constant, thus enabling a comparison of county results with minute as well as large differences in the level of industrialization accounted for. On the basis of these data taken as a whole, for a given level of

TABLE 4

LOADINGS ON THE INDUSTRIALIZATION FACTOR FOR ALL COUNTIES IN ENGLAND, WALES, SCOTLAND, NORTHERN IRELAND AND SOUTHERN IRELAND (N = 118)

Variable[a]	1851	1861	1871	1881	1891	1901	1911	1921	1931	1951	Absolute Mean Over Time
(1) Manufacturing Occs.	0·832	0·852	0·869	0·912	0·936	0·898	0·809	0·754	0·863	0·842	0·857
(2) Agricultural Occs.	−0·871	−0·845	−0·858	−0·935	−0·929	−0·862	−0·833	−0·620	−0·920	−0·831	0·850
(3) Proportion 65 and Over	−0·696	−0·431	−0·666	−0·687	−0·612	−0·766	−0·834	−0·643	−0·679	−0·697	0·671
(4) Decennial Pop. Growth	0·641	0·667	0·712	0·796	0·747	0·770	0·775	0·176	0·632	0·482	0·640
(5) Marriage Rate	0·666	0·588	0·711	0·798	0·811	0·605	0·644	0·468	0·402	0·655	0·635
(6) Urbanization	0·538	0·547	0·556	0·624	0·598	0·626	0·694	0·561	0·772	0·687	0·620
(7) Infant Mortality	0·823	0·398	0·661	0·754	0·754	0·802	0·776	0·719	−0·111	−0·119	0·592
(8) Birth Rate	0·474	0·709	0·728	0·840	0·334	0·854	0·784	0·798	−0·117	−0·016	0·565
(9) Ethnic Diversity	0·609	0·752	0·668	0·598	0·555	0·560	0·452	0·227	0·238	0·160	0·482
(10) Population	0·310	0·263	0·322	0·396	0·404	0·393	0·407	0·353	0·535	0·436	0·383
(11) Comm. and Prof. Occs.	0·402	0·172	0·274	0·509	0·406	0·360	0·397	−0·037	0·613	0·510	0·368
(12) Irish Born	−0·331	−0·345	−0·342	−0·514	−0·498	−0·436	−0·444	−0·108	−0·442	−0·219	0·368
(13) Roman Catholic	−0·342	−0·338	−0·328	−0·471	−0·478	−0·397	−0·416	−0·080	−0·399	−0·207	0·346
(14) Established Church	0·236	0·241	0·317	0·502	0·522	0·403	0·440	0·040	0·438	0·203	0·334
(15) Religiosity	−0·166	−0·284	−0·301	−0·408	−0·498	−0·110	−0·465	−0·311	−0·132	−0·361	0·304
(16) English Born	0·083	0·056	0·176	0·335	0·401	0·259	0·347	0·006	0·692	0·278	0·263
(17) Foreign Born	−0·012	0·259	0·243	0·157	0·244	0·152	0·291	0·117	0·502	0·248	0·223
(18) Celtic Speakers	−0·223	−0·192	−0·186	−0·203	−0·167	−0·176	−0·229	−0·184	−0·332	−0·292	0·218
(19) Sex Ratio	−0·152	−0·054	0·117	0·098	0·135	0·079	−0·018	−0·193	−0·307	−0·281	0·143
(20) Female Domestics	−0·104	−0·170	−0·136	0·108	0·032	−0·080	−0·078	−0·365	−0·163	−0·049	0·129
(21) Nonconformity	0·228	0·216	0·107	0·095	0·086	0·130	0·124	0·095	0·043	0·082	0·121
(22) Employment	0·002	0·130	0·269	−0·135	−0·049	0·157	0·002	0·016	0·328	0·026	0·075
(23) Welsh Born	0·125	0·176	0·116	0·148	0·132	0·110	0·118	0·049	−0·022	−0·002	0·098
(24) Scottish Born	0·164	0·169	0·079	0·069	−0·006	0·095	0·010	0·071	−0·253	−0·057	0·131
(25) City Size	0·116	0·073	0·082	0·087	0·073	0·058	0·034	0·031	0·108	0·085	0·075
(26) Civil Service Occs.	0·104	0·034	−0·057	−0·029	−0·056	0·047	0·002	0·043	0·234	0·104	0·071
(27) Population Density	0·074	0·023	0·042	0·054	0·063	0·066	0·059	0·038	0·150	0·134	0·070

a All variables, save (4), (10), (25) and (27), are proportional to country population.

industrialization in a particular county in a specific year, the regression equation predicts an estimated level of *per capita* income. Figure 2 shows those counties whose *mean* level of *per capita* income for all eight observations in time was overestimated on the basis of the industrialization variables.[14] In other words these are counties which are relatively poor given a particular level of industrialization. The preponderance of shaded areas in the Celtic regions is unmistakable, with the single exception of the southern Scottish lowland agricultural counties. Similarly, large areas in England have positive residuals from the regression equation.

RELATIVELY DISADVANTAGED COUNTIES, 1851-1961

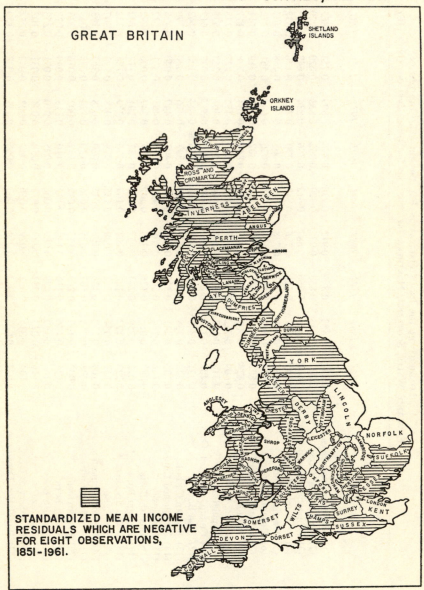

STANDARDIZED MEAN INCOME RESIDUALS WHICH ARE NEGATIVE FOR EIGHT OBSERVATIONS, 1851-1961.

FIGURE 2

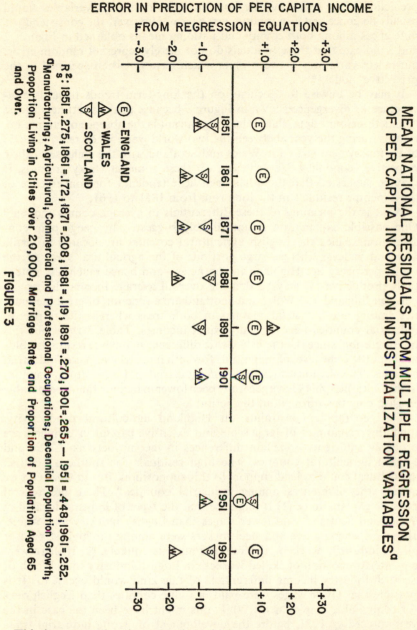

FIGURE 3

This is a map showing counties which are more or less disadvantaged throughout the whole period. Figure 3 shows residuals from the predicted *per capita* income averaged for counties within England, Wales, and Scotland, at each point in time. It enables us to look at trends of income convergence over time which the over-all county means in Figure 2 obscure. The most notable feature of Figure 3 is the persistence of Wales and Scotland beneath the English mean residual incomes, save the exceptions of 1891, when the Welsh, and 1951, when the Scottish residual values were highest. In linear regression analysis the residual obtained from the prediction of *per capita* income from the industrialization variables would usually be conceived as a random error term. However, the consistency of differences among both county and national means obtained in Figures 2 and 3 indicate that these residuals do not merely represent random error, but reflect variations between units which have not been specified in the predictive model.[15]

It may be unwise to speculate on the long-term trends towards convergence or divergence shown in Figure 3 because of the spottiness of the twentieth-century data. Particularly significant is the absence of county tax returns during the years between the two world wars, when relative levels of unemployment soared in Wales and Scotland with the collapse of their respective economies. Nevertheless, on these somehat shaky grounds, it may be suggested that there has been little tendency for convergence of these income residuals in the long run, from 1851 to 1961.

What is the meaning of these differentials in average county income? One possible explanation is immediately suggested by geographic considerations. Since the English agricultural counties are located in fertile Lowland valleys, whereas large portions of the agricultural areas of the Celtic periphery are Highland in character—and hence much less potentially productive—it may be that the over-all average income differences between England and Wales and Scotland are a function of great inequalities among non-industrial counties in both areas whereas the respective industrial counties have virtually equal incomes. Table 5 rules out this interpretation, since the English–Celtic difference in income residuals holds at about the same level of magnitude for both industrial and non-industrial counties. This demonstrates that *both* industrial and agricultural counties in the Celtic periphery have generally been lower in income than comparable English counties throughout the period.

The geographic constraints on Highland agricultural productivity, inhibiting economies of large scale and extensive capital investment, are probably sufficient to explain differences in income between Celtic and English agricultural counties. The high residuals for southern Scottish agricultural counties lend support to this supposition. But to what can we ascribe the differences among industrial counties? There are several possible explanations. (1) It might be that the *types* of industry located in Wales and Scotland paid lower wages than English industry as a whole. However, since miners and steelworkers were among the highest paid of all the industrial workers, this interpretation is unlikely. (2) If there were a greater proportion of skilled workers in English industry than Welsh or Scottish industry income differentials of this kind would occur. (3) It is possible that lower wages were paid in Celtic counties than English ones for comparable employment. While this might have been the case in the years preceding 1921, before the development of strong industrial trade unions, it is much less likely by 1951 and 1961 when collective bargaining was carried out on a national basis. (4) Increasing unemployment following World War I in the Celtic industrial counties, and the relative collapse of Celtic industry compared with English industrial production could account for the discrepancy in income in more recent years. Unemployment in Wales and Scotland continued to be significantly above the national average at the end of the 1960s [*Hammond, 1968*].

TABLE 5

MEAN RESIDUALS FROM PREDICTED PER CAPITA INCOME BY MULTIPLE REGRESSION

Industrial Counties In	1851	(N)	1861	(N)	1871	(N)	1881	(N)	1891	(N)	1901	(N)	1951	(N)	1961	(N)
England	+1·35	2	−0·67	3	+0·65	4	+1·42	6	+1·09	8	−0·58	10	+2·39	16	+4·82	16
Wales	—	—	−1·60	1	−2·40	1	−4·10	2	−0·65	2	−3·10	2	−13·30	2	−22·04	2
Scotland	−0·25	2	−1·07	3	−0·20	3	−0·19	7	−0·47	6	+0·07	9	+1·21	8	−4·82	8
All Industrial Counties	+0·55	4	−0·97	7	−0·05	8	−0·07	15	+0·29	16	−0·54	21	+0·82	26	−0·21	26
Non Industrial Counties In																
England	+0·61	38	+1·08	37	+0·75	36	+0·57	34	+0·20	32	+0·56	30	−0·17	24	+11·47	24
Wales	−0·83	13	−1·40	12	−1·55	12	−1·11	11	+1·52	11	−0·76	11	−4·56	11	−19·79	11
Scotland	−0·74	31	−0·52	30	−0·49	30	−0·24	26	−1·03	27	+0·05	24	+1·31	25	−2·09	25
All Non Industrial Counties	−0·13	82	+0·10	79	−0·08	78	+0·02	71	−0·07	70	+0·15	65	−0·36	60	+0·09	60

M

CONCLUSION

Though it has been determined that regional structural irregularities have persisted—even when taking comparable levels of industrialization into account—for over a century between England and the Celtic periphery, the significance of this fact is not at all clear. Since regional structural equality was not a natural outcome of the extension of markets into the periphery, the central government was urged, through political pressure, to take an active role in the redistribution of resources and economic opportunities to these areas. At two stages in recent years, 1945–48, and in the 1960s, the British government has made regional development a high priority in its domestic programme [*McCrone, 1969, p. 271*], in response to political mobilization in depressed areas. Sizeable incentives were extended to industrial firms willing to locate in areas such as South Wales and Scotland. Despite these programmes, the need for regional development has not subsided. This is a problem of decisive interest because it challenges many of the assumptions inherent in development theory—notably those stressing the inevitably revolutionary consequences of industrialization in specific territories.

Economists distinguish between two types of causes of regional economic differences. *Structural disadvantages* in a given region occur when its dominant industry begins to decline basically because of an inability to compete with new producers in the international market. Wales and Scotland have been areas of declining industry, particularly coal, and shipbuilding since the collapse of the international markets for these export commodities after 1921. A second source of regional differences lies in *locational disadvantages* which are thought to be characteristic of specific regions. A firm may, for example, refuse to be located far from its target market, or in an area where labour productivity is supposedly low—despite incentives from the central government.

Whereas the diagnosis of an industry in decline is essentially objective and in this sense not prone to argument among qualified observers, the striking element in the notion of locational disadvantage is its inherently *subjective* quality.[15] True, transport costs are a factor in the decision to locate new industry, though they are far less important now than at any previous time. But the decision to relocate an industry is far more complex than the simple question of transport costs would suggest. There are other considerations, some of which may be subject to *ethnocentric bias*. A survey of corporate decisions rejecting the establishment of Scottish branches or outright relocation cited the importance of criteria of

> the supposed remoteness of Scotland from the main markets and centres of supply . . . but (there was also) **unwillingness to enter an unfamiliar social environment and the belief that Scottish labour was intractable and not highly productive** [*Brown, 1969, p. 778, emphasis added*].

Hence even the active intrusion of the central government into the market-place has failed to bring about substantial improvement in redressing regional structural inequality. Hirschman [*1958 p. 185*] comments that the mere fact that an *ethnically non-distinctive* region has been backward for a period of time may create an image of it in dynamic areas which actually serves to preserve and contribute to regional differences by ideological means:

The successful groups and regions will widely and extravagantly proclaim their superiority over the rest of the country and their countrymen. It is interesting to note that to some extent these claims are self-enforcing. Even though the initial success of these groups may often be due to their luck or environmental factors such as resource endowment, matters will not always be left there. Those who have been caught by progress will always maintain that they were the ones who did the catching: they will easily convince themselves, and attempt to convince others, that their accomplishments are primarily owed to their superior moral qualities and conduct.

It has long been recognized that definitions of cultural inferiority have a way of becoming self-fulfilling prophecies, thereby legitimizing the institutionalization of inequality between collectivities.[17] Since most of the investment capital in the British Isles is concentrated in England, we might at least question whether or not social definitions such as these, when they are tinged with ethnic prejudice against the 'Celts' of the British periphery, affect the concrete decisions of individual investors. Such ethnic discrimination was characteristic of English attitudes towards the Celtic areas in the nineteenth century and earlier,[18] further, actual English decisions to invest in Wales and Scotland were conditional upon the realization of political stability, in practice involving the suppression of Celtic culture in Highland areas. While this argument is highly inferential, subsequent analysis has lent it some empirical support. Within Welsh and Scottish counties the prevalence of Celtic culture, as indicated by Welsh- and Gaelic-speaking and religious nonconformity, is negatively associated with *per capita* income throughout the period [*Hechter, 1971c*]. These findings have been demonstrated to be independent of differences in the level of county industrialization.

In fine, continuing Celtic economic backwardness might be seen as an outcome of many individual decisions which affect the Celtic regions directly and indirectly, but which are, in themselves, not part of a planned or even consciously stated policy aiming at the exploitation of the Celtic periphery. The resulting pattern of economic disadvantages in the Celtic lands may in fact be the socially unanticipated result of the aggregate of these individual decisions. In this way the present form and future direction of social life in the Celtic regions may be very largely influenced by market considerations in the United Kingdom as a whole, as well as the social definitions of significant actors in England with no necessary interest in or commitment to development in the periphery. The phenomenon of Celtic nationalism may be seen in this context as a political response to the continuation of regional inequality.

APPENDIX

A Note on the Per Capita *Income Variable*

Historical estimates of national and regional income accounts are necessarily of doubtful accuracy since the techniques of accounting are of recent vintage, and hence the statistics upon which proper accounts rest were not collected. Despite these limitations there have been two kinds of attempts at national income estimation for nineteenth-century Britain. Estimates for the early part of the century have been garnered from various contemporary writers interested in measuring the growing wealth of the realm [*Deane, 1956*].

The second method has relied heavily on income tax statistics supplemented by estimates of the national wage bill, agricultural income and productivity, and other types of income excluded from the tax returns [*Feinstein, 1961*]. In the course of a tortuous development the income tax went through many revisions which make the historical series discontinuous and generally incomparable over time [*Stamp, 1927*]. Changes in the exemption limits have to be laboriously calculated if the absolute growth of the national income is desired. If one is interested in the absolute value, in real income, of the tax assessment the *net* return must be calculated. However, net returns have been published only since the twentieth century. Although the net value for each schedule has been estimated back to 1855 there is no means by which these statistics can be determined for constituent regions.

Since we are not particularly interested in the growth of county incomes over time, but rather in the estimation of the relative *shares* of national income distributed in counties and regions, the gross measurements are of some value. By holding exemption rates constant for all four regions in given years we obtain a crude measure of the regional distribution of income at one point in time.

There are further difficulties for the period 1851–1911. The income tax was composed of five separate schedules, A through E, corresponding to different sources of income. Only three of these schedules, A, B, and D, relating to income from rents, farms, and industry respectively, were published in county returns. The missing schedules, C and E, refer to income from foreign investment and government salaries. They tend to make up about 15 per cent of the total tax bill through the nineteenth century, and perhaps 20 per cent by 1911. Since there is no way to obtain a county breakdown for these sources of income we have ignored them in creating the variable, making the assumption that *per capita* returns for these schedules are equal for all counties and regions. There is abundant reason to question this assumption. London has long been the centre of both Britain's administration and finance, hence England's share of schedules C and E should be significantly higher than those of Wales, Scotland, and most especially, Ireland. Thus this indicator probably underestimates English income.

In the construction of the variable, exemption rates were standardized at each decennial period according to the analysis of J. C. Stamp. Estimates of Ireland's 'true taxability' were taken from Stamp's calculations. For our purposes we have assumed that tax evasion for the counties occurred at a constant rate.

The income variable for the years 1951 and 1961 is somewhat different, in that it represents total county net income before taxes. These data were collected and published in county returns by the Board of Inland Revenue, and have been previously used to estimate regional income inequality [*Williamson, 1965*].

NOTES

1. Note the following clear statement by Frederick Engels:

'Since the end of the Middle Ages, history had been moving towards a Europe made up of large, national states. Only such national states constitute the normal political framework for the dominant European bourgeois class (*Bürgertum*) . . . the existence of a mass of petty German states with their many differing commercial and industrial laws was bound to become an intolerable fetter on this powerfully developing industry and on the growing commerce with which it was linked—a different rate of exchange every few miles, different regulations for establishing a business everywhere, literally everywhere, different kinds of chicanery, bureaucratic and fiscal traps, even in many cases still, guild restrictions against which not even a license was of any avail. . . . The ability to exploit the massive labour force of the fatherland in unrestricted fashion was the first condition for industrial development, but wherever the patriotic manufacturer sought to concentrate workers from all over Germany, there the police and Poor Law authorities stepped in against the influx of immigrants' [*Engels, 1968, pp. 29–32*].

2. This position tends to be taken by classically inclined economists and by the more sociologically minded political scientists. Classical economic theory holds that the market serves to reallocate factors of production such that factor prices equilibrate in both regions. While this may not lead to an immediate movement towards regional equalization of *per capita* incomes, in the long run such a trend should emerge according to this theory.

Political scientists such as Karl Deutsch [*1966*] feel that increases in total transactions between regions lead to higher levels of integration, implying more regionally homogeneous levels of social and economic development. The ideational content of interregional transactions is particularly stressed by the 'Political Culture' school of comparative politics [*Almond and Verba, 1963*].

3. The distinction was first drawn by Halford Mackinder [*1902*]. See also Thirsk [*1967*] and Emery [*1967*]. For another geographer's division of the British Isles, emphasizing the prevalence of North–South conflict in all regions, see Heslinga [*1962*].

4. 'In two important respects economic legislation was thus less influenced by municipal policy than on the Continent. First, all branches of industry were uniformly regulated throughout the country and great care was taken to maintain a regular supply of labor for agriculture. Secondly, the agents which the law prescribed for the administration of its rules were the same for town and country. . . . Its chief innovation in contrast with the medieval order lay in its uniform and well-planned character, and the monarchy, knowing what it was about, was able to stamp this character on the whole system.' [*Heckscher, 1962, Volume I, pp. 233*]

5. For an interesting empirical study of the regional redistribution of wealth following the Industrial Revolution see Buckatzsch [*1950*]. Read [*1964*] provides useful information on the changing influence of the northern cities in English history.

6. While we have adopted the logic of Friedlander's [*1902*] cutoff points to distinguish between industrial and non-industrial counties, the definition we have used is slightly different from his. Friedlander's variable is the percentage *of all adult males* engaged in non-agricultural occupations, while ours is the percentage of all *employed* adult males in such occupational categories. Our definition is somewhat more stringent, and therefore results in slightly fewer 'industrial counties' than does Friedlander's. Since the *Censuses of England and Wales and Scotland* did not publish occupational statistics by county in 1961, Figure 1 was constructed for that year with the assumption that the 1951 figures were the best estimates for 1961. Both Ireland and Northern Ireland did publish such statistics.

7. The decennial time series for this and all subsequent indicators, broken down by nation, may be obtained by writing the author.

8. The Scottish educational system was the first public institution of its kind in Europe, and for a time, its best. Scotland had, as a result, a much higher level of literacy than England throughout the eighteenth century as well [*Stone, 1966*]. Scotland boasted five universities, two of them outstanding in their day, Edinburgh and Glasgow, at a time when England's two were relatively moribund. The consequence of this was that in the eighteenth century the English aristocracy sent its sons to backward Scotland for an education. Explanations of Scotland's remarkable educational history tend to fall back on the Calvinistic zealousness of the post-Reformation period, though there has been some question about the moral and intellectual rectitude of the eighteenth century Kirk.

9. The definition of V_w:

$$V_w = \sqrt{\dfrac{\sum\limits_i (y_i - \bar{y})^2}{N}} \Big/ \bar{y}, \text{ where } N = \text{number of counties}$$

A similar measure which is weighted by population has been employed in cross-national studies where the areal units for which statistics are selected vary considerably. This is not the case in intra-national comparisons.

10. If we look at the V_w for counties, instead of regions, the curvilinear relationship holds:

Year	Vw in per capita income	N
1851	0·36	86
1861	0·32	86
1871	0·33	86
1881	0·34	86
1891	0·40	86
1901	0·48	86
1951	0·30	86
1961	0·26	86

11. The first discussion of the colonial political economy stressing 'dualism' was by J. H. Boeke [1953]. Thereafter, particularly emphasizing cultural institutions, J. S. Furnivall [1948], brought into currency the notion of 'plural societies'. Georges Balandier [1951] was simultaneously working out the specifics of the type of development found in the 'colonial situation'. Subsequent studies have tended to split the problem of colonial development into largely cultural [van den Berghe, forthcoming] and more strictly political economic facets [Rhodes, 1970]. Celso Furtado [1967, p. 129] presents a concise description of the evolution of the phenomenon:

'The third line of expansion of the European industrial economy was towards already inhabited regions, some of which were densely populated, whose old economic systems were of various, but invariably pre-capitalistic types. The contacts between the vigorous capitalistic economies and these regions of long-standing habitation did not occur in a uniform manner. In some cases interest was limited to the opening up of lines of trade. In others there prevailed right from the start a desire to encourage the production of raw materials for which demand was increasing in the industrial centres. The effect of the impact of capitalist expansion on the archaic structures varied from region to region, being conditioned by local circumstances, the type of capitalistic penetration, and the intensity of the penetration. The result, however, was almost always to create hybrid structures, part tending to behave as a capitalistic system, part perpetuating the features of the previously existing system. The phenomenon of underdevelopment today is precisely a matter of this type of dualistic economy.'

12. However, a consideration of New Zealand's difficulties during the negotiations on British entry into the Common Market suggests this is an overly optimistic assessment of the economic well-being of such economic systems.

13. The inclusion of Ireland and Northern Ireland into the multiple regression reveals that Northern Ireland is the most disadvantaged of all regions in the British Isles from 1861–81, with roughly double the negative residual of Wales. Surprisingly, Ireland's income residuals are *higher* than those of Wales in these years perhaps reflecting the common British complaint of the time that she was proportionally undertaxed [Stamp, 1927].

14. Since the variability of the *per capita* income variable is greater in 1951 and 1961, when it is based on total county income, than in the preceding years, it was necessary to standardize county income residuals at each observation to avoid a bias in the computation of longitudinal means.

15. One of the missing factors in the determination of county income is *cultural*: the degree to which given counties are anglicized [Hechter, 1971c].

16. A. O. Hirschman [1958, pp. 184–85] puts this somewhat differently:
'Thus investors spend a long time mopping up all the opportunities around some "growth pole" and neglect those that may have arisen or could be made to arise else-

where. What appears to happen is that *the external economies due to the poles, though real, are consistently overestimated by the economic operators*. The reason for this tendency . . . must be sought in the realm of social psychology.'

17. The social mechanisms of such institutionalization are very engagingly discussed by Robert K. Merton [*1957, pp. 421–36*].

18. For the medieval period see Jones [*1971*]; through the eighteenth century see Snyder [*1920*]; while Coupland [*1954, pp. 186–195*] is illuminating for the nineteenth.

REFERENCES

Almond, G., and Verba, S., 1963, *The Civic Culture*, Princeton: Princeton University Press.

Alonso, W., 1964, 'Location Theory' in J. Friedmann and W. Alonso, eds., *Regional Development and Planning*, Cambridge: M.I.T. Press.

Baer, Werner, 1964, 'Regional Inequality and Economic Growth in Brazil'. *Economic Development and Cultural Change*, 12, 3.

Balandier, Georges, 1951, 'La Situation Coloniale: Approche Théorique', *Cahiers Internationaux de Sociologie*, 11.

Boeke, J. H., 1953, *Economics and Economic Policy of Dual Societies*, New York: Institute of Pacific Relations.

Brown, A. J., 1969, 'Surveys of Applies Economics: Regional Economics, with Special Reference to the United Kingdom', *The Economic Journal*, 79, No. 316.

Buckatzsch, E. J., 1950, 'The Geographical Distribution of Wealth in England, 1086–1843', *Economic History Review*, 2nd Ser., 3.

Carmichael, S., and Hamilton, C. V., 1967, *Black Power: The Politics of Liberation in America*, New York: Random House, London: Jonathan Cape.

Coupland, Reginald, 1954, *Welsh and Scottish Nationalism*, London: Collins.

Deane, Phyllis, 1956, 'Contemporary Estimates of National Income in the First Half of the Nineteenth Century', *Economic History Review*, 2nd Ser, 8.

Deutsch, Karl, 1966, *Nationalism and Social Communication*, Cambridge: M.I.T. Press.

Dos Santos, Theotonio, 1970, 'The Structure of Dependence', *The American Economic Review*, 60, 2.

Emery, F., 1967, 'The Farming Regions of Wales', in J. Thirsk, ed., *The Agrarian History of England and Wales*, Volume IV, Cambridge: Cambridge University Press.

Engels, Frederick; 1968, *The Role of Force in History*, New York: International Publishers.

Feinstein, C. H., 1961, 'Income and Investment in the United Kingdom, 1856–1914', *The Economic Journal*, 71, No. 282.

Fisher, F. J., 1954, 'The Development of the London Food Market, 1540–1640', in E. M. Carus–Wilson, ed., *Essays in Economic History*, Volume I, London: Edward Arnold Ltd.

Friedlander, Dov, 1970, 'The Spread of Urbanization in England and Wales, 1851–1961'. *Population Studies*, 24, 3.

Furnivall, J. S., 1948, *Colonial Policy and Practice*, Cambridge: Cambridge University Press.

Furtado, Celso, 1967, *Development and Underdevelopment*, Berkeley: University of California Press.

Geertz, Clifford, 1963, 'The Integrative Revolution: Primordial Sentiments and Civic Politics in the New States', in C. Geertz, ed., *Old Societies and New States*, New York: Free Press.

González-Casanova, Pablo, 1965, 'Internal Colonialism and National Development', *Studies in Comparative International Development*, 1, 4.

Gray, H. L., 1915, *English Field Systems*, Cambridge: Harvard University Press.

Hammond, Edwin, 1968, *An Analysis of Regional Economic and Social Statistics*, Durham: Rowntree Research Unit, University of Durham.

Harman, Harry, 1960, *Modern Factor Analysis*, Chicago: University of Chicago Press.

Hechter, Michael, 1971a, 'Towards a Theory of Ethnic Change', *Politics and Society*, 1.

Hechter, Michael, 1971b, 'Regional Inequality and National Integration: the Case of the British Isles', *Journal of Social History*, 5, 1.

Hechter, Michael, 1971c, 'The Political Economy of Ethnic Change: the Celtic Periphery in the British Isles', paper read at the Annual Meeting of the American Anthropological Association, New York, November.

Heckscher, Eli, 1962, *Mercantilism*, London: George Allen and Unwin.

Heslinga, M. W., 1962, *The Irish Border as a Cultural Divide*, Assen. Netherlands: Van Gorcum.

Hicks, J. R. 1959, *Essays in World Economics*, Oxford: Clarendon Press.

Hirschman, Albert O., 1958, *The Strategy of Economic Development*, New Haven: Yale University Press.

Homans, G. C., 1957–58, 'The Frisians in East Anglia', *Economic History Review*, 2nd Ser., 10.

Homans, G. C., 1969. 'The Explanation of English Regional Differences', *Past and Present*, 42.

Jones, W. R., 1971, 'England Against The Celtic Fringe: a Study in Cultural Stereotypes', *Cahiers d'Histore Mondiale*, 13, 1.

Lasuén, J. R., 1962, 'Regional Income Inequalities and the Problems of Growth in Spain', Regional Science Association: *Papers*, 8.

Mackinder, Halford, 1902, *Britain and the British Seas*, New York: D. Appleton.

Mendenhall, Thomas, C., 1953, *The Shrewsbury Drapers and the Welsh Wool Trade*, London: Oxford University Press.

McCrone, Gavin, 1969, *Regional Policy in Britain*, London: George Allen and Unwin.

Merton, Robert K., 1957, 'The Self-Fulfilling Prophecy', in *Social Theory and Social Theory and Social Structure*, New York: Free Press.

Myrdal, Gunnar, 1957, *Rich Lands and Poor*, New York: Harper and Row.

Perroux, Francois; 1955, 'Note sur la notion de pole de croissance', *Matériaux pour une analyse de la croissance economique*, Cahiers de l'Institut de Science Economique Apliquée, Série D, 8.

Read, Donald, 1964, *The English Provinces, 1760–1960: A Study in Influence*, London: Edward Arnold, Ltd.

Rhodes, R. I., ed., 1970, *Imperialism and Underdevelopment*, New York: Monthly Review Press.

Smith, Adam, 1950, *The Wealth of Nations*, London: Methuen.

Snyder, Edward D., 1920, 'The Wild Irish: a Study of Some English Satires Against the Irish, Scots, and Welsh', *Modern Philology*, 17, 12.

Stamp, J. C., 1927 *British Incomes and Property*, London: P. S. King and Son, Ltd.

Stone, Lawrence, 1966, 'Literacy and Education in England, 1640–1900', *Past and Present*, 33.

Tachi, M., 1964, 'Regional Income Disparity and Internal Migration of Population in Japan', *Economic Development and Cultural Change*, 12, 2.

Thirsk, Joan, 1967, 'The Farming Regions of England' in J. Thirsk, ed., *The Agrarian History of England and Wales*, Volume IV, Cambridge: Cambridge University Press.

van den Berghe, P. L., forthcoming, 'Pluralism', in J. J. Honigman, ed., *Handbook of Social and Cultural Anthropology*.

Williamson, Jeffrey G., 1965, 'Regional Inequality and the Process of National Development: a Description of the Patterns', *Economic Development and Cultural Change*, 13, 4, Part 2.

Zipf, G. K., 1941, *National Unity and Disunity*, Bloomington: Indiana University Press.